ARCHAEOLOGY AND CELTIC MYTH

Archaeology and Celtic myth: an exploration

JOHN WADDELL

FOUR COURTS PRESS

Typeset in 10.5 pt on 12.5 pt EhrhardtMTPro *by*
Carrigboy Typesetting Services for
FOUR COURTS PRESS LTD
7 Malpas Street, Dublin 8, Ireland
www.fourcourtspress.ie
and in North America for
FOUR COURTS PRESS
c/o ISBS, 920 NE 58th Avenue, Suite 300, Portland, OR 97213.

A catalogue record for this title is available
from the British Library.

ISBN 978-1-84682-494-4

This publication was grant-aided by the Publications Fund of
National University of Ireland, Galway.

Printed in England
by Antony Rowe, Chippenham, Wilts.

Contents

Acknowledgments

I am deeply grateful to the Society of Antiquaries of Scotland whose invitation to deliver the Rhind Lectures in Edinburgh in early 2014 provided the motivation for the preparation of this work, which, in addition to some new study, has allowed me to expand on a number of recently published papers. This has been an interdisciplinary task that would not have been possible without the invaluable advice of Máirín Ní Dhonnchadha, Professor of Old and Middle Irish and Celtic Philology in the National University of Ireland Galway. I owe a similar debt of gratitude to Conor Newman, who has pioneered the exploration of the archaeology and mythological associations of the Tara landscape. Jane Conroy deserves special thanks for her support. The responsibility for all shortcomings is mine alone.

Another significant stimulus was 'The Connacht Project' in the National University of Ireland Galway. This is an interdisciplinary research initiative under the direction of Professor Ní Dhonnchadha that investigates aspects of the early Irish literary evidence relating to the ancient province of Connacht. This extraordinarily rich material includes early medieval world literature such as *Acallam na Senórach* (Tales of the Elders of Ireland) and the *Táin Bó Cúailnge* (The Cattle Raid of Cooley) as well as Patrician texts and bardic poetry. The archaeological component of this project addresses the challenges posed by a number of western sites and monuments, like the royal complex of Rathcroghan, where myth, history and archaeology converge.

Carleton Jones, Robin Bendrey and Jim Mallory were generous sources of useful information and Luis Berrocal-Rangel kindly allowed me to read his illuminating study of '*chevaux-de-frise*' prior to publication. Angela Gallagher assisted with the preparation of the illustrations. I am very grateful to her and to many others for their help in this regard.

The sources of the illustrations are as follows: (figures) 3.1: B. Raftery 1983; 3.2:1–3: E.M. Jope 2000; 3.2:4: I. Stead & K. Hughes 1997; 3.3:1–2: F. Kaul 1998; 3.3:3: E. Aner & K. Kersten 1976; 3.4:1: P. Patay 1990; 3.4:2: S. Wirth 2006; 3.4:3–4: E. Sprockhoff 1955; 3.4:5: C. Rolley 2003; 3.5:1: J. Meduna & I. Peskar 1992; 3.5:2: H.N. Savory 1976; 3.5:3: M. Duignan 1976. 4.1: J. Waddell et al. 2009; 4.2: J. Waddell et al. 2009 and S. Ferguson 1864; 4.3: J. Waddell 2010; 4.4: M. Cahill & M. Sikora 2011 and J. Coles & A.F. Harding 1979; 4.5: J. Biel 1982 and R.J. Harrison 2004; 4.6: G. Eogan 2001. 5.1: C.J. Lynn 2003 (reproduced with the permission of the Controller of HMSO); 5.2: C.J. Lynn 1986; 5.3: H. Zimmer 1955; 5.4:1: W. Kimmig 1988; 5.4:2: P.-M. Duval 1987; 5.4:3: I. Marazov 1989; 5.5: A: C.J. Lynn 1997 (reproduced with the permission of the Controller of HMSO); 5.5:B: J.P. Mallory & T.P. McNeill

1991; 5.5:C: J. Auboyer 1959. 6.1: F. Guizot, *L'histoire de France* (1872). 7.1: A. Corns et al. 2008 and the Discovery Programme; 7.2: L. Hansen 2010; 7.3: J. Biel 1982; 7.4: R. Dehn et al. 2005; 7.5: K. Parfitt 1995. (Plates) 1: T.H. Roosevelt 1907; 2 and 3: courtesy of Geraldine Stout from G. Stout 2002; 4: C.J. Lynn 2003 (reproduced with the permission of the Controller of HMSO); 5: E. Hull 1909; 6: T.H. Roosevelt 1907; 7 photo: Gerry Bracken 1989 and J. Waddell et al. 2009; 8: courtesy of Landesmuseum Württemberg, Foto: P. Frankenstein, H. Zwietasch, Landesmuseum Württemberg, Stuttgart; 9: C. Rolley 2003 and Collections du musée du pays Châtillonnais: Trésor de Vix; 10: photo: Eamonn O'Donoghue 2005.

Illustrations

FIGURES

COLOUR PLATES

(between p. 48 and p. 49)

Preface

When Stuart Piggott published his *Ancient Europe* in 1965 he described this monumental survey of European prehistory from the beginnings of agriculture to classical antiquity as a personal estimate of certain factors that, in his opinion, had contributed to the character of the ancient world that lay behind early historical Europe. This was a study based on the Rhind Lectures three years before and in it he argued that medieval and modern Europe was not wholly the product of the Roman tradition. The essential rural economy of what was to become historical Europe had, he suggested, roots that struck very deep in prehistoric antiquity. Innovation and radical change were exceptional, the conservatism of barbarian Europe, as he called it, led to the preservation of accustomed modes and the retention and transmission of tradition down the generations.[1]

It is fair to say that his model of innovating and conserving societies was very much in the cultural-historical tradition of the time but, as Richard Bradley has observed, it anticipated some of the ideas of interest in contemporary archaeology.[2] However, Piggott's notion of the retention and transmission of tradition, not just over centuries but over millennia, is well worth examining. This question inevitably arises in a study that attempts to correlate archaeology and myth – for myth was a feature of all societies and, as we shall see, early Irish myth was a pre-eminent medium for the transmission of cosmographic beliefs and concepts of kingship.

This study is an exploration and its central premise is that elements of pre-Christian Celtic myth preserved in medieval Irish literature shed light on older traditions not just in Ireland but elsewhere in Europe as well.

As an archaeologist with no expertise in the study of myth and a complete deficiency in Old and Middle Irish, I am very conscious of the dangers and difficulties of this sort of exercise. In my defence, however, I call Karl Valentin. He was one of the leading comedians in Weimar Germany and one of his stage sketches showed him searching for his house keys in a pool of light cast by a street lamp. A policeman comes to his aid and eventually asks the worried Valentin where exactly he had lost his keys. He points to a dark corner of the stage and when asked why he has not searched there replies 'There is no light over there'. This anecdote was recounted some fifty years ago by the Welsh scholar Alwyn Rees in a spirited defence of the far-ranging study of comparative mythology and he thought it an apt illustration of an academic

---

1 S. Piggott, *Ancient Europe* (1965), p. 258. 2 R. Bradley, 'Stuart Piggott' in I.A.G. Shepherd & G.J. Barclay (eds), *Scotland in ancient Europe* (2004), p. 6.

unwillingness to explore beyond the circle of light of one's own discipline.[3] It is true, in these post-processual times, that transdisciplinary studies are now far commoner. Much interesting work on archaeology and myth has been done in Scandinavia in recent decades for instance. But the risks of venturing well outside one's area of expertise have not diminished. The many references to the scholarly contributions of acknowledged specialists in other fields are just one indication of my debt to them.

This enquiry mainly focuses on aspects of the mythology associated with four well-known Irish archaeological landscapes: Newgrange and the Boyne Valley, and the royal sites of Rathcroghan in Co. Roscommon, Navan in Co. Armagh, and Tara in Co. Meath. Ironically, the archaeological and mytho-logical importance of the Navan and Tara landscapes failed to afford them much protection from officially sanctioned vandalism and destruction in recent decades. In the 1980s, extensive limestone quarrying near Navan Fort endangered the environs of that famous monument. While the fort itself was a protected site, the landscape had no protection. At one point, a 30m-deep quarry face encroached to within some 40m of the enclosure bank. Despite concerns, quarrying was allowed to continue in 1984 with the tacit support of the planning service and the Historic Monuments branch of Northern Ireland's Department of the Environment. A twenty-two-day-long planning enquiry then found in favour of the quarry owner but the exceptional level of public protest eventually forced the London government to refuse planning consent.[4]

Twenty years later, Tara's landscape would face a similar threat. Even though the name of Lug, the greatest of the Celtic gods, is associated with a large ringfort called Rath Lugh just north-east of the Hill of Tara in the Gabhra Valley, this was no protection to the surrounding *ferann ríg*, Tara's medieval royal demesne. The early years of the new millennium saw the construction of a motorway that now sunders this landscape and just skirts the ringfort. The motorway proposal prompted an international controversy and the pre-development excavations, not surprisingly, did produce some significant outcomes but at an utterly unacceptable cost. The results gave the lie to the claim by the motorway supporters that the sites in the valley were not associated with the famous hilltop monuments.[5]

The mythological associations of these celebrated complexes will allow us to pursue the archaeological implications of several mythic themes in early Irish literature, namely sacral kingship, a sovereignty goddess, solar cosmology and

3 A.D. Rees, 'Modern evaluations of Celtic narrative tradition' in *Proceedings of the Second International Congress of Celtic Studies 1963* (1966), p. 31.   4 B. Bender, 'The politics of the past: Emain Macha (Navan), Northern Ireland' in R. Layton et al. (eds), *Destruction and conservation of cultural property* (2001), pp 199–211.   5 C. Newman, 'Misinformation, disinformation and downright distortion: the battle to save Tara, 1999–2005' in C. Newman & U. Strohmayer, *Uninhabited Ireland* (2007); 'In the way of development: Tara, the M3 and

the perception of an Otherworld, in an attempt to demonstrate that these concepts shed some light on features of Irish and European prehistory. Conversely, occasionally archaeology may illuminate some aspects of myth.

Tomás Ó Cathasaigh once wrote:

> what is remarkable about the Irish situation is the extent and richness of the vernacular literature which has come down to us from the early medieval period. Much of this literature is firmly rooted in ancient myth and remains robustly pagan in character; it has been used, along with other evidence, to build up at least a partial picture, not only of the pagan religion of the Irish, but also that of the Celts, and it has even been laid under contribution in the comparative study of Indo-European mythology.[6]

If this is so, the archaic mythic themes in this material have the potential to shed light on older European belief systems. The mythic elements are scattered across the whole corpus from saga literature to place-lore to hagiography. Excerpts are given here in translation but a few are presented in the original Old Irish or Middle Irish as well to illustrate the nature of a body of material that often presents daunting scholarly challenges (ch. 1). Though a common practice in Celtic studies, I avoid acronyms and, with the exception of the well-known *Táin Bó Cúailnge* (The Cattle Raid of Cooley), usually cite the title of texts both in the original and in translation. The structure of the book reflects its origins in a series of half a dozen lectures. These addressed a number of overlapping themes with some inevitable repetition, which, I hope, has now been minimized.

Though well aware of the many millennia that separated the construction of the Boyne tombs and their appearance in medieval tales, M.J. O'Kelly, when he published his excavations at Newgrange, was also inspired to wonder if the first seeds of the oral traditions behind its rich mythology had been planted in the Neolithic.[7] His work demonstrated that this was a monument intimately linked to the utilization of solar phenomena and the mythological themes we shall examine associated with Newgrange and the River Boyne (ch. 2) focus on the manipulation of time, on the power of secret knowledge and on the part the sacred river played in the creation of the megalithic structure. Here, archaeology and myth converge. If, as seems likely, some features of these myths have millennia-old Indo-European roots, then their transmission over a great timespan is a testimony to the hold they once had on the human mind. That some archetypal subjects might have such a long lifespan in pre-literate

the Celtic Tiger' (forthcoming, 2014).   6 T. Ó Cathasaigh, 'Pagan survivals: the evidence of early Irish narrative' in P. Ní Chatháin & M. Richter (eds), *Irland und Europa* (1984), p. 291. 7 M.J. O'Kelly, *Newgrange: archaeology, art and legend* (1982), p. 48.

times is entirely plausible. For instance, a widespread cosmological belief about the celestial voyage of the sun may be detected at different times in various parts of Europe over a period of some two thousand years and the archaeological evidence – solar symbols on metalwork – extends from Ireland to central Europe (ch. 3). Here we have one striking example of Piggott's concept of the retention and transmission of tradition.

Anyone who has stood on the stony ground of the great fort of Dún Aonghasa on the Aran Islands and witnessed the dramatic sight of the setting sun sinking in the Atlantic must get a sense of the questions this spectacle could have raised in the pre-modern mind. Here began the nocturnal journey of the sun through the netherworld to its rebirth in the east. A belief in an Otherworld, a persistent theme in early Irish literature, finds expression not only in some of the prehistoric solar imagery but in other ways in the archaeological record where there is some evidence the Otherworld was considered a reversed or inverted reflection of this one (ch. 4). This concept is found in early literature including a text that seemingly refers to a natural cave with a man-made souterrain at Oweynagat in Rathcroghan that is remembered as an entrance to this supernatural realm. This is by no means the only piece of archaeological evidence that offers a glimpse of this ancient belief. The Otherworld was never far away at Navan Fort and the kingship ceremonial associated with Macha, its horse goddess and goddess of sovereignty, is examined in chapter 5. If, as seems possible, horse sacrifice and the sacred marriage (often called by the Greek term *hieros gamos*) between king and goddess were a part of these rites, then we have a manifestation of an Indo-European tradition that may once have had a wide European currency.

Another goddess, Maeve of Rathcroghan (Medb of Crúachain), introduces us to a further aspect of the sovereignty figure (ch. 6), namely her association with drinking ritual. Although Medb is popularly remembered as the fickle initiator of the great cattle-raid in the epic *Táin Bó Cúailnge* (The Cattle Raid of Cooley), her name, generally thought to be related to the word mead, is an indication that she was originally a primeval goddess with an Indo-European dimension who – representing the sovereignty of the land – bestowed a drink on he who would be king in an acknowledgment of his right to rule. There is no shortage of evidence for drink-related activity in prehistory and it is possible that the evidence for drinking ceremonial in some exceptional female burials reflects the woman's role in such a ritual affirmation of male rule. This rite may also have been a part of that sacred marriage between king and goddess echoes of which survived in features of medieval royal inauguration. Such a symbolic union is one indication of the former sacred character of a king whose authority derived from the Otherworld.

The institution of sacral kingship, closely associated with Tara, is explored in chapter 7. There is no denying the difficulties of recognizing this phenomenon in the archaeological record, witness the reluctance to use the term king rather than chief, and kingdom rather than chiefdom in archaeological studies. However, the fact that it may have been a widespread Indo-European institution and its prominence in early Irish tradition suggest that we should at least try to identify it. Some elite male interments, like the famous Iron Age burial at Hochdorf, deserve to be considered as illustrations of this phenomenon.

That myth may provide new perspectives on archaeological issues is not in doubt. One of the remarkable features of Dún Aonghasa is the presence of a *chevaux-de-frise* outside one of its ramparts. Such bands of upright stones are generally believed to have had a defensive role, retarding the approach of an attacking force. In a major study of this phenomenon, Luis Berrocal-Rangel shows that these stones probably had an equally important symbolic purpose. He cites the Greek myth of the foundation of Thebes by Cadmus who, instructed by the oracle at Delphi to found a town, encountered a dragon guarding a spring. When the hero killed the dragon, Athena appeared and told him to sow the dragon's teeth. He did so and a group of fully armed men sprang from the ground. Five of these supernatural *Spartoi*, the fierce 'sown men', helped him found the city. Berrocal-Rangel argues that the clusters of upright stones found at Bronze Age and Iron Age forts in various parts of Europe were not just a hindrance but also had a symbolic protective role. It is an intriguing thought that the prehistoric significance of Dún Aonghasa was enhanced by the presence of a phalanx of formidable stone warriors.[8]

8 L. Berrocal-Rangel, 'New interpretations on upright stone bands: *"chevaux-de-frise"* in western Europe' (forthcoming).

CHAPTER I

Confronting ancient myth

Archaeologists working in Ireland occasionally face some quite unusual challenges. Those who have studied the archaeology of the celebrated Hill of Tara, for instance, have not only had to address the interpretative problems posed by a range of enigmatic earthworks but have also been confronted by a series of monuments and a landscape that bear an inordinate weight of myth and legend. As Conor Newman wrote in the preface to his major survey of that royal site undertaken for the Discovery Programme, 'In myth Tara is a stage whereon some of the major dramas of the Irish heroic age were played out, when Irish men and women sparred with the gods and touched immortality'.[1] Chris Lynn, who prepared Dudley Waterman's meticulous excavations at Navan Fort for publication, also had to engage with the fact that this famous enclosure had long been identified with the legendary Emain Macha, a royal centre that figured prominently in the group of heroic tales commonly called the Ulster Cycle.[2] So too with the survey I and my colleagues have undertaken at Rathcroghan in the west of Ireland, a complex of monuments with a rich mythology and closely associated with the epic *Táin Bó Cúailnge* (The Cattle Raid of Cooley), the principal story in that Ulster Cycle.[3]

It is impossible to ignore the mythic dimension of these places. The challenges they pose are many and obviously any attempt to reconcile prehistoric archaeology and medieval myth might justifiably be seen as a foolhardy if not a futile exercise. It is, of course, true that the stories associated with places like these do indicate the importance they had in the medieval mind but whether or not they illuminate aspects of an older world has been much debated. For example, writing of early Irish narrative literature, the author of one study of European paganism has declared:

> Its oldest manuscripts, however, only go back to the twelfth century, long after the end of paganism; the texts are of limited usefulness and it is largely wishful thinking to suppose that much material earlier than the early Middle Ages has survived in this tradition: they may preserve some useful social detail, for instance testifying to the existence of druids and prophets, but considerably less on pagan religious attitudes.[4]

---

[1] C. Newman, *Tara: an archaeological survey* (1997), p. xi. [2] C.J. Lynn, *Excavations at Navan Fort* (1997). [3] J. Waddell et al., *Rathcroghan, Co. Roscommon* (2009). [4] K. Dowden, *European paganism* (2000), p. 16.

The well-known phrase 'a window on the Iron Age' formed the subtitle of K.H. Jackson's Rede Lecture in Cambridge in 1964, which he titled *The oldest Irish tradition: a window on the Iron Age*.[5] In it he argued that some Irish medieval literature, and in particular the Ulster Cycle, depicted a pre-Christian Iron Age world. For him, the *Táin* with its heroic warriors, endemic warfare and archaic material civilization – as he put it – did reflect a genuine Iron Age. He did not, of course, imply that the main protagonists in this tale, Queen Maeve or Medb of Connacht and the Ulster hero Cú Chulainn, were historical figures, though this was the firm belief of earlier generations. Early in the twentieth century, William Ridgeway, a former professor of Greek in Queen's College, Cork, who was appointed Disney Professor of Archaeology in Cambridge in 1892, attempted to demonstrate that the world of the *Táin* was the world of La Tène Iron Age Celts. He accepted the traditional date around the beginning of the Christian era for the events recounted in this epic. He noted how the tall, fair-haired physique, and the arms and dress of the warriors of the *Táin* agreed with descriptions of the Gauls, of the Celts of northern Italy and the Danube region, and of the Belgic tribes described by Julius Caesar. There was, he asserted, a striking correspondence between these material remains and the culture depicted in the *Táin* and it could be justifiably inferred that there had been an invasion of Celtic peoples from Gaul in the centuries immediately before the birth of Christ.[6] This view was shared by archaeologists such as R.A.S. Macalister and nationalist writers like Aodh de Blácam, who had also declared that this material was 'a window into the early Iron Age'.[7]

These tales provided a beguiling picture of a former Heroic Age and for one eminent writer they told of an Ireland 'in which still obtained ancient customs that had vanished elsewhere even from the memory of man' and they were especially admirable for 'their exaltation of the glorious courage of men and of the charm and devotion of women'.[8] Ó Cathasaigh has proposed that there have been three broad approaches to the study of early Irish tradition, namely the mimetic, the mythological and the textual. In this, the mimetic, this literature is seen as a reflection of real circumstances or events.[9]

Jackson presented his lecture and undertook its publication to direct the attention of archaeologists and others to the exceptional wealth of early Irish vernacular writing, this 'archaic fragment of European literature' as he described it. Since components of Irish La Tène art survive into the early medieval period, he thought it reasonable that the memory of other pre-Christian traditions might have survived too. But his thesis has not fared well. It has been questioned on linguistic, chronological and archaeological grounds.

5 K.H. Jackson, *The oldest Irish tradition* (1964).   6 W. Ridgeway, 'The date of the first shaping of the Cuchulainn saga', *Proceedings of the British Academy* 2 (1906), 135–68.   7 A. de Blácam, *Gaelic literature surveyed* (1929), p. xi.   8 T. Roosevelt, 'The ancient Irish sagas', *Century Magazine* 73 (1907), 336.   9 T. Ó Cathasaigh, 'Pagan survivals' in P. Ní Chatháin & M. Richter (eds), *Irland und Europa* (1984), p. 296.

Just to illustrate one aspect of the latter, Jim Mallory, in a seminal paper in 1982, demonstrated how the swords described in the *Táin*, far from being La Tène-type weapons, were comparable to swords of the Viking period and generally later than the eighth century AD. In short, the swords of the Ulster Cycle are the swords familiar to the medieval redactors of these tales. Further study confirmed this picture of an early medieval date for much of the material culture of the *Táin*, 'demonstrably or probably' later than the fourth century AD. According to Mallory, the learned class who contributed to the formation of this epic literature were both producing an historical fiction and attempting to portray a past world. This was a complex world that may have included some memory of what constituted antiquity.[10]

Other writers have critiqued Jackson's approach, arguing that early Irish epic literature was not a legitimate source for the study of pagan Celtic society either in Ireland or in Celtic Europe. The Ulster Cycle was considered an early medieval literary composition.[11] This was a part of the scholarly debate between 'nativists' and others about the degree to which pagan oral traditions contributed to the literary corpus. John Koch reviewed the near total demolition of Jackson's case and had to conclude that the only really salvageable part of Jackson's work was the memorable subtitle. Nonetheless, it did seem likely that some features (such as head-hunting, chariotry, feasting and the champion's portion) might well have been a part of a pre-Christian world.[12] Since the *Táin* was a literary creation that grew over centuries, Ruairi Ó hUiginn was correct in claiming

> it is quite evident that the events and society portrayed in the Ulster Cycle do not reflect a picture of Irish society at the time of Christ ... Neither, however, are they an accurate picture of life in Early Christian Ireland, contemporaneous with their time of writing.

But as he also said, it may be that some of the archaic features found in it and in other tales are archaisms handed down orally and some of these are inherited myth.[13]

It is interesting to observe that while it was Jackson's belief that this epic literature might shed some light on the Iron Age, he was cautious about the study of myth. The mythological content of the medieval literary tradition was, he thought, just 'a gold-mine for the speculation of scholars'. Elsewhere, writing of the Mabinogion, he declared that mythological interpretations 'can be tailored to fit anything, and hence they are a favourite device in the hands of

---

10 J.P. Mallory, 'The world of Cú Chulainn' in J.P. Mallory (ed.), *Aspects of the Táin* (1992), pp 103–59. 11 N.B. Aitchison, 'The Ulster Cycle', *Journal of Medieval History* 13 (1987), 87–116. 12 J.T. Koch, 'Windows on the Iron Age, 1964–1994' in J.P. Mallory & G. Stockman (eds), *Ulidia* (1994), pp 229–42. 13 R. Ó hUiginn, 'The background and development of *Táin Bó Cúailnge*' in J.P. Mallory (ed.), *Aspects of the Táin* (1992), p. 55.

the unscholarly'.[14] But, as we shall see, it is the mythic component of early Irish and Welsh tradition that provides some important insights into older collective beliefs and practices.

Students of cognitive archaeology who seek to understand the ideology, religious concepts, cosmology and symbolic structures of past societies appreciate the difficulty in determining past ways of thought from the material evidence in the archaeological record. However, symbolic behaviour has been recognized again and again. Bradley's identification of the relationship between prehistoric rock art and the situation of these carvings in the landscape is a case in point. Some ritual imperative lay behind their location; they emphasized the significance of special places, but this obviously was only a part of the story. Their purpose was to convey other messages too and, as he notes, some of the motifs employed may have been inspired by shamanic activities.[15]

It has been often said that archaeologists introduce the word ritual when all other explanations fail. Perhaps this is too cynical, for the term is often used with good justification. Clearly, the identification of ritual in an archaeological context is not an easy or straightforward task and even the definition of the term presents great difficulties.[16] It is widely accepted as an action that addresses some supernatural entity or power in either a sacred or a secular environment, but any more precise identification of the actors and procedures involved is often impossible. What prompted a particular ritual activity in prehistory and the identification of the belief systems that lay behind it present significant interpretative challenges. The use of ethnographic analogy may remind us of neglected aspects of human behaviour, broaden the imagination and help to test our modern western ways of thinking. As Julian Thomas has said, it has an important role 'in troubling and disrupting what we think we already know'.[17] It is possible to use parts of medieval Irish literature in this way.

There are other possibilities, however, for the archaic mythic substrata in this material are well worth exploring because they offer a window on older belief systems. As Colin Renfrew has observed, most societies of which we are aware had mythic accounts of how things came to be and, while we have no direct access to such narratives formulated during the prehistoric past, we do have access to the material traces of how these societies tried to make sense of their world.[18] Some of the mythic themes encountered in early Irish tradition are of great antiquity and, I suggest, they provide us with indirect access to some older European beliefs. There are myths that supply some insights into archaeological matters or, at the very least, encourage us to consider new or different interpretations. Some archaeological evidence may illuminate aspects

14 K.H. Jackson, *The international popular tale and early Welsh tradition* (1961), p. 129. 15 R. Bradley, *Rock art and the prehistory of Atlantic Europe* (1997).   16 E. Kyriakidis (ed.), *The archaeology of ritual* (2007), passim.   17 J. Thomas, *Archaeology and modernity* (2004), p. 241.   18 C. Renfrew, *Prehistory: the making of the human mind* (2007), p. 182.

of some myths. It is necessary to emphasize, however, that this is neither a study of myth nor a study of the cognitive models of the medieval Irish. It is an exploration of some instances where prehistoric archaeology and ancient myth appear to converge.

Some of these mythic themes may be very old indeed. Most European languages belong to that language family called Proto-Indo-European or simply Indo-European. The earliest member of this family for which we have linguistic evidence is Hittite recorded in cuneiform script on clay tablets in Anatolia around 1700BC. The oldest texts, in Indo-Iranian, are in Vedic Sanskrit and appear later in the second millennium BC, as does Mycenean Greek. Celtic and Italic languages are attested in the first millennium BC. Students of comparative linguistics and mythology have from time to time identified shared and often complex themes and characteristics in Celtic and Vedic tradition, for example. These features, it is argued, are a part of a common Indo-European inheritance and are thousands of years old. They are either so numerous, unusual or relatively precise as not to be accidental and are unlikely to have been transmitted over such a great geographical distance in more recent times.

THE LITERARY CORPUS

Early Irish literature is by far the most substantial body of written material in a vernacular tongue in western Europe. Unique in volume and scope, it is composed in Old Irish (roughly AD600–900) and Middle Irish (approximately AD900–1200). No brief summary (and certainly not one offered by an archaeologist) can hope to do justice to the enormous array of manuscript material represented and to the formidable body of scholarship devoted to it.[19] It is a challenge to specialist and non-specialist alike. For the latter, sometimes dependant on unreliable nineteenth-century translations, difficulties are compounded by divergent interpretations and by the fact that there may be multiple recensions of a particular text. As Donnchadh Ó Corráin has observed, 'the different recensions of the same text are not usually capricious synchronic variants but different versions developed to suit the changing circumstances which come about with the passage of time'.[20]

While the survival of archaic mythic themes and pagan concepts is not in doubt, it is not always easy to distinguish a genuine archaism from a medieval

19 General surveys include P. Ó Riain, 'Early Irish literature' in G. Price (ed.), *The Celtic connection* (1992), pp 65–80; J. Carney, 'Language and literature to 1169' in D. Ó Cróinín (ed.), *A new history of Ireland* (2005), pp 451–510; M. Ní Bhrolcháin, *An introduction to early Irish literature* (2009). 20 D. Ó Corráin, 'Historical need and literary narrative' in D. Ellis Evans et al. (eds), *Proceedings of the Seventh International Congress of Celtic Studies*

borrowing or invention. Myths undoubtedly had important cultural meanings for medieval folk because they sometimes expressed concepts that described acceptable social norms and beliefs. Those that conflicted with contemporary Christian mythology were either deliberately assigned to a pagan past or subjected to a process of amendment or selection. John Carey has stressed that medieval Ireland's literary legacy is the result of an ancient and evolving tradition in which inherited materials may have been combined, recombined, adapted and transmuted, and archaism and innovation must constantly be weighed against one another.[21] It is evident that the study of Irish prehistory fascinated the medieval Irish and in the great twelfth-century undertaking the *Lebor Gabála* (The Book of Invasions), we are given an account of the history of Ireland from the time of the biblical deluge that has been described as

> a fantastic compound of genuine racial memories, exotic Latin learning and world history derived from Orosius and Isidore of Seville, euhemerised Celtic mythology, dynastic propaganda, folklore and pure fiction.[22]

Modern scholars have generally divided the narrative literature into four groups of tales: the Ulster or Heroic Cycle, the Mythological Cycle, the Finn Cycle and the Cycle of the Kings, a division based for the most part on the identity of the protagonists. The exploits of a number of pseudo-historical and historical kings are narrated in the Kings' Cycle and include various stories about Cormac mac Airt, the greatest of Tara's kings, who supposedly ruled in the second or third century AD. The Finn or Fenian Cycle centres on the deeds of heroes such as Finn mac Cumaill – a figure with many mythological qualities. He and his band of warriors are prominent in the lengthy late twelfth- or early thirteenth-century text *Acallam na Senórach* (Tales of the Elders of Ireland), in which the few surviving and very old members of the *fian* of Finn mac Cumaill describe events of the past in a sequence of dialogues with St Patrick. It was once thought that the tales of these youthful warriors were modelled on Viking raiders but it now appears that the *fian*, a war-band mainly composed of unmarried and landless young men, is a romanticized version of a widespread male institution found in various Indo-European societies.

Among the texts we will refer to, the *Táin Bó Cúailnge* is the best known tale of the so-called Ulster or Heroic Cycle, which also includes *Fled Bricrenn* (Bricriu's Feast) with its beheadings and competition for the champion's portion. The Mythological Cycle includes two versions of *Cath Maige Tuired* (The Battle of Moytura), an epic battle between the pagan gods of Ireland that has been compared to the battle between the Asuras and Devas in Vedic India,

(1986), p. 144.   21 J. Carey, 'Myth and mythography in *Cath Maige Tuired*', *Studia Celtica* 24–5 (1990), 53–69.   22 F.J. Byrne, *Irish kings and high-kings* (1973), p. 9.

and other stories such as *Tochmarc Étaíne* (The Wooing of Étaín) and *De Gabáil int Sída* (The Taking of the Otherworld Mound). In fact, the mythological material is to be found in varying degrees over the entire corpus of these sagas and in the topographical, ecclesiastical, legal, genealogical and historical literature. The *dindshenchas* tradition or lore of famous places is a particularly rich mythological source. This topographical material, explaining how numerous places got their names, is preserved in prose and metrical versions in manuscripts such as the twelfth-century Book of Leinster. This *dindshenchas* has been described as the 'mythical geography of the country'.[23]

Many important studies of this vast literary field have, of course, been undertaken. Much of this, in Ó Cathasaigh's terminology, has been textualist in which the focus of study is analysis of the text itself. T.F. O'Rahilly was a redoubtable exponent of the mythological approach. His *Early Irish history and mythology*, published in 1946, clearly revealed the strong mythological component in early Irish literature. While historical figures may in time metamorphose into mythical heroes, he exposed the fallacy at the heart of a euhemeristic tradition that preferred to see most of its mythic characters as historical personages.[24] He demonstrated the widespread nature of a belief in the Otherworld and explored with enthusiasm, as we shall see, the theme of solar symbolism.

The Rees brothers' 1961 *Celtic heritage* was a significant contribution to comparative studies of Irish and Welsh tradition, drawing occasional parallels with Indian institutions and mythology. The latter was a theme pursued by Myles Dillon in the 1940s and in a posthumously published study on the survivals of Indo-European speech and society. The broader Celtic world has not been neglected either and Proinsias Mac Cana published a wide-ranging survey of Irish and Continental material in his *Celtic mythology* in 1970, equating several Irish deities with their Gaulish counterparts. For instance, the name of Lug, the pre-eminent god in Irish tradition and a major figure in *Cath Maige Tuired* (The Second Battle of Moytura), is to be found in place-names such as Lugdunum (Lyon). He was equated with Mercury by Julius Caesar.[25] Anne Ross and Miranda Green have been to the fore in exploring many of the correspondences between archaeological material, classical sources and mythological references in the Celtic world.[26]

---

23 M.-L. Sjoestedt, *Gods and heroes of the Celts, translated by Myles Dillon* (1949), p. 1. 24 T.F. O'Rahilly, *Early Irish history and mythology* (1946). 25 G. Hily, *Le dieu celtique Lugus* (2012), pp 3, 121. 26 A. & B. Rees, *Celtic heritage* (1961); P. Mac Cana *Celtic mythology* (1970); A. Ross, *Pagan Celtic Britain* (1967); M. Green, 'Back to the future: resonances of the past in myth and material culture' in A. Gazin-Schwartz & C. Holtorf (eds), *Archaeology and folklore* (1999), pp 48–66; M. Green, *An archaeology of images* (2004) and references.

THE CELTIC WORLD

The term 'Celtic world' requires some explanation because it has been claimed in some archaeological circles that the ancient Celts were never a cultural entity but are a construct of modern times. Particular and understandable emphasis has been given to the archaeological diversity that is such a striking feature of the world of the Celtic-speaking peoples of the first millennium BC. These folk are known to have occupied large areas of Continental Europe in the latter part of this millennium and there is no dispute that Ireland and Britain were Celtic-speaking lands at this time too. Even though they were linguistically related, it is debatable if the peoples whom the Greeks called Celts ever considered themselves to belong to an ethnically identifiable group. Yet linguistic compatibility must have facilitated communication and relationships, and provided a sense of group identity. That said, the modern ethnic definition of the ancient Celts is indeed a recent concept. The nineteenth century saw the development of both the genetic family tree model of linguistic development and the idea of distinct biologically defined racial groups.

The Celts were given an archaeological identity with the discovery of characteristic artefacts in a great cemetery at Hallstatt, near Salzburg, in Austria and at La Tène, on Lake Neuchâtel, in Switzerland. These artefacts were part of the body of evidence that enabled the construction of the first detailed chronology of the 'Iron Age', which was divided into the two main phases named after these two sites. The discovery of La Tène swords, or brooches, or art, was then considered to be the material remains of the Celtic peoples known to Greek and Roman writers. Whether in central Europe or in Ireland, La Tène-type material was simple confirmation of the presence of Celts and an illustration of how these people shared not just a material cultural assemblage but religious beliefs and social structures as well.

This cultural-historical approach appeared to demonstrate the spread of Celtic peoples across a wide area of Europe from a Celtic 'homeland' that was usually placed in the region of the upper Rhine and Danube where the La Tène art style developed. The concept of a Celtic world extending from Ireland to central Europe and beyond is therefore of relatively recent vintage and the extent to which, in this world, there were common factors in material culture, in rural economy and in social institutions is now the subject of some healthy scrutiny thanks to the 'Celtoscepticism' of some writers – to use the term coined by Patrick Sims-Williams.[27] This sceptical approach is encapsulated in the inventive titles of works such as Malcolm Chapman's *The Celts: the construction of a myth* (1992), Simon James' *The Atlantic Celts: ancient people or*

---

27 P. Sims-Williams, 'Celtomania and Celtoscepticism', *Cambrian Medieval Celtic Studies* 36 (1998), 1–35.

modern invention? (1999) and *The Celts: origins, myths and inventions* by John Collis (2003).

Despite their common linguistic inheritance, which is not a modern myth, there are great variations in material culture, subsistence and economy discernible across the Celtic world and the supposed homogeneity once implied by the adjective 'Celtic' is now being questioned by archaeologists conscious of these contrasts and concerned that its too ready acceptance has diverted attention from the difficult questions posed by difference and diversity. Even though one scholar declared almost a century ago 'the term Celtic is indicative of language, not of race', many commentators have not given due emphasis to the significance of the emergence of a common language family, or indeed to the evidence for shared beliefs and mythologies among the insular and Continental Celtic-speaking peoples.[28] While a measure of linguistic harmony may not mean cultural accord in every respect, it is worth recalling the statement by Tacitus in his *Agricola* that in the first century AD there was no great difference in language and religion between Britons and Gauls.[29]

In Ireland, archaeological investigations at sites like Tara, Rathcroghan and Navan have helped to direct greater attention to their literary dimensions and mythological associations. The study of the Navan landscape in particular has generated a large body of work on the Ulster Cycle adding to the very extensive corpus of study on that cycle alone. Thanks to the work of many scholars it is now possible to take a deeper look at some of the mythic themes and their possible archaeological implications.

MYTHIC THEMES

The principal tale, the *Táin Bó Cúailnge*, begins in Rathcroghan. In the second recension of that epic preserved in the Book of Leinster, it commences with the famous pillow talk between Ailill and Medb 'when their royal bed had been prepared for them in Ráth Crúachain in Connacht'.[30] This account of bulls and battles recounts how the 'the men of Ireland' from Connacht, Leinster and Munster, under the leadership of Medb, undertake a *táin bó* or cattle raid into Ulster. Their objective is to seize the Donn Cúailgne, the brown bull of Cooley, so that Medb will have a bull to match the great white-horned bull, Findbennach, owned by her husband. But the men of Ulster, ruled by their king Conchobor, whose court is at Emain Macha or Navan Fort, have been cursed and suffer an annual debility, a weakness that means only the warrior Cú Chulainn (pl. 1), who was not Ulster-born, can defend the province.

28 The quotation is Eoin MacNeill's in his *Phases of Irish history* (1919), p. 3.   29 H. Mattingly, *Tacitus. The Agricola and the Germania* (1970), p. 62.   30 C. O'Rahilly, *Táin Bó Cúalnge from the Book of Leinster* (1967), p. 137.

Numerous fights with Medb's warriors culminate in the final battle when the Ulstermen, now recovered, are victorious. The superhuman Cú Chulainn, mortally wounded in single combat, dies heroically, facing his enemies and bound upright to a pillar stone. The epic ends with a lengthy battle between the two bulls in which they traverse the whole of Ireland with the Donn Cúailgne as the eventual victor. Passing Rathcroghan with the mangled remains of Ailill's prize bull on his horns, he scatters the body parts of the Findbennach in various places across Ireland before reaching his homeland in Cooley, Co. Louth, where, in his fury, he slaughters some of its inhabitants before collapsing and dying.

While the tale relates the events of a heroic past, it is, in its medieval form, a sophisticated literary creation that evolved over centuries. Latin had a considerable influence on native vernacular literature and the *Táin* contains heroic motifs found in Virgil's *Aeneid* and in the *Thebaid* and *Achilleid* of Statius. It is now clear, for example, that time and again the deeds of Cú Chulainn recall those of Achilles.[31] That aspects of Cú Chulainn's story should also appear to echo features of the life of Christ is not surprising either, since this literature was very much the product of a literate and consciously Christian environment.[32] Yet it is obvious that the *Táin*, like other stories, is permeated with mythic allusions, some of them offering intriguing glimpses into beliefs that were a part of an older Indo-European world, that of a linguistic family that included Celtic, Germanic, Indian, Iranian and others.

Some ancient myths were a part of a sacred narrative, perhaps a cosmogonic account of the beginning of the world or a cosmological tale that describes humanity's role in and experience of that world. This mythic realm is often peopled by gods and goddesses and is a stage for the deeds of other supra-human figures too. In ancient Greece, myth was seen as 'an oral, poetic performance, informed by memory and appropriate for celebrating the gods' and 'reserved for stories that are moral in their content, reverent in their attitude, and socially beneficial in their consequences'.[33] Mythic themes take many forms and even the countless remnants that survive in modern folklore should not be dismissed as the mere residue of primitive stories.

Some recurring motifs in Irish tradition may be especially revealing in so far as they reflect the hold these topics once had on archaic European thought processes and the roles they played in attempts to understand those enduring questions about the beginnings of things, about human existence and the ultimate destiny of humanity. As Mac Cana wrote, the negative, pejorative sense attached to the word 'myth', as a false report or story, began with the Greek philosophers and continued with Christian writers who equated it with

31 B. Miles, *Heroic saga and classical epic in medieval Ireland* (2011), p. 145.   32 K. McCone, *Pagan past and Christian present in early Irish literature* (1990), p. 197.   33 B. Lincoln, *Theorizing myth* (1999), pp 28–9.

the falsehood of pagan belief. In its primary sense, however, myth is an account of cosmic and cultural beginnings 'underpinning the institutions that ensure the survival and well-being of society, and representing in symbolic terms man's relationship with his environment and the supernatural powers who act upon it'.[34]

Another writer, Jaan Puhvel has clearly explained its importance and its function:

> Myth in the technical sense is a serious object of study, because true myth is by definition deadly serious to its originating environment. In myth are expressed the thought patterns by which a group formulates self-cognition and self-realization, attains self-knowledge and self-confidence, explains its own source and being and that of its surroundings, and sometimes tries to chart its destinies. By myth, man has lived, died and – all too often – killed. Myth operates by bringing a sacred (and hence essentially and paradoxically 'timeless') past to bear preemptively on the present and inferentially on the future ('as it was in the beginning, is now, and ever shall be'). Yet in the course of human events societies pass and religious systems change; the historical landscape is littered with the husks of desiccated myths. … Yet equally important is the next level of transmission, in which sacred narrative has already been secularized, myth has been turned into saga, sacred time into heroic past, gods into heroes and mythical action into 'historical' plot.[35]

As we shall see, though depicted as a dominant but capricious war-leader in the *Táin*, Queen Medb was originally a goddess of sovereignty whose name and function have an Indo-European dimension, and that cataclysmic battle of the two bulls is a distorted reflection of elements of an Indo-European myth of creation. Another mythological incident in the epic is an appearance by the god Lug. His coming in answer to a desperate Cú Chulainn's cry for help is a dramatic intervention at a moment of great confusion on the battlefield with the war goddess Nemain adding to the terror. This is a literary stratagem that confers a divinely ordained heroic status on the hero.[36]

Lug has a role in the birth of Cú Chulainn as well. The triple conception of the hero is described in one of the *remscéla* or introductory tales to the epic. It is a relatively short story that survives in two versions in several manuscripts and is believed to have been written in the first half of the eighth century.

---

34 P. Mac Cana, *The cult of the sacred centre* (2011), p. 25.   **35** J. Puhvel, *Comparative mythology* (1987), p. 2.   **36** A. Dooley, *Playing the hero: reading the Irish saga Táin Bó Cúailnge* (2006), p. 128, subjects this episode to a detailed literary analysis.

Compert Conculainn (The Birth-tale of Cú Chulainn) begins:

> Láa n-áen ro bátar mathi Ulad im Chonchobar i n-Emain Macha. No
> thathigtis énlaith mag ar Emuin. Na gelltis, conna facabtais cid mecnu na
> fér ná lossa hi talam. Ba tochomracht la hUltu anaicsiu oc collud a
> n-hírend. Imlaat nói cairptiu dia tofund láa n-and, ar ba bés léu-som
> forim én. Conchobar dana hi sudiu inna charput, ocus a fiur Deichtire,
> ossí maccdacht ...

> One day the nobles of Ulster were around Conchobar in Emain Macha.
> A birdflock used visit the plain in front of Emain. They used graze it
> until they left not even roots nor grass nor herbs in the ground. The
> Ulstermen were troubled to see them destroy their land. One day they
> harness nine chariots to pursue them, for it was a custom with them to
> hunt birds. Conchobar was there too in his chariot, and his sister
> Deichtire, and she was of childbearing age ...[37]

At first glance, this appears to be a slightly fantastical account in which
Deichtire, after various vicissitudes, finally gives birth to a son who will, of
course, become known as Cú Chulainn. A simplified version forms the first
chapter of Lady Augusta Gregory's celebrated book *Cuchulain of Muirthemne*,
published in 1902. This was a hugely influential work based on older scholarly
translations and it popularized the epic adventures of the heroes of ancient
Ulster. In a preface, William Butler Yeats declared that this was the best book
to come out of Ireland in his lifetime and that in her work she was giving
Ireland 'its *Mabinogion, its Morte d'Arthur, its Niebelungelied*'. He added, with a
poetic flourish, 'to us Irish these personages should be more important than all
others, for they lived in the places where we ride and go marketing, and
sometimes they have met with one another on the hills that cast their shadows
upon our doors at evening'.[38]

   Marion Deane has shown just how complex this short birth-tale is.[39] The
land at Emain Macha has been laid waste by a flock of birds. Deichtire and
Conchobar, king of Ulster, follow the birds southwards in his chariot
accompanied by the warriors of Ulster. Nine score beautiful birds, each pair

37 M. Deane, 'From sacred marriage to clientship: a mythical account of the establishment
of kingship as an institution' in R. Schot et al. (eds), *Landscapes of cult and kingship* (2011),
pp 1–21; text from E. Windisch, *Compert Conculainn* (1880), with spelling of personal
names emended.   38 A. Gregory, *Cuchulain of Muirthemne* (1902), pp viii, xvii.   39 M.
Deane, 'Dangerous liaisons', *Proceedings of the Harvard Celtic Colloquium* 23 (2003), 52–79;
'*Compert Conculainn*: possible antecedents?' in J.E. Rekdal & A. Ó Corráin (eds), *Proceedings
of the Eighth Symposium of Societas Celtologica Nordica* (2007), 61–85; 'Kingship: a
valedictory for the sacred marriage' in R. Ó hUiginn & B. Ó Catháin (eds), *Ulidia 2* (2009),
pp 326–42; 'From sacred marriage to clientship' (2011).

linked by a silver chain, lead the hunting party far from the wasteland until they lose sight of the flock and as night descends and as snow falls, they seek refuge in a *brug*, a great house, where they find abundant hospitality for all their number. Here, a woman is about to give birth to a boy and at the moment of his birth a mare gives birth to twin foals.

The child is nursed by Deichtire who, it transpires, is not just midwife but also mother to the child. The child is taken to Emain Macha where he falls ill and dies. A sorrowful Deichtire drinks from a copper cup and a small creature leaps from the cup to her mouth each time she sips. In her sleep she is addressed by Lug mac Ethnend who advises her that it was he who deliberately caused the devastation of the land around Emain to bring the assembly to this particular place. He tells her that she had spent the night with him, that he was the father of the child of her first pregnancy who died, but she would now be pregnant by him again. He also proclaimed *bai in mac altae, ocus ba hé tatharla inna broind* ... (he was the boy who was reared, and it was he who had come into her womb ...). He states that the foals were reared for the boy. She contrives to miscarry the child so she can remarry without liability. It appears too that Conchobar, when drunk, used to sleep with his sister. He marries her to Súaltaim mac Róig and she becomes pregnant again. A child is born and named Sétanta who will in time be renamed Cú Chulainn.

The fact that Deichtire is impregnated twice by Lug and then by Súaltaim is, not surprisingly, just one of several details unseen or transformed by Lady Gregory. Far from being a normal family scenario, this is a straightforward birth narrative on only one level. According to Deane, several mythic themes are embedded here. Deichtire appears as both midwife and mother in the episode in the *brug* and Lug is represented as the child of her first pregnancy (the boy who was reared) and both father and son of the second. Lug's union with Deichtire was incestuous, as was her relationship with Conchobar. Deane argues that this incestuous element serves to emphasize the distinction between nature and culture and represents an imaginary moment of transition when social norms prohibiting incest are introduced. I would add that incest was also probably seen as an act that marked the marginal status of king or deity outside the social order just as incestuous origins might be a characteristic of a hero.

A medieval audience would not have seen anything implausible or incongruous here, for the symbolic significance and societal implications of various details and the apparent contradictions would have alerted them to deeper meanings and resonated in ways that we can only dimly apprehend. Deane shows how the mythic dimension here correlates human actions and cosmic forces: a contest between husband and lover for a woman is paralleled by a contest between various elements of light for possession of the earth. The sacral nature of Conchobar's kingship would have been readily apparent too

and Deichtire's name, as Deane remarks, would have had a dual reference to a goddess of the land and the Otherworld (containing *tír* – land – and *dag-thír* or *deg-thír* – goodly land).

The seasonal pattern of the tale would have been well understood. The land lies waste at the beginning of winter and the sacred king Conchobar and the god Lug are both contenders for the kingship and for the fruits of the land represented by the goddess of sovereignty. The theme of a wasteland, common in Irish tradition, reflects the want of a righteous king who will restore its fertility, something Conchobar has clearly failed to preserve. Conchobar and Lug are, in varying degree, a personification of sun, sky or light and represent the fluctuating power of the sun. The departing sun and the migrating birds are harbingers of winter, Conchobar is in decline and Lug is in the ascendant. As snow falls and night descends, the sun enters the Otherworld. Lug's second impregnation of Deichtire and his declaration that he was both father and son makes sense when it is remembered that the sun generates itself and all other life. After her miscarriage, when 'she discharged the living contents of her belly', she was fully restored just as the earth with the returning sun disgorges itself of its produce and becomes sound again.

On the human level, however, Lug's conduct and Deichtire's unregulated fertility pose difficulties for her Ulster kin; an illegitimate child would present problems. Furthermore, Lug's role in the destruction of the royal territory threatened Conchobar's sovereignty. As an exemplary myth that explains the origins of particular customs and offers a model for desirable behaviour, the narrative then recounts Conchobar's return to power and its consequences. He does not engage in a sacred marriage with the goddess of sovereignty to ensure the well-being of his kingdom, but ratifies his role as a political leader by entering a contract with someone without the kin-group. He enhances his prestige and power by restructuring the laws of nature and, in establishing a marriage contract with Súaltaim to look after his affairs, he initiates the contractual relationship of clientship as a royal institution.

This interpretation of the birth-tale of Cú Chulainn introduces a modern reader to themes such as solar imagery linked to kingship and divinity, a sovereignty goddess associated with land and prosperity, sacral kingship and the Otherworld. These loom large in early Irish tradition and in different ways may have left their mark in archaeological contexts not just in Ireland but further afield.

CHAPTER 2

The Otherworld hall on the Boyne

The River Boyne rises near Carbury Hill in Co. Kildare and enters the Irish Sea south of the promontory of Clogher Head and just east of Drogheda, flowing through the fertile lands of Co. Meath. A great loop in the river near the village of Slane contains the famous prehistoric complex dominated by the great passage tombs of Newgrange, Dowth and Knowth (pl. 2). The landscape and the river itself are extraordinarily rich in mythological associations. This mythological past was just one of the challenges faced by O'Kelly when he began his major excavation campaign at Newgrange in the early 1960s.[1]

The huge mound of Newgrange was built on the highest point of a low ridge and the entrance to the tomb is on the south-east facing the Boyne. Like its counterparts at Knowth, upstream and 1km to the north-west, and Dowth a little under 2km to the north-east, its construction was an immense undertaking by a stone-using farming people. The excavations provided the first accurate plan of the celebrated monument and much detail about its construction, art and date. This approximately circular mound measures 85m in maximum diameter and about 11m in height; it covers almost 0.4 hectare (one acre) and is composed mainly of water-rolled stones. It is surrounded by a continuous line of ninety-seven large kerb stones, many of which bear decoration.

Thanks to radiocarbon dating of organic samples retrieved in the course of the excavations, we now know that the tomb chamber was built over five thousand years ago shortly before 3000BC. The 19m-long passage is lined with forty-three large upright orthostats and roofed with massive transverse slabs, the largest of which weighs an estimated ten tons. With its two lateral cells and one terminal cell, the chamber is of the common cruciform plan and is roofed with a very fine 6m-high corbelled vault. It seems that the eastern cell was the more important; it is larger than the others and contains the most decoration. Four large and slightly hollowed 'basin stones' occur in the chamber; such stones are known in other passage tombs and they possibly once contained the burnt or unburnt bones of the dead.

Because the tomb has been open since at least the late seventeenth century, little has survived of the original contents. Excavation in the chamber recovered some cremated bone (of four or five people) and the position of these bone fragments suggested to O'Kelly the possibility that the burial

1 M.J. O'Kelly, *Newgrange* (1982).

deposits were once placed in the basin stones. Objects found with the bones are typical of Irish passage tombs and include stone beads and pendants, fragments of bone pins and some small balls of polished stone (including a conjoined pair).

O'Kelly's discovery of what has been called the 'roof-box' above the entrance to the passage indicates that the face of the mound turned inwards at the entrance to permit access to this feature, which is formed by a gap between the first two roof-slabs of the passage. At dawn on the midwinter solstice, the shortest day of the year, the rays of the rising sun shine through the roof-box and briefly illuminate the chamber (pl. 3). The spectacle occurs for over a week before and after the solstice and lasts for a little over a quarter of an hour. Only on the solstice itself does the beam extend to the end cell. Indeed, it has been calculated that at the time the tomb was built, the beam of sunlight would have bisected the chamber and illuminated the end recess. Clearly the orientation of the tomb was of great importance to those who had access to the monument and solar phenomena had a very important place in their magico–religious beliefs and practices. Complex rites outside and inside the tomb were presumably timed to coincide with this midwinter event and probably occurred at other times too.

Solar ritual has been claimed elsewhere in the Boyne Valley. Two tombs are known on the western side of the large mound at Dowth and the setting sun in winter seems to illuminate the interior of the southernmost of these.[2] However, equinoctial alignments proposed at Knowth are doubtful.[3] In any event, it is not certain that these points in the year when day and night have equal lengths were significant times in the calendar of a farming community. It is also possible, of course, that our modern emphasis on astronomical precision is misplaced. As Robert Hensey reminds us, the experience of sunlight penetrating the darkness of a monument may have been a major ritual event in itself. The sun could have been perceived as a witness and a metaphor for truth or sacred knowledge.[4] As the creator of life, we should remember too that it may have been seen as an expression of sexual potency.

Excavation at Newgrange revealed that a considerable amount of material had collapsed from the mound, a layer of cairn stones 8 to 10m wide lay outside the kerb that retained the mound, and this led O'Kelly to suggest that a sloping wall of stones, almost 3m high, had rested on top of the kerb stones and that the original mound was steep-sided and flat-topped. On the south-east, a lot of angular pieces of quartz were found at the base of the collapse and he further argued that the mound, in the area of the entrance at least, was

---

2 A. Moroney, 'Winter sunsets at Dowth', *Archaeology Ireland* 13:4 (1999), 29–31.   3 F. Prendergast & T. Ray, 'Ancient astronomical alignments: fact or fiction?', *Archaeology Ireland* 16:2 (2002), 32–5.   4 R. Hensey, 'The observance of light: a ritualistic perspective on "imperfectly" aligned passage tombs', *Time and Mind: the Journal of Archaeology, Consciousness and Culture* 1 (2008), 319–30.

faced with sparkling white quartz and oval granite stones. The monument that the visitor sees today is based on this assessment. This drum-shaped reconstruction with a quartz façade is controversial and it has been proposed that the quartz and granite were laid down as a platform in front of the tomb. While O'Kelly believed Newgrange to be a single-period monument (even if its construction took several decades), turf lines recorded by him in the cairn material may in fact represent layers of vegetation that denote a long and complicated multi-period process of enlargement, perhaps over many hundreds of years.[5] The site is likely to have been a place of pilgrimage for a protracted period of time.

The cairn, it has been estimated, contains about 200,000 tons of stony material, much of it water-rolled stone transported from the river terraces of the Boyne about 1km to the south. Its stone construction is in interesting contrast to the alternating layers of stone and earth that form the great mound at Knowth. Some of the rounded stones, such as examples of granite, may have been deliberately selected many kilometres to the north from the northern shores of Dundalk Bay and transported south. Some of the quartz may have come from the Wicklow Mountains. Altogether, the tomb and the kerb that retains the mound comprise over five hundred very large stones, mostly massive greywacke slabs (a type of sandstone) and these represent the largest category by far of the imported stone used. Their most likely source is 16km to the north-east on the coast near the village of Clogherhead, just north of the mouth of the Boyne, where exposed rock would have been quarried with relative ease.[6]

Ease of extraction may not have been the only factor, of course; the seashore may have been perceived as a liminal zone that conferred a special meaning on the stones and they may have been thought to have a magical quality even before they were incorporated in the tomb.

Excavation to the south of the passage tomb revealed later activity beyond the limits and on top of the material that had slipped from the mound. There was evidence of considerable occupation: hearths, numerous pits, post-holes and stake-holes, short stretches of foundation trenches, concentrations of sherds of early Bronze Age Beaker pottery, flints and animal bones were found. One of several pits produced charcoal that was radiocarbon dated to 2488–2284BC and a bronze axehead that seems to have been an offering made somewhat later in the earlier Bronze Age. The animal remains were preponderantly those of domesticated cattle and pig, with the latter the dominant species. These may be the remains of ceremonial feasts in front of the tomb around the

5 P. Eriksen, 'The great mound of Newgrange', *Acta Archaeologica* 79 (2008), 250–73.
6 M. Corcoran & G. Sevastopulo, 'The origin of the greywacke orthostats and kerbstones at Newgrange and Knowth, Brú na Bóinne', Heritage Council March 2008 Seminar, www.heritagecouncil.ie/seandalaiocht/hci-irish-page/bru-na-boinne-research-framework-project/march-2008-seminar/?L=3, accessed 17 Dec. 2012.

end of the third and at the beginning of the second millennium BC. Other ceremonies were undoubtedly associated with pit and timber circles identified near the great mound. Whether the tomb was accessible is not known. Nothing was found within it to indicate later usage but, of course, there are many rituals that might leave no archaeological trace.

Also found were some bones of horse (some 1% of the total). These were once thought to be one of the exotic novelties, like metalworking, that seemed to coincide with the appearance of Beaker pottery. Radiocarbon dating of some teeth has demonstrated that they actually date to the first two centuries AD.[7] Iron Age activity is also attested here by the discovery over the years of various finds of Romano-British date – many of them from the area of the entrance to the tomb. These include part of a Bronze Age gold torc, originally of thirteenth-century BC date and bearing a much later and unintelligible Roman inscription, twenty-five coins ranging from the time of Domitian (AD81–96) to Arcadius (*c*.AD385), and some bronze brooches, glass beads and gold rings and bracelets.[8] Most if not all of these were votive offerings placed before the monument and the whole assemblage, and the goldwork in particular, represent an exceptionally significant pattern of deposition. The horse bones, of course, raise the possibility of equine rituals.

THE MYTHIC DIMENSION

When he published his account of the 1962–75 excavations in 1982, O'Kelly entitled his book *Newgrange: archaeology, art and legend* and, in a six-page chapter, felt obliged to address the fact that Newgrange and the other great tombs of the Boyne complex figured prominently in early Irish mythology. As he noted, medieval tradition recorded that Brug na Bóinne (the Otherworld mansion or hall of the Boyne) was the dwelling place of the Tuatha Dé Danann (the people of the goddess Danu) including the great god Dagda and his son Óengus. It was also appropriated by the early kings of Tara as the supposed burial place of their pagan ancestors. The Dagda and Óengus are both alluded to in *Tochmarc Étaíne* (The Wooing of Étaín), in which it is said the Brug belonged to Elcmar who was married to Bóand, the goddess of the River Boyne.

O'Kelly thought it possible that Newgrange's association with the chief of the gods and his son was one reason for the enduring sanctity of the monument and its focus as an offering place in Roman times. He wondered if

---

7 R. Bendrey et al., 'The origins of domestic horses in northwest Europe', *Proceedings of the Prehistoric Society* 79 (2013), 91–103. 8 R.A.G. Carson & C. O'Kelly, 'A catalogue of the Roman coins from Newgrange, Co. Meath', *Proceedings of the Royal Irish Academy* 77C (1977), 35–55. The inscription on the torc reads *SCBONS.MB*.

there was any connection between one of the traditional attributes of the Dagda as a sun god (as asserted by scholars such as T.F. O'Rahilly) and the yearly visitation of the sun to the tomb. He has nothing to say about the mythology associated with the River Boyne, but it is surely here that the Newgrange story begins.

Though often described as a cemetery, the bend of the Boyne is more than a collection of individual tombs. It is well known that the building of prehistoric monuments established or enhanced the importance of particular locations and created a new sense of order in the landscape. A cluster of small tombs at Knowth and a small tomb to the west of Newgrange may mark the beginning of small-scale monument construction in the bend of the river and in sympathy with the terrain. A later phase witnessed the emergence of the huge and complex tombs at Newgrange, Knowth and Dowth, with a greater interest in display and visibility in both art and architecture.

The great tombs now dominated the area and became the focal monuments for other small tombs and for ceremonial activities that ordered space, time and mind. Stefan Bergh has remarked that such large monuments are characterized by constructional complexity and a high investment in labour. They reflect a competitive socio-religious milieu in which certain knowledge was probably the preserve of a minority who, in their ability to predict some celestial events, appeared to control time – the ultimate expression of power. As he has written, a site like Newgrange was 'a monument of secrets'.[9] In these large monuments, rituals were based on mystery.

Large circular enclosures like a great earthwork just east of Dowth (Site Q) and various monuments in the vicinity of Newgrange demonstrate the continued importance of this sacred landscape at least to the end of the third millennium BC. While the modest early tombs effectively sanctified the landscape, it is possible that it was the river itself that first made this part of the Boyne Valley consecrated ground. The river's mythical beginnings are surprising.

The prose *Dindshenchas* records the creation of the river at its source at the well of Nechtan near Carbury Hill in Co. Kildare, where the Boyne has a prominent part in the initiation of a mythopoeic process:

> Boand ben Nechtain m*ei*c Labrada dodceha*id* docum in tobar diam[air]
> bui i n-urlaind in Sídha Nechtain. Ca*ch* óen fodriced ni ticed uad can
> maidsin a da rosc *acht* min[i]ptis hé Nech*tan* 7 a tri déogbaire .i. Flesc 7
> Lam 7 Luam a n-anmand.
> Fe*cht* and mu*s*luid Boand la dim*us* do cobfis cum*ach*ta in tobair, 7 asbe*rt*
> nad búi cum*ach*ta diamair co*n*nise*d* cumac a delba, 7 imsói tuaithbel in

---

9 S. Bergh, 'Design as message: role and symbolism of Irish passage tombs' in A. Rodríguez Casal (ed.), *O Neolítico Atlántico e as orixes do megalitismo* (1997), p. 149.

tob*uir* fo*th*ri, 7 máidhid *t*ri tonna tairsi don tob*ur*, 7 fosruidbed a sliasait 7 a [leth]laim 7 a lethsuil. Imsói di*diu* fo*r* teche*d* a haithisi co fairgi 7 an uis*ce* anadíaidh co hInbe*r* mBóinne, 7 ba hísin m*áthair* Oeng*us*a m*eic* in Dag*da*.

Vel ita: Bó ainm in [t]srotha 7 Find aband Sl*ébe* Guaire, 7 dia comr*ac* mole is ainm Boand (rectius Bófind) ...

Bóand wife of Nechtán son of Labraid went to the secret well which was in the green of Síd Nechtaín. Whoever went to it would not come from it without his two eyes bursting, unless it were Nechtán himself and his three cupbearers, whose names were Flesc and Lám and Luam.

Once upon a time Bóand went through pride to test the well's power, and declared that it had no secret force which could shatter her form, and thrice she walked withershins round the well. (Whereupon) three waves from the well break over her and deprive her of a thigh and one of her hands and one of her eyes. Then she, fleeing her shame, turns seaward, with the water behind her as far as Boyne-mouth, [where she was drowned]. Now she was the mother of Oengus son of the Dagda.

Or thus: *Bó* the name of the stream [of Síd Nechtain] and *Find* the river of Sliab Guairi, and from their confluence is the name *Bóand* [= Bó + Find] ...[10]

Here we have a tale of the imprudent visit to the forbidden well by Bóand, the wife of the god Nechtan, who three times fails to take the auspicious sunwise circuit, moving instead counter-clockwise around it. As a result, she suffers grievously for her curiosity. Three great waves erupt from the well, depriving her of an eye, a thigh and a hand. She flees and is drowned at the mouth of the Boyne river that is formed by this cataclysmic event. Two explanations are given for the name of the holy river, however; in one it is named after the river goddess Bóand herself and in another after the conjunction of the rivers *Bó* and *Find*. As Mac Cana has written, the generation of variants like this is a characteristic feature of myth, where different accounts may confirm and complement rather than contradict one another.[11] In a longer version in the eleventh-century metrical *Dindshenchas*, parts of the river are given fifteen different names and – clearly influenced by Christian monastic learning – the Boyne flows to join the Severn, the Tiber, the Jordan and others, becoming part of the great universal river that ultimately reaches 'the paradise of Adam'.[12] A similar explanation about the

10 Wh. Stokes, 'The prose tales of the Rennes Dindsenchas', *Revue celtique* 15 (1894), 315.
11 P. Mac Cana, 'Place-names and mythology in Irish tradition' in G.W. MacLennan (ed.), *Proceedings of the First North American Congress of Celtic Studies* (1988), p. 335.   12 E. Gwynn, *The Metrical Dindshenchas Part 3* (1913), 27; an emended translation is given by M.

origins of the River Shannon in the prose *Dindshenchas* seems to be borrowed from that of the Boyne.

The great scholar of comparative mythology, Georges Dumézil, identified a relationship between the Boyne story and the myth of Apam Napat in Indo-Iranian tradition. He was struck by such parallels at either extreme of the Indo-European world, a situation that appeared to exclude any possibility of horizontal transmission.[13] While aspects of Dumézil's work are debated, it is widely accepted that there are common traits to be found in many Indo-European mythologies. In the *Rig Veda*, Apam Napat is a water divinity who emits a brilliant burning force; in short, he is associated with fire and water. In the Iranian Avesta, he has similar associations as guardian of a lake containing the Xvarnah, a brilliant 'light of glory' that is a symbol of royal power. Various attempts to seize this forbidden prize cause the lake to overflow, creating a number of rivers, one of which continues to preserve the divine light.

While the Irish tale contains no mention of a fiery essence in Nechtan's well, Dumézil claimed that there must have been some such force to burst a wrongdoer's eyes. Patrick Ford then ingeniously proposed that this force was the illuminating brilliance of wisdom. He cites several instances where wells are described as a source of knowledge, including a tract in which the waters of Segais had a hazel tree growing above them. The nuts that fell therein furnished mastery of poetry to whoever drank there (and Segais is another name for the part of the Boyne that flows from the well of Nechtan).[14]

Thus there are several common themes in the Indo-Iranian and Irish traditions: these include a burning or brilliant element hidden in waters, this constituent is attainable only by those who are qualified. It is forbidden to those who are not. Three attempts are made to retrieve the Xvarnah and Bóand circles the well three times in an inauspicious direction, and illegitimate attempts to retrieve the element result in the overflowing of the waters.[15]

If, as seems likely, the story of the origins of the Boyne is part of an Indo-European tradition, then the sanctity of the river and a particular association with secret knowledge is of great antiquity. The very name, probably originally Bou-vinda, is thought to mean cow white goddess and a similar compound occurs in Sanskrit as Go-vinda, reflecting the prestige of cattle in both Indian

Herbert, 'Society and myth, *c.*700–1300' in A. Bourke et al. (eds), *The Field Day anthology of Irish writing*, 4 (2002), p. 254. 13 G. Dumézil, 'Le puits de Nechtan', *Celtica* 6 (1963), 50–61. Also G. Dumézil, *Mythe et épopée*, 3 (1973), p. 34 and at p. 67, where he suggests that the Roman legend of the overflow of Lake Albano near Rome might be a part of this tradition, but on this see M.L. West, *Indo-European poetry and myth* (2007), p. 277. 14 P.K. Ford, 'The Well of Nechtan and "La Gloire Lumineuse"' in G.J. Larson (ed.), *Myth in Indo-European antiquity* (1974), pp 67–74. On the well of Segais, see T.F. O'Rahilly, *Early Irish history and mythology*, p. 322; V. Hull, 'Early Irish *Segais*', *Zeitschrift für celtische Philologie* 29 (1962–4), 321–4. 15 E.B. Findly, 'The "Child of the Waters": a revaluation of Vedic Apam Napat', *Numen* 26 (1979), 164–84.

and Irish tradition.[16] While the bovine component is not in doubt, it has been proposed that '-vind' derives from an Indo-European form meaning knowledge or discovery.[17]

The Boyne's connection with the attainment of knowledge is echoed in Fenian tradition in the tale of Finn mac Cumaill's acquisition of the skills of healing and poetry from the salmon of knowledge that was to be found in a pool in the river.[18] Newman has indicated that the name Nechtan may be linked with the River Níth, a river that springs from a well on Tara. Though the etymology is obscure and debated, as Dumézil and others have said, both Níth and Nechtan may have Indo-European roots derived from *neigw-t-*, Sanskrit *nikta-*, 'washed, purified', Old Irish *necht-* or from Indo-European *new-* 'new, vigorous, fresh'.[19]

O'Kelly briefly alluded to the fact that the Dagda and Óengus are two divine personages associated with Newgrange. Carey, in an innovative study correlating archaeology and myth, has explored some of the textual references that touch on Brug na Bóinne.[20] In a short tale entitled *De Gabáil int Sída* (The Taking of the Otherworld Mound), the Dagda ('the good god', also called Eochaid *Ollathair*, 'Eochaid the great father') distributes the Otherworld mounds among his followers. He gives a mound called Síd Rodrubán to Lug for instance, but keeps several including Newgrange for himself. He gives nothing to his son Óengus ('the Mac Óc' or 'the young son'), who seeks a dwelling of his own. Óengus is granted a night and a day in the Brug but takes possession of it, declaring 'night and day are the whole world and that is what has been given to me'. In the twelfth-century Book of Leinster, the events are described as follows:

> There was a famous king over the Túatha Dé in Ireland.
> His name (was) Dagán. Great, then, was his power, even though it belonged to the Mac Míled after the conquest of the country, for the Túatha Dé destroyed the corn and the milk round about the Mac Míled until they made the friendship of the Dagda. Afterwards, he saved their corn and milk.

16 T.F. O'Rahilly, *Early Irish history and mythology*, p. 3; M. Dillon, *Celts and Aryans* (1975), p. 12.   17 H. Wagner, *Studies in the origins of the Celts and of early Celtic civilization* (1971), p. 23.   18 J.F. Nagy, *The wisdom of the outlaw* (1985), pp 34, 214; D. Ó hÓgáin, *Fionn mac Cumhaill* (1988), p. 55.   19 C. Newman, 'The sacral landscape of Tara' in R. Schot et al. (eds), *Landscapes of cult and kingship* (2011), p. 37; G. Dumézil, *Mythe et épopée*, 3, p. 35; also C.-J. Guyonvarc'h, 'Annexes étymologiques du commentaire. Nechtan (*Nept-ono-*) ou "le fils de la soeur"', *Celticum* 15 (1966), 377–82; G.S. Olmsted, *The gods of the Celts and the Indo-Europeans* (1994), p. 398; C. Jendza, 'Theseus the Ionian in Bacchylides 17 and Indo-Iranian Apām Napāt', *Journal of Indo-European Studies* 41 (2013), 431–57.   20 J. Carey, 'Time, memory and the Boyne necropolis', *Proceedings of the Harvard Celtic Colloquium* 10 (1990), 24–36.

Now when he was king at first, his might was vast, and it was he who apportioned out the fairy mounds to the men of the Túatha Dé, namely Lug Mac Ethnend in Síd Rodrubán, (and) Ogma in Síd Aircelltrai, but for the Dagda himself Síd Leithet Lachtmaige, Oí Asíd, Cnocc Báine, (and) Brú Ruair. As, however, they say, he had Síd In Broga from the beginning.

Then Mac Oac came to the Dagda in order to petition for land after it had been distributed to each one. He was, moreover, a fosterling to Midir of Brí Léith and to Nindid, the seer.

'I have none for thee', said the Dagda. 'I have completed the division'.

'Therefore let be granted to me', said the Mac Ooc, 'even a day and a night in thy own dwelling'.

That then was given to him.

'Go now to thy following', said the Dagda, 'since thou hast consumed thy (allotted) time'.

'It is clear', said he, 'that night and day are (the length of) the whole world, and it is that which has been given to me'.

Thereupon the Dagda went out, and the Mac Ooc remained in his Síd. Wonderful, moreover, (is) that land. Three trees with fruit are there always, and a pig eternally alive, and a roasted swine, and a vessel with marvellous liquor, and never do they all decrease.[21]

A version of how Óengus gained possession of the Brug is also told in *Tochmarc Étaíne* (The Wooing of Étaín), perhaps first written in the ninth century. Here we learn that he was conceived by the Dagda with the goddess Bóand (also known as Eithne), who was the wife of a certain Elcmar, and that Óengus was conceived and born in the one day. He was 'begotten at the break of day and born betwixt it and evening'.[22] In *Tochmarc Étaíne*, Elcmar (another name for Nechtan) occupies the Brug and the Dagda tells Óengus how to deceive him into yielding possession. He is to seek kingship for a day and a night in the Brug but this is to mean for all eternity, for 'it is in days and nights that the world is spent'. Elcmar is tricked in this fashion and has to move to another Otherworld mound at nearby Cleittech somewhere on the Boyne.

In a third late tale, *Altram Tighe Dá Mheadar* (The Fosterage of the House of Two Vessels), Óengus gains the Brug by placing Elcmar under an enchantment that will last until the end of time 'until heaven and earth are mingled together, and until sun and moon are mingled together'.[23] As Carey

---

21 V. Hull, 'De Gabáil in t-Sída (concerning the seizure of the fairy mound)', *Zeitschrift für celtische Philologie* 19 (1933), 53–8. For another translation entitled 'The Taking of the Hollow Hill' by J. Carey, see J. T. Koch & J. Carey (eds), *The Celtic heroic age* (1995), p. 134. 22 O. Bergin & R.I. Best, 'Tochmarc Étaíne', *Ériu* 12 (1938), 143. A translation by J. Carey is to be found in Koch & Carey, *The Celtic heroic age*, p. 135. 23 Translation: L. Duncan,

demonstrates, these three versions share a common theme: Óengus wins the Brug through the power of the word, through verbal dexterity or magic, which, significantly, involves the manipulation of time.

Knowth too has its mythological associations, including an allusion in a twelfth-century bardic poem where 'the cave of Knowth' is instanced as an entrance to the Otherworld, to Emain Ablach, the Arthurian Avalon.[24] A statement in the metrical *Dindshenchas* declares that this was 'the hill of Buí', the burial place of one of the wives of the great god Lug. Her name may be derived from *Buvya, meaning 'the cow-like one'.[25] Ó Cathasaigh has gathered some disparate strands of evidence in early literature to argue that this Buí is a manifestation of the goddess of sovereignty, the personification of the land and its fertility, and the source of the power of sacral kingship.[26]

Dowth, known in early literature as both Dubad and Síd mBresail (the Otherworld mound of Bresal) features in *Tochmarc Emire* (The Wooing of Emer), where the warrior Cú Chulainn travels 'between the god and his prophet' that is between *'Mac Óg i Síth in Broga'* (Newgrange) and *Síth mBresail* (Dowth).[27] In the metrical *Dindshenchas*, this Bresal is credited with the building of the great tumulus and once again the manipulation of time occurs. His sister casts a spell that fixes the sun in the sky so that a day might last indefinitely and allow the task to be completed. Bresal lustfully commits incest with her and the spell is broken and the sun departs. Since the construction work has been darkened (*ro dubad*), 'Dubad (darkness) shall to be the name of this place forever'.[28] It is a remarkable coincidence, as Carey says, that these legends should reflect control over time and that archaeological excavation has revealed solar ritual at Newgrange. Like O'Kelly, he notes that they raise the question whether tales recorded in medieval times might echo the beliefs of Neolithic tomb-builders millennia before.

It is difficult for the modern mind to grasp the impact the appearance of the solstice sun must have had for those who witnessed it. For the prehistoric spectator, this was the rebirth of the sun, the equivalent of the Resurrection for the medieval Christian, and a mystical happening of such significance that it too should be recounted generation after generation. There is evidence that Newgrange was the location of occult practices in the eleventh century AD (see

'Altram Tige Dá Medar', *Ériu* 11 (1932), 209.   24 F.J. Byrne, 'Historical note on Cnogba (Knowth)', *Proceedings of the Royal Irish Academy* 66C (1968), 383–400.   25 H. Wagner, 'Origins of pagan Irish religion', *Zeitschrift für celtische Philologie* 38 (1981), 6.   26 T. Ó Cathasaigh, 'The eponym of Cnogba', *Éigse* 23 (1989), 27–38.   27 A.G. van Hamel, *Compert Con Culainn and other stories* (1933), p. 37. C. Swift, 'The gods of Newgrange in Irish literature and Romano-Celtic tradition' in G. Burenhult & S. Westergaard (eds), *Stones and bones* (2003), p. 58, argues the absence of firm evidence to equate *Síth in Broga* with Newgrange.   28 E. Gwynn, *The Metrical Dindshenchas Part 4* (1924), p. 272; J. Carey, 'Time, memory and the Boyne Necropolis', 27; M.J. O'Kelly & C. O'Kelly, 'The Tumulus of Dowth, County Meath', *Proceedings of the Royal Irish Academy* 83C (1983), 147.

below) when the monument was probably a place of ritual and myth telling. Its associated myths may have been retold, reshaped and developed over many generations, but retained the fundamentally important elements that reflected its sacred beginnings.

THE TRANSMISSION OF TRADITION

The longevity of potent myths anchored to a monument like Newgrange need not surprise. Enduring monuments like this could well be the focus for the preservation of remnants of the beliefs of a pre-literate society, just as the myths associated with natural and other man-made features in the landscape survive in an attenuated fashion in the place-lore of the *dindshenchas*. Thomas has observed (writing of some Neolithic monuments in south-west Scotland) that 'durable monuments, principally those composed of earth and stone, had a mnemonic capacity. Their continued presence and reuse brought the past into the present ... '.[29]

When writing of the royal site of Rathcroghan, I speculated that a person standing on the great focal mound in that complex in later prehistoric times would have had a view of a landscape saturated with meaning. More than twenty-five burial mounds would have been visible from this vantage point and were testimony to the funerary importance and sanctity of the place as a whole in later prehistory. They proclaimed the relationship of the community to land and ancestors and probably served as mnemonic devices for remembering the past and for structuring oral history. The relatively inconspicuous nature of most of them today belies their ancient significance and we may be reasonably sure they were points of reference in both a ritual and a mythological landscape in which territorial and genealogical rights were expressed in both monument and oral tradition.

If the dates of these various mounds span one or even two millennia, then a visitor to Rathcroghan at the dawn of the Christian era may have been confronted by a landscape associated with a mix of mythical and historical personages. Some recent burial places will have been credited to persons still in living memory, perhaps extending several generations back into mythical time, but the conception of a historical past was in all likelihood constrained in such a pre-literate society.[30] As Mircea Eliade and others have reported, in such societies the recollection of a real person or a historical event would survive in popular memory for two or three centuries at most when the individual would then be assimilated to their mythical model – such as a hero.

29 J. Thomas, 'The identity of place in Neolithic Britain' in A. Ritchie (ed.), *Neolithic Orkney* (2000), p. 86.   30 J. Waddell et al., *Rathcroghan, Co. Roscommon* (2009), p. 205.

An event would be identified with a category of mythical action – such as a fight with a monster.[31]

However it does not always follow that oral tradition becomes unstable or corrupt within a few hundred years, it can have a much longer historical dimension. This would appear to be the case among the Tlingit people of south-eastern Alaska, for example, where tales such as 'The First War in the World', recorded early in the twentieth century (about a memorable early battle), relate events associated with settlements and places in the Dundas Bay region. Geological studies have determined that this area was available for settlement on glacial sediments at the quiescent glacier front shortly after AD1000 but was engulfed by the advancing ice during the following Little Ice Age. The ice began to retreat some time before AD1794 and recent decades have seen the identification of settlements and topographical features referred to in Tlingit oral tradition in this area.

Excavation at one settlement associated with the celebrated conflict demonstrated that it was founded around AD1150 and vacated several centuries later as the ice advanced. It has been possible to establish a correlation between oral tradition and landscape changes such as glacial advance, rising sea levels, settlement and population displacement. Archaeological excavation and radiocarbon dating have all helped to provide a broad chronological framework for these events. Even though some chronological inconsistencies occur in oral narratives (several battles are probably compressed in that story of the inception of Tlingit warfare for instance), oral tradition is judged to be strongly historical for some 850 years. Among the factors that probably contributed to this historical conservatism are the role these traditions played in maintaining group identities, perpetuating rights to land and resources, and structuring social interaction.[32]

Undoubtedly, the monuments and landscape of the Boyne Valley were also the subject of numerous oral narratives that bore witness over a very long timespan to events and people of an ancestral past. But it is quite an exceptional place because no other megalithic complex has such a rich surviving mythology, though in a few cases elsewhere scraps of folklore have lingered to this day. A cluster of cairns on the summit of Knockma, near Tuam in Co. Galway, is almost certainly a small passage tomb cemetery. In modern times, its folklore was dominated by the figure of Finnbheara, a fairy chieftain with a habit of enticing beautiful women to his Otherworld domain. In medieval literature, he figures briefly in several tales including *Altram Tighe Dá Mheadar* (The Fosterage of the House of Two Vessels), where he pays a visit to Óengus in the Brug to see the womenfolk there:

31 M. Eliade, *The myth of the eternal return* (1971), p. 43; R. Bradley, *The past in prehistoric societies* (2002), p. 8.   32 A.L. Crowell & W.K. Howell, 'Time, oral tradition and archaeology at Xakwnoowú', *American Antiquity* 78 (2013), 3–23.

> ... tainig Finnbharr Meadha o Sidh maelcnocach Meadha gunuigi in
> mBrug os Boinn d'fechain an banntrachta sin ...

> ... so came Finnbarr Meadha from the bleak-hilled Sidh Meadha, to the
> Brugh by the Boyne to see those women ... .[33]

The passage-tomb cemetery at Loughcrew, Co. Meath, is known as *Sliabh na Caillí*, 'the hag's mountain'. It has several hilltop cairns attributed to the Cailleach Bhéarra and supposedly created by stones dropped from her apron.[34] In modern folklore, stories of this female figure are widespread in Ireland and in Gaelic Scotland and she is sometimes linked to megalith construction as at the well-known megalithic tomb at Labbacallee (*Leaba na Caillí*, 'the hag's bed') in Co. Cork.

It is of interest that Loughcrew should also be one of those megalithic sites where, as at Newgrange and Knowth, later Iron Age activity is attested. Thousands of fragments of small bone slips were recovered from one of the passage tombs here and, far from being a craftsman's 'trial pieces', they are much more likely (given their context) to have had some cultic purpose, as Barry Raftery noted.[35] Some bear La Tène art usually dated on rather uncertain stylistic grounds to about the first century AD. The great majority of these small slips are plain, however, and were produced by carefully shaping and polishing pieces of cattle rib-bones and they may have been used in some divinatory practice. Tacitus records a ritual akin to casting the bones in his *Germania*:

> For omens and the casting of lots they have the highest regard. Their
> procedure in casting lots is always the same. They cut off the branch of a
> nut-bearing tree and slice it into strips; these they mark with different
> signs and throw them completely at random onto a white cloth. Then the
> priest of the state, if the consultation is a public one, or the father of the
> family if it is private, offers a prayer to the gods, and looking up at the
> sky picks up three strips, one at a time, and reads their meaning from the
> signs previously scored on them.[36]

---

33 L. Duncan, 'Altram Tige Dá Medar', 193, 212. Folklore: R. Lynch, *The Kirwans of Castlehacket, Co. Galway* (2006). The claim that Knockma was Cúil Cheasra, the burial place of Cesair, granddaughter of Noah, who came with her entourage to Ireland before the Deluge, is a seventeenth-century antiquarian invention. H. Morris, 'Dun na mBarc and the Lady Ceasiar', *Journal of the Royal Society of Antiquaries of Ireland* 63 (1933), 81, has argued that a large prehistoric mound at Knockadoobrosna, near Boyle, Co. Roscommon, is a likely contender for the burial place of Cesair. On Cesair, see: J. Carey, 'Origin and development of the Cesair legend', *Éigse* 22 (1987), 37–48.   34 E. Hull, 'Legends and traditions of the Cailleach Bheara or Old Woman (Hag) of Beare', *Folklore* 38 (1927), 244.   35 B. Raftery, 'Iron Age Ireland' in D. Ó Cróinín (ed.), *A new history of Ireland* (2005), p. 159.   36 H. Mattingly, *Tacitus*, p. 109.

The occasional reuse of prehistoric burial mounds and cairns for ironworking seems to be a further ritual use of such sites. Invariably and unfortunately undated, this sort of magical metallurgy has been recorded at a number of megalithic tombs and one early medieval blacksmith who practised his skills at Tara was described as 'a man learned in occult arts and a prophet of note …'[37] One wonders if some of the Iron Age interest in Neolithic chambered tombs in the north of Scotland, identified by Richard Hingley, had occult purposes too.[38]

The repeated reuse of megalithic tombs in later prehistory may have been a widespread phenomenon, but one not often explored or easily recognized. There is intriguing evidence from one of the monuments in the passage-tomb cemetery at Carrowmore, Co. Sligo. A boulder circle (no. 26) may once have had a central chamber and some cremated bone and a fragment of a mushroom-headed antler pin probably came from this destroyed feature. A ditch inside the boulder circle and a setting of four posts inside a gap in the circle date to about the sixth century BC, as do three cultivation ridges and deposits of three different kinds of cereals (barley, rye and oats) found in a nearby pit. The excavator interpreted this as ritual cultivation for sacrificial purposes within the modified monument.[39]

Another sort of adaptation took place at a passage tomb at Kiltierney, Co. Fermanagh. In the first century BC or the second century AD a ditch was dug around the monument, the mound was enlarged and nineteen small mounds averaging about 3m in diameter and 1m high were built around its circum-ference just outside the ditch, forming, in effect, a discontinuous outer bank in ring-barrow fashion. Some cremated burials were placed in shallow pits in the augmented original mound and one was accompanied by a bronze fibula and four glass beads. Some cremated bone was found beneath some of the small satellite mounds and one produced a cremation, an iron fibula and burnt fragments of decorated bronze, possibly part of a mirror handle.[40]

There is one other outstanding Irish example of repetitious reuse. A fascinating sequence of votive offerings was identified by William O'Brien in a small nondescript tomb in Altar townland, near Schull, in west Cork. The monument, a wedge tomb, seemed to have been aligned on Mizen Peak 13km to the south-west and it has been suggested that this was an orientation towards the setting sun at the feast of Samhain. Excavation produced some evidence of burial, a little cremated bone of a human adult was found near the entrance and a single unburnt tooth was recovered. No artefacts were found. At first glance, these results might be considered unpromising but a programme of radiocarbon dating of a number of samples from a few carefully selected

37 B.G. Scott, *Early Irish ironworking* (1990), pp 149, 185.   38 R. Hingley, 'Ancestors and identity in the later prehistory of Atlantic Scotland', *World Archaeology* 28 (1996), 231–43. 39 G. Burenhult, *The archaeological excavation at Carrowmore, Co. Sligo* (1980), p. 37; S. Bergh, *Landscape of the monuments* (1995), p. 190.   40 A. Hamlin & C. Lynn (eds), *Pieces of*

contexts provided unexpected and exciting insights into a protracted pattern of ritual usage.

It revealed a remarkable depositional sequence: the unburnt tooth dated initial activity to 2316–1784BC; charcoal from a small pit near the centre of the chamber was dated to 1250–832BC and might indicate some sort of depositional practice that could have included offerings of food or some other perishables; charcoal found near the rear of the chamber provided slightly later dates of 998–560BC and 766–404BC. More charcoal from a small pit on the south side of the chamber was dated to the period 356BC–AD68 and a deposit of periwinkle and limpet shells inside the entrance was of later date: 2BC– AD230. A pit in the centre of the chamber contained various deposits of shells (periwinkle and limpet) and fish-bones (wrasse and eel). Three dates for the upper fill place some of this activity in the second century AD. The initial rites at Altar seems to have involved just the deposition of token deposits of human remains but the placing of food offerings, including fish and shellfish, appears to have figured prominently in later times. Clearly it was regarded as a sacred place over a remarkably long span of time and the events that took place within the chamber, as O'Brien suggested, were probably intended to mediate with the Otherworld.[41]

Like some of the folklore attached to prehistoric monuments in various countries, the few tales ascribed to Loughcrew and those associated with Knockma are probably the folkloric remnants of a richer mythic past, now utterly lost to us.[42] If so, then this is a telling reminder of just how exceptional is the mythology of the Boyne, linked as it is both to the river and to individual monuments. The river, as we have seen, was a source of secret knowledge and its goddess was the mother of the god of Newgrange. In brief, the Boyne had a creative part in the story of the tomb, a role also expressed in the very stones used in its construction.

ACTS OF CREATION

It will be remembered that O'Kelly estimated that the mound of Newgrange contained about 200,000 tons of stony material, much of it transported from the river terraces of the Boyne about 1km away. Indeed, he thought that a water-filled feature[43] near the river might have been the quarry used. It is much more likely that the exposed riverbank was a readily accessible source. Furthermore, if the great greywacke stones were sourced on the coast at

the past (1988), p. 24.   **41** W. O'Brien, *Sacred ground: megalithic tombs in coastal south-west Ireland* (1999), pp 91, 201.   **42** For example in Britain, see L.V. Grinsell, *Folklore of prehistoric sites in Britain* (1976) and in the southern Netherlands, N. Roymans, 'The cultural biography of urnfields', *Archaeological Dialogues* 1 (1995), 2–24.

Clogherhead, then they were most likely transported by water southwards along the coast to the river mouth and then up the Boyne to Newgrange. If this was the case, the river played a fundamental part in the actual creation of the monument. It had a magical role too – as a source of esoteric knowledge. This wisdom was the basis of the power of the initiates who used the monument to display their ability to predict solar events and who appeared to control the very course of the sun. Furthermore, before Newgrange, it is quite possible that the river had a similar role in facilitating the construction of the first megalithic tomb in the area, wherever that was. Thus we should consider the hallowed river to be the primary sacred feature in this landscape.

As the Indo-European roots of the creation myth of the river show, some mythic themes may have an especially long lifespan. As we shall see (in ch. 3), archaeological evidence demonstrates that a belief in the heavenly voyage of the sun to the Otherworld was a part of European cosmology for almost two thousand years. Since the enlargement of Newgrange and the ceremonial activity there may have spanned a millennium, the river myth could have been grafted to the story of the mound many generations after its primary building phase when, however, the immense feat of its construction was still remembered.

It is quite conceivable that figures such as the Dagda (whose epithet *Ollathair*, 'the great father', is similar to that used of the Indo-European 'father god' as in Latin *Iuppiter* and Vedic *Díaus pítar*),[44] Óengus and Bóand or their precursors – and events associated with them – were a part of the beliefs of those who frequented Newgrange over such a long timespan. Aspects of their myths may well be incorporated in constructional and morphological elements of the monument. Though difficult – if not impossible – to identify with any certainty, it is possible too that secret knowledge, solar concepts and even such mythic events as the triple waves that created the Boyne are encoded in the passage tomb art. The answer to the question may always elude us but maybe this primordial catastrophe is represented by the well-known triple spiral motif.

The creation myth of the River Boyne and the river's particular association with secret knowledge assuredly has a bearing on the Newgrange tale, just as the solar phenomena there, centred on the periodic penetration of sunlight, is reflected in the monument's association with the Dagda who, among his various manifestations, was a solar deity and was also renowned for his wisdom and sexual prowess.[45]

Important medieval settlement has been recorded at Knowth, and judging from the souterrain discovered at Dowth, settlement took place there too in

43 Illustrated in G. Stout, *Newgrange and the Bend of the Boyne* (2002), fig. 26.   44 Also in Greek, Luvian and Hittite: C. Watkins, *How to kill a dragon* (1995), p. 8.   45 T.F. O'Rahilly, *Early Irish history and mythology*, p. 469; E.A. Gray, *Cath Maige Tuired* (1982), p. 121.

early medieval times. These locations, no doubt, give their inhabitants status and legitimacy. The attachment of souterrains to the northern tomb at Dowth and to both the western and eastern passage tombs at Knowth is much more than just evidence of domestic activity. The power of the Otherworld was still appreciated in the early medieval period and the attachment of a souterrain to a sacred place probably means that the practice of subterranean storage had a ritual dimension too. The very act of underground deposition was probably associated with a belief in the protective capabilities of the chthonic powers. The notion that the Knowth tombs were still places of potent magic for some in or about the eighth century is supported by the presence of a series of inscribed names in insular script and a number of ogam inscriptions found for the most part in or near the chamber areas. The latter inscriptions are cryptic ogams and their enigmatic status seems to imply that they had a special meaning for the elite few who might understand them.[46]

Newgrange, however, was different and remained inviolate and undisturbed by Iron Age and early medieval settlement. As we have seen, Romano-British offerings demonstrate that it was a focus of votive gifts in the early centuries AD. That it was a place of occult deeds almost a thousand years later suggests that it was still venerated in medieval times. A great plague in 1084 prompted the following interesting entry in the Annals of Tigernach:

> A great pestilence in this year, which killed a fourth of the men of Ireland. It began in the south, and spread throughout the four quarters of Ireland. This is the causa causans of that pestilence, to wit, demons that came out of the northern isles of the world, to wit, three battalions, and in each battalion there were thirty and ten hundred and two thousand, as Oengus Óc, the son of the Dagda, related to Gilla Lugan, who used to haunt the fairy-mound every year on Halloween …[47]

It is particularly striking that half a millennium after the introduction of Christianity some of the old gods were evidently acknowledged and, even more noteworthy, that this Gilla Lugan should still apparently be a regular and persistent visitor to the Otherworld mound of Óengus at the great feast of Samhain, when he evidently communed with the son of the Dagda. Whether his visits involved entering the tomb we do not know, but the Otherworld Hall of Óengus evidently retained its potent magic in the eleventh century.

Within a century or so, Newgrange would become a part of the extensive farmlands of the Cistercian abbey of Mellifont. In time, it would acquire its

46 C. Swift, 'Commentary: the Knowth oghams in context' in F.J. Byrne et al., *Excavations at Knowth 4* (2008), p. 127; the location of the inscriptions in both tombs is shown on p. 91.
47 Wh. Stokes, 'The Annals of Tigernach. Fourth fragment', *Revue celtique* 17 (1896), 416.

present English name, the name of the ancient Brug dimly preserved in place-names like Breo Park and the Ford of Brow on the River Boyne.[48] However, the sacred knowledge that the mound embodied and the role the river played in its making would still survive in mythic guise in medieval texts. Newgrange is particularly significant, therefore, because it is an instance where there is some agreement between prehistoric archaeology and ancient myth – both appear to tell a similar story about the creation and usage of the monument.

48 G. Stout, *Newgrange* (2002), p. 67 and fig.11.

CHAPTER 3

The elusive image

If figures like Conchobar, king of Ulster, and the god Lug were both personifications of the sun, then solar imagery was a subtle but potent metaphor in early Irish literature. Many writers have believed that Lug, whose name means brightness or light, was a solar figure,[1] but unambiguous evidence for a solar cult is still hard to identify in early texts. True, T.F. O'Rahilly did claim, in his monumental *Early Irish history and mythology*, that the statement by St Patrick, in his *Confessio*, that 'the splendour of the material sun, which rises every day at the bidding of God, will pass away, and those who worship it will go into dire punishment', was incontrovertible historical proof, from an unimpeachable authority, that the pagan Irish worshipped the sun. He argued with great erudition that numerous mythic figures were ultimately the expression of a pre-eminent solar deity. He suggested that the sun-god, the lord of the Otherworld, was known by many names in Ireland and combined the attributes of figures such as the Dagda or Eochaid *Ollathair* ('Eochaid the great father') who 'used to rule the weather and the crops', the one-eyed Balar, Nuadu and many others. The name of the legendary king Eochaid *Ánchenn* ('Eochaid of the glowing head') was, he thought, one piece of evidence that the head was a symbol of the sun.

O'Rahilly believed that one Mac Cécht was a euhemerization of Dian Cécht, a physician and god of healing, who may have been a sun god because he appeared as a traveller of the heavens journeying all over Ireland before morning. The latter's name is usually considered to combine the words 'swift' and 'power', but for O'Rahilly 'swift' might also signify 'quickly revolving' like a wheel.[2] He thought a certain Mac Roth, a messenger of Ailill and Medb in the first recension of the *Táin Bó Cúailnge*, was a solar symbol because he circled the island in a single day like the sun: *Mac Roth, techtaire Ailella 7 Medba – is é timchellas Hérind i n-óenló* (Mac Roth, the messenger of Ailill and Medb – he it is who could go all round Ireland in one day).[3]

Solar symbolism has also been associated with kings of Tara. One of the seven taboos 'that the sun should not rise while he is in bed in the plain of Tara', and another prohibition on Conaire Mór in the tale *De Shíl Chonairi Móir* (Of the Seed of Conaire Mór) that the sun should neither set nor rise on

---

1 References: T.F. O'Rahilly, *Early Irish history and mythology*, p. 513 (who disagreed); D. Gricourt & D. Hollard, 'Lugus et le cheval', *Dialogues d'histoire ancienne* 28 (2002), 126.
2 T.F. O'Rahilly, *Early Irish history and mythology*, pp 58ff, 292, 304, 469–70, 472, 519.
3 C. O'Rahilly, *Táin Bó Cúailnge* (1976), p. 39.

him in Tara, have been considered an indication of the solar nature of Tara's kings as the representatives of the sun on earth.[4]

Such brief allusions are slender evidential threads for a solar cult, but one Mug Ruith has a larger literary presence. He appears as a euhemerized magician or wonder-working druid with an amalgam of pagan and Christian traits. According to O'Rahilly, he was originally a solar deity whose name was Roth (wheel) and was associated with the *roth rámach* (oared wheel), the 'oars' supposedly being the rays of the sun. Mug Ruith figures prominently in the thirteenth- or fourteenth-century *Forbais Dromma Damgaire* (The Siege of Druimm Damgaire also called the Siege of Knocklong)[5] and in a ninth-century poem *Mug Ruith, rígfhili cen goí* (Mug Ruith, a royal poet without falsehood).[6]

Mug Ruith's exploits in the Siege of Druimm Damgaire represent an instance of the protection of kings by supernatural means found in several early medieval texts.[7] His name means 'slave of the wheel' and 'day and night were equally bright' to those who travelled in his chariot (*ba comhsolus la ocus aghaidh don lucht no bidh ann*). In defending a Munster king against an unjust attack by Cormac mac Airt, king of Tara, the feats of this formidable practitioner of magical arts included the creation of a well to provide water, the generation of a black mist with his breath and, dressing in his shaman-like druidic costume of bull hide with bird mask, the production of a fire-storm to force the retreat of Cormac's warriors:

> Tucad tra a seche thairb maeil uidhir co M*ogh* R*uith*, 7 a encennach alath brec con-a foluam*ain* ethaidi, 7 a aidme draidh*echta* ar cena. *Ocus* dosrala suas a comuidecht na teined ind aeor 7 i firmi*mint* 7 gabust*ar* ac sodh 7 ag bual*adh* na tein*ed* budh t*huaidh*, 7 ro chan in reth*oric*-so: 'Saigti druadh dolbaim-si, 7 *rel.*'

> The bull-hide from a horn-less brown bull belonging to Mogh Ruith was now brought to him along with his speckled bird-mask with its billowing wings and the rest of his druidic gear. He proceeded to fly up into the sky and the firmament along with the fire, and he continued to turn and beat the fire towards the north as he chanted a rhetoric: 'I fashion druids' arrows ...'[8]

While his supernatural qualities are not in doubt, Mug Ruith is a less than convincing solar symbol though at first glance the *roth rámach* (oared wheel)

4 H. Wagner, *Studies in the origins of the Celts*, p. 58 n. 2.   **5** S. Ó Duinn, *Forbhais Droma Dámhgháire* (1992).   **6** J. Carey, 'An Old Irish poem about Mug Ruith', *Journal of the Cork Historical and Archaeological Society* 110 (2005), 113–34.   **7** B. Slavin, 'Supernatural arts, the landscape and kingship in early Irish texts' in R. Schot et al. (eds), *Landscapes of cult and kingship*, p. 83.   **8** Text: M.-L. Sjoestedt, 'Forbuis Droma Damhghaire', *Revue celtique* 43

might seem a promising motif to pursue. Because of his heathen history, medieval writers, in combining native and Christian lore, credited Mug Ruith with being an assistant of the heretical Simon Magus (who also had the ability to take to the air) and, even worse, with the horrific crime of beheading John the Baptist.[9] The apocalyptic appearance of the *roth rámach*, bringing death and destruction, was seen as vengeance for this sin and what aspects of this puzzling artefact should be accepted as pagan cult emblem or apocryphal invention is difficult to say. As we have seen, O'Rahilly thought it a solar symbol, as have others, but other proposals include a flying machine, a ritual whirling bull-roarer and a comet.[10] While the figure of Mug Ruith probably represents genuine native tradition, his association with the *roth rámach*, whatever it was, is difficult to explain; it may have been, like his bull hide and bird mask, a part of his druidic apparatus.

It is not at all surprising that Mac Cana in his *Celtic mythology* saw little or no evidence of solar mythology in early Ireland. He thought that Patrick's condemnation of sun worship was one of the theological commonplaces he acquired during his religious training. In a succinct appraisal, he wrote:

> if one excludes this, then in all the substantial remains of Irish tradition there is hardly any worthwhile evidence of a cult of the sun. There is, it is true, an abundance of solar symbolism, or motifs that lend themselves to such an interpretation, and there are gods who, like the Gaulish Apollo, are associated with attributes of the sun; but one can scarcely speak of sun-worship as such without doing violence to the extant traditions of Ireland and Wales.[11]

Even more recently the very scant evidence in literary and epigraphic sources for a solar cult among the Continental Celts has prompted an equally negative conclusion.[12]

In some circles, a belief in the importance and ubiquity of solar mythology has really never recovered from the over-enthusiastic advocacy of the subject by that great Victorian student of Sanskrit studies and professor of Comparative Philology at Oxford, Max Müller. The school of solar mythologists he

(1926), 62, 110 (quotations); English trans.: S. Ó Duinn, *Forbhais Droma Dámhgháire*, pp 59, 103.   9 A.M. O'Leary, 'Mog Ruith and apocalypticism in eleventh-century Ireland' in J.F. Nagy (ed.), *The individual in Celtic literatures* (2001), p. 51.   10 K. Müller-Lisowski, 'La légende de St Jean dans la tradition irlandaise et le druide Mog Ruith', *Études celtiques* 3 (1938), 57; E. O'Curry, *Lectures on the manuscript materials of ancient Irish history* (1861), p. 401 (flying machine); R.A.S. Macalister, 'Temair Breg', *Proceedings of the Royal Irish Academy* 34C (1919), 351 (bull-roarer); P. McCafferty & M. Baillie, *The Celtic gods* (2005), p. 83 (comet). E. Gwynn, *The Metrical Dindshenchas Part 4*, p. 426, saw Mog Ruith's association with this object as the result of etymological speculation.   11 P. Mac Cana, *Celtic mythology* (1970), p. 32.   12 A. Hofeneder, 'Vestiges of sun worship among the Celts', *Pandanus '10* 4:2 (2010), 85–107.

represented has even been described as dangerous to the sanity of the modern reader.[13] K.H. Jackson too had a dim view of solar mythology, remarking that 'sun-gods are still with us, lurking nowadays on the outer fringes of scholarship'.[14] To some degree all of this must have encouraged Mac Cana's rather negative assessment of the admittedly tenuous literary evidence.

The condemnation of sun worship by St Patrick, however, was not necessarily a formulaic utterance and the scarcity of unambiguous traces of a sun cult in early literature may well be a testimony to the censorious abilities of Christian editors and to the very potency of the pagan beliefs they encountered in the tales they recorded. Indeed, Mac Cana would later admit that this was very likely to have been the case:

> Anthropologists have shown that Christian missionaries elsewhere have tended to concentrate their fire on ritual and certain other areas of belief which conflicted with central tenets of Christianity while at the same time tolerating the continuance of less crucial areas of popular indigenous religion … It is hardly surprising therefore that Irish monastic redactors, for all their inherited empathy with native tradition in general, did not chose to record substantive accounts of native cosmology and eschatology, though it should be said that there are indeed many scattered fragments that point to the existence of such mythologies in pre-Christian oral literature.[15]

Here we surely have the reason for the absence of any extensive trace in early Irish literature of those great myths about the creation and end of the world that are such a feature of other Indo-European mythologies. Just how a cosmogonic theme has been reworked almost out of all recognition is illustrated by the curious finale to the *Táin Bó Cúailnge*, where the dismembered parts of the defeated Connacht bull Findbennach are scattered by the Donn Cúailnge, the bull of Cooley, to create features of the Irish landscape (Athlone or Áth Luain, the ford of the haunch, being just one example). This is a distorted reflection, it seems, of elements of an Indo-European myth of creation where the theme of dismemberment figures in naming or origin legends.[16]

SOLAR JOURNEYS

There is, of course, a large body of archaeological evidence to support the thesis of a widespread solar cult of some description. It is true, as Mac Cana admitted, that there is an abundance of solar motifs in Continental Europe in

13 R.M. Dorson, 'The eclipse of solar mythology', *Journal of American Folklore* 68 (1955), 393.   14 K.H. Jackson, *The international popular tale* (1961), p. 39.   15 P. Mac Cana, *The cult of the sacred centre* (2011), p. 221.   16 B. Lincoln, *Priests, warriors and cattle* (1981), p. 87; P. Mac Cana, 'Place-names and mythology in Irish tradition' in G.W. MacLennan (ed.), *Proceedings of the First North American Congress of Celtic Studies* (1988), p. 339.

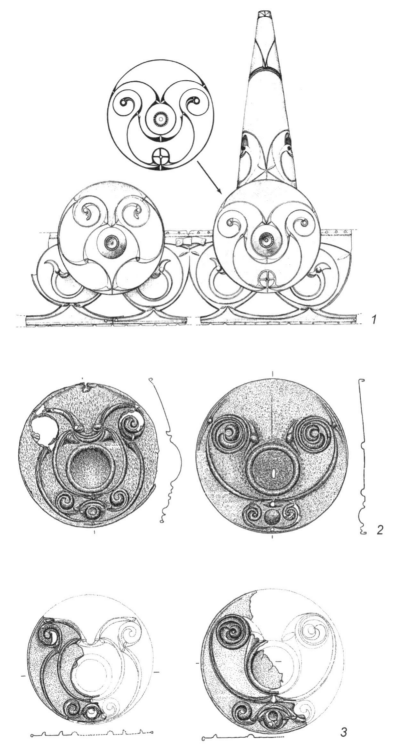

3.1, 1. Solar imagery on the Petrie Crown: a solar boat with bird's heads on prow and stern is depicted on the right-hand disc, reversed bird's heads occur on an openwork bronze band behind the discs and the solar roundel on the left-hand disc seems to be set in an inverted vessel. 2. Pair of bronze discs from Monasterevin, Co. Kildare: the stylized solar boat on the disc on the right has reversed bird's heads. 3. Pair of bronze discs from Co. Armagh: the stylized solar boat on the disc on the right also has reversed bird's heads. Various scales.

particular. While the occasional triskele, swastika or wheel motif may have had a diversity of meanings, perhaps a charm or a good-luck talisman to ward off evil, it is now possible to identify one quite complex symbol in both prehistoric Europe and pre-Christian Ireland that was not just a mere charm but was the expression of a religious cosmology. This, the combination of a representation of a boat and an associated sun disc, is a depiction of the solar boat carrying the sun across the heavens.

In Ireland, the most obvious expression of this motif is to be found on the so-called Petrie Crown. This object (fig. 3.1) got its name because it was once in the collection of the nineteenth-century antiquary George Petrie, who did not record its provenance so we know nothing about the circumstances of its discovery. Like the bronze crown found on the skull of an adult male buried with sword and shield at Mill Hill, near Deal, in east Kent, it probably was a high-status or even kingly head-piece (ch. 7).[17]

The Petrie Crown is fragmentary, now consisting of a band of openwork sheet bronze with a pair of slightly dished discs attached to the front. Each disc, some 5cm in diameter, apparently supported a conical bronze horn, one of which survives. The band, the discs and the horn, are each very skilfully decorated with a symmetrical design of thin and elongated trumpet curves, some terminating in different sorts of bird's heads.

The design on the disc below the surviving horn is particularly interesting because the bird's head terminals flank a circle set in a crescent form. This is not, as was once claimed, a face with an upturned curling moustache but a solar symbol, a representation of the solar boat with bird's head prow and stern that conveyed the sun across the sky. The sun ship appears in two different guises on the Petrie Crown and finds its clearest and fullest expression on this disc where a wheel motif in the boat and below the roundel gives emphasis to the solar symbolism. On the other disc, the bird's heads and the roundel are well delineated but the boat motif appears inverted.

A pair of large bronze discs found together at Monasterevin, Co. Kildare, has given the name Monasterevin type to a group of four complete and three fragmentary discs (fig. 3.1). Made of sheet bronze, these discs are usually slightly concave and range in diameter from about 25cm to just over 30cm. Their purpose is unknown. Decoration is similar but not identical and consists of bold repoussé work up to 1cm high. The overall pattern is a fairly consistent one: a large central circle or roundel, varying from a slight concavity to a deep bowl-shaped hollow, is placed within a symmetrical field of trumpet curves forming an approximately U-shaped or semi-circular arrangement with spiral terminals. Though nothing is known about the circumstances of their discovery,

---

17 I.M. Stead, 'The metalwork' in K. Parfitt, *Iron Age burials from Mill Hill, Deal* (1995), p. 72.   18 R. Ó Floinn, 'Notes on some Iron Age finds from Ireland' in G. Cooney et al. (eds), *Relics of old decency* (2009), pp 99–210.

in addition to those from Monasterevin, it seems as if examples from Co. Armagh and possibly from Lismore, Co. Waterford, were found in pairs too.[18] This pairing, as we shall see, is highly significant.

Not surprisingly, given the positioning of a pair of spirals above a circle, several writers have seen great staring faces or grotesque faces or even an open-mouthed fish in this design. But once again, it is a solar boat that is represented.[19] Compared with the Petrie Crown, however, the designs on all these Monasterevin-type discs are more stylized and the paired bird heads are reduced to abstract curving features.

In the past, when compared to the Petrie Crown, the images on these discs would have been judged to be a severe case of stylistic disintegration or typological regression, a sad process of degeneration charted by John Evans, who applied Darwinian principles in his numismatic studies of native versions of the gold stater of Philip II of Macedon. This was famously illustrated by Grahame Clarke as an example of typological devolution. As the latter put it, 'in the hands of artificers, to whom the naturalistic rendering of Philip's head had no particular significance other than as a mere mark of identification, the design rapidly disintegrated ...'[20] Various writers have since pointed out that these native coins in both Britain and Gaul were not always the debased products of clumsy engravers, nor were they always a deliberate abstraction. Real choices about design and content were deliberately made.[21]

While not denying the existence of incompetent artists and copiers, the technical calibre of the Irish decorated bronzes confirms that something much more significant may be taking place in this fissioning process whether on coin or disc. As Clifford Geertz has remarked, to approach 'primitive art' from the side of Western aesthetics leaves us with an externalized conception of the phenomenon supposedly under intense inspection but actually not even in our line of sight.[22]

On these discs, the artist seems to be seeking to hide the solar symbol or more likely trying to reduce it to its essential elements. In doing so, they are giving greater emphasis to its inherent strength. In a very deliberate act, a traditional symbol is altered to give it a new or different or more powerful meaning. Just as repetition, such as triplism, may accentuate the power of an image, so dissection may expose its inner qualities. The possibility that both the sun ship and a human face are depicted should not be discounted either – this art is multivalent with several potential readings.

19 J. Waddell, 'The elusive image' in G. Cooney et al. (eds), *Relics of old decency* (2009), pp 341–9. **20** G. Clarke, *Archaeology and society* (1960), p. 135. **21** P.-M. Duval, *Monnaies Gauloises et mythes celtiques* (1987), p. 91; S. Scheers, 'Celtic coin types in Britain' in M. Mays (ed.), *Celtic coinage: Britain and beyond* (1992), p. 41; J. Creighton, 'Visions of power', *Britannia* 26 (1995), 289. **22** C. Geertz, *Local knowledge* (1983), p. 98.

3.2, 1. The Battersea shield with solar imagery on lower roundel highlighted; the solar image on the upper roundel is inverted. 2. Aylesford bucket. 3. Unprovenanced Gibbs mirror. 4. Mirror from Aston, Herts. Various scales.

This elusive image of the solar boat is not confined to Ireland. It is to be found on British metalwork of the last century BC and the early centuries AD as well. It is a noteworthy detail on the celebrated Battersea shield (fig. 3.2, 1) where, along with swastika-like motifs, it is a prominent feature on the two smaller circular panels. It figures in a minor way on the decorated bronze band on the Aylesford bucket, where two pairs of bird-like creatures surround a whirligig (fig. 3.2, 2). It occurs in an attenuated form on the unprovenanced Gibbs mirror and on the Aston, Hertfordshire, mirror (fig. 3.2, 3–4) for instance. Now it is a moot point whether the decoration on these mirrors was meant to be viewed with the object held handle up or handle down, but since this solar image was equivocal depending on how it was presented this may be irrelevant. What is striking is that this motif, the 'lyre-loop with flanking coils' in Jody Joy's terminology, is the basis for the extremely complex designs on a number of other mirrors such as those from Birdlip, Gloucester, and Portesham, Dorset, as he has demonstrated.[23] On these remarkable pieces, the solar motif has all but disappeared or has been deliberately secreted in an ornate composition.

On items like the Battersea shield, solar imagery is also represented by the swastika and elsewhere it is encoded in motifs such as whirligigs, triquetras and triskeles, as Miranda Green has shown.[24] Like the solar boat, these motifs are further indicators of widespread and deeply rooted belief systems that evidently transcend the numerous regional archaeologies and identities that make up the Iron Age of these islands and adjacent parts of Continental Europe. Vincent and Ruth Megaw have emphasized the importance of a visual symbolism that reflected a form of communication and a wide community of concepts and ideas.[25]

The manufacture of objects like the Petrie Crown, the Monasterevin-type discs and the Battersea shield represents craftsmanship of the highest quality in which religious and secular concerns are combined. The religious dimension is indicated by the solar symbolism employed in an exercise that was certainly a sacred task in which every detail of the composition may have been imbued with significance. The technical skills deployed must have been an expression of status and prestige for whoever commissioned them.

In contrast to the relatively overt depiction of the solar boat at an earlier date in the Bronze Age, the insular artists in late prehistory now very clearly sought to manipulate the traditional image. This stylization was in all probability a very deliberate process of mystification and disarticulation to

23 J. Joy, 'Reflections on Celtic art' in D. Garrow et al. (eds), *Rethinking Celtic art* (2008), p. 85; *Iron Age mirrors* (2010), p. 32.   24 M. Green, *The sun-gods of ancient Europe* (1991), p. 48.   25 J.V.S. & M.R. Megaw, 'Cheshire cats, Mickey Mice, the new Europe and ancient Celtic art' in C. Scarre & F. Healy (eds), *Trade and exchange in prehistoric Europe* (1993), 219–32; R. & V. Megaw, 'Through a window on the European Iron Age darkly', *World Archaeology* 25 (1994), 287–302.

capture its essential elements. In doing so, they may have given greater emphasis to its inherent strength and, equally purposefully, they may have sought to introduce a deliberate ambiguity in an imagery of exclusion that might be understood by a select few and be intentionally multivalent. Those who saw grotesque human heads or faces in the Monasterevin-type discs, for example, could have just engaged in one potential reading. Whatever the reason, there was a deliberate attempt to obscure or conceal the solar motif.

Since it seems as if it may have been taboo to utter the name of the great god Lug, perhaps a similar taboo applied to the overt depiction of the symbol of a solar deity? While the name Lug, the bright or shining one, as we have seen, has often been considered to reflect his solar nature, it has been proposed that he was originally a god by whom people swore an oath. Thus a formula such as *tongu do dia toinges mo thuath* ('I swear to the god to whom my people swear') found in the Ulster Cycle was an oath (**lugiom* in Common Celtic) to a god whose name had to be avoided because others might learn to use it to their own advantage.[26]

The celestial voyage of the sun is not the only theme represented on these discs and on the Petrie Crown. In the pair of baroque roundels containing a solar boat and multiple swastikas on the Battersea shield (fig. 3.2), it is significant that the uppermost is inverted, and this inversion could be a reference to the Otherworld. The inverted boat on one of the pair of discs on the Petrie Crown is yet another example of this contrapuntal imagery that seems to offer contrasting explicit and implicit readings corresponding to the upper world and the lower one.

The Otherworld had many manifestations in early Irish literature (and we will explore it in chapter 4). It may be a land under the earth or the *síd* (otherworldly) mound, a land beneath lakes or the sea, or an island. Often seen as a land of peace and plenty and a place of perpetual feasting, it was also a timeless region and, sometimes, the mirror image of the human world. Allusions to this nether world seem to be a part of much of the solar symbolism known at an even earlier date in Bronze Age Europe, often indicated by reversed or inverted motifs.

The Nordic Bronze Age has an exceptional iconographic repertoire on stone and bronze. This has enabled various commentators to suggest the existence of a complex solar cosmography in which boats, solar imagery, human figures, horses and fish may figure. Flemming Kaul, for example, has demonstrated that a cyclical story is illustrated on a series of bronze razors. On these a solar boat is sometimes depicted travelling from left to right, that is from east to west as one faces south, in its day-time journey across the heavens. In addition, it may be shown moving in the reverse direction from right to left,

26 J.T. Koch, 'Further to *Tongu do dia toinges mo thuath* etc.', *Études celtiques* 29 (1992), 253.

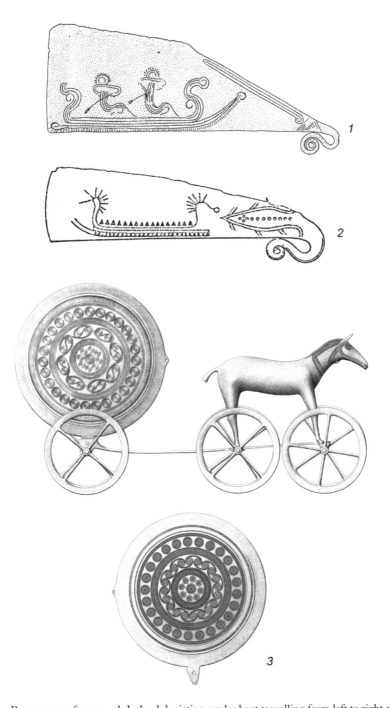

3.3, 1. Bronze razor from south Jutland depicting a solar boat travelling from left to right and containing two human figures, possibly two aspects of the sun god. 2. Bronze razor from Møn, southern Zealand, showing a boat with horse-head prow and stern sailing towards the left followed by a fish. 3. The Trundholm 'chariot of the sun'. The gilded face of the bronze sun disc is mainly decorated with concentric circle motifs and is drawn by the horse from left to right that is from east to west. The bronze face (below) bearing concentric circle motifs and a design of linked spirals is to the fore when the vehicle is drawn from right to left.

which represents its night-time journey through the underworld from whence it emerges at dawn to resume its cosmic course.[27]

This is to be seen on razors like that from south Jutland with an image of a boat that contains two human figures, sometimes considered twin solar deities, who are clearly paddling the vessel from left to right (fig. 3.3). In contrast, another example from southern Zealand with horse-head prow and stern is sailing from right to left and is followed by a fish. According to Kaul, this is a ship of the night and the underworld and such left-sailing vessels, where they can be identified in Denmark, are never associated with solar images.

The famous 'chariot of the sun' from Trundholm in Denmark is undoubtedly the best known Bronze Age solar symbol, one that very graphically illustrates the sacral function of the horse at this time (fig. 3.3). As suggested by Hans Drescher many years ago, the gold-plated bronze disc, mounted on a wheeled vehicle, is drawn by a horse from left to right and depicts the sun's westward route across the heavens in the northern hemisphere. When reversed, the back of the bronze disc, which was apparently never gold-covered, is pulled by the horse from right to left and this – it is now generally believed – represents the sun's nocturnal journey under the land or under the sea towards the dawn in the east.[28]

It is interesting to note that the decoration differs slightly on the two faces; the number of concentric circle motifs varies and spiral motifs, in linked pairs, only occur on the bronze nocturnal face. Numerical and calendrical interpretations have been considered[29] but whatever the explanation, the contrasting decorative detail seems to imply that different meanings are reflected in the designs on either face. The apparent depiction of different aspects of the sun on the one object and the representation of an Otherworldly dimension to solar myth on this Nordic metalwork are especially interesting because they explain some features of sun symbolism elsewhere in Europe.

Examples of images of a boat with bird's head prow and stern and an associated sun disc, the *Vogel-Sonnen-Barke*, are widely distributed in central Europe in particular in the late Bronze Age and early Iron Age.[30] Some classic illustrations occur on a small number of bronze buckets of Hajdúböszörmény type in Hungary, where the sun is shown as a disc or a boss prominently placed in a boat with duck or swan heads at either end. A sheet bronze bucket in a private collection, possibly in Austria, bears embossed solar boat imagery in a broad frieze that circumscribes its upper body. The decoration on this, the Vienna situla as Stefan Wirth calls it, essentially consists of two zones of solar

27 F. Kaul, 'Bronze Age tripartite cosmologies', *Praehistorische Zeitschrift* 80 (2006), 235–46.
28 H. Drescher, 'Neue Untersuchungen am Sonnenwagen von Trundholm', *Acta Archaeologica* 33 (1962), 42; F. Kaul, *Ships on bronzes* (1998), p. 30. 29 K. Randsborg, 'Opening the oak-coffins', *Acta Archaeologica* 77 (2006), 68. 30 S. Wirth, 'Vogel-Sonnen-Barke' in H. Beck et al. (eds), *Reallexikon der Germanischen Altertumskunde* 32 (2006), 552–63.

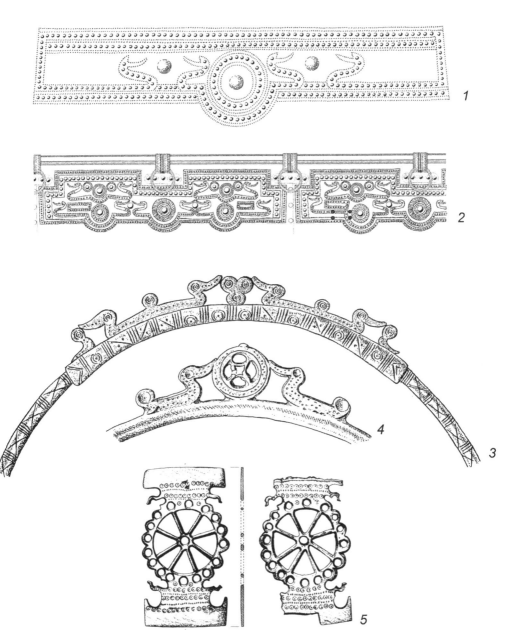

3.4, 1. Detail of decoration on a bronze bucket of Hajdúböszörmény type from Nyírlugos, eastern Hungary, with a solar boat with bird's head prow and stern and sun disc flanked by smaller boats with reversed bird's heads. 2. The frieze of two rows of solar boats one above the other on the Vienna situla. 3. Solar boat on a bronze torc from Attancourt, Haute-Marne. 4. Solar symbolism on a bronze torc from the Marne region. 5. Two of the bronze mounts on the wagon from the Vix burial with solar symbol and bird's heads. Various scales.

boats, one above the other, all sailing around the circumference of the vessel, in a continuous symmetrical composition that, in its mirror imagery, evokes the sun's journey above and below the horizon (fig. 3.4, 2). As he points out, this is a cosmological narrative that recalls the diurnal and nocturnal voyages of the sun and the various representations of the sun that occur had different meanings.[31]

In certain cases, the Otherworldly solar voyage appears to be implied by reversal or inversion. In some designs, as on the Vienna situla and on a vessel from Nyírlugos, eastern Hungary (fig. 3.4, 1), a central image is flanked by smaller boat images with inturned bird's heads, the position of the sun being depicted as a small boss. These opposed or reversed birds are possibly intended to denote a nocturnal Otherworld ship and the complete image presents an abbreviated version of the story of the cosmic eternal return of the sun that affirms that day is not conquered by night.

Inverted boats may tell a similar tale of Otherworldly significance. Unlike designs with reversed bird's heads, images of upturned solar boats are rare, but they do occur. They are to be found, for example, paired keel-to-keel with stylized upright craft in a frieze of embossed designs on a Hallstatt-period bronze bucket from Kleinklein in Austria, keel-to-keel on the plate of a bronze neck ring from Fangel Torp, Odense, Denmark, and on a bronze shield in Copenhagen.[32] Keel-to-keel examples are also to be found in Scandinavian rock art and may represent, as Kristian Kristiansen claims, upper and lower realms.[33]

A journey to an inverted Otherworld is probably signified in the seven openwork bronze plaques that decorated each side of the wooden super-structure of the wagon in the Vix burial. This last voyage of the high-status woman laid on this vehicle is reflected in the symbolism of the solar wheel with pairs of bird's heads above *and* below (fig. 3.4, 5). This Otherworld will be explored in the following chapter and her special status will be examined in chapter 6.

From an insular perspective, the Vienna situla is important in another respect because it belongs to the Hosszúpályi variant of the Kurd type, a bucket form represented by well-known finds in Ireland in the Dowris, Co. Offaly, deposit (fig. 4.3, 1) and in Wales from Nannau, near Dolgellau, in Merioneth.[34] If plain bucket Hosszúpályi forms like these could be transmitted from central Europe to the far west, associated ideas and beliefs might also be shared. A solar cosmology may have been associated with prestigious bucket fashions.

31 S. Wirth, 'Le mystère de la barque solaire' in L. Baray (ed.), *Artisanats, sociétés et civilisations* (2006), pp 331–45.   32 Kleinklein: G. Prüssing, *Die Bronzegefässe in Österreich* (1991), p. 50, no. 104; Fangel Torp: F. Kaul, *Ships on bronzes* (1998), no. 128; Copenhagen shield: Wirth, 'Le mystère de la barque solaire' (2006), 342, fig. 10.   33 K. Kristiansen, 'Rock art and religion' in A.C. Fredell et al. (eds), *Representations and communications* (2010), p. 102.   34 S. Gerloff, *Atlantic cauldrons and buckets* (2010), p. 238.

The dating of the Dunaverney flesh-hook with its small model birds to the late Bronze Age *c.*1000BC is obviously important because it indicates that bird imagery had a long prehistory in Ireland. It seems that a family of swans and cygnets and a pair of ravens are represented on this object and this may imply that other binary opposites, such as birds of air and birds of land, were a part of insular belief systems at this early date.[35] Given the association of war goddesses like the Morrígan with black birds in Irish tradition, it is possible that a distinction between black and white birds like swans and ravens was particularly important over several millennia.[36]

The solar boat occasionally occurs in Continental La Tène imagery in northern France. Among a series of bronze torcs, for example, one from Attancourt bears a pair of sun ships, each with bird's head prow and stern and containing a sun disc; both flank a triple roundel, possibly a triple sun, in such a way as to offer a version of the reversed bird image. Reversed birds confront a wheel-shaped sun symbol on an unprovenanced example from the Marne region (fig. 3.4, 3–4).

BINARY OPPOSITES AND OTHERWORLDLY BIRDS

Accepting that discs from Monasterevin and from Armagh were indeed found as pairs, then their respective complementarity presents more than just solar imagery; there may be Otherworldly references here as well. The pairing of these discs is significant: if placed side-by-side, one disc in each pair has one solar boat with out-turned bird's heads while its counterpart has reversed heads – a detail repeated in the small design below each boat. As with the reversed images on the late Bronze Age Nyírlugos bucket, the disc with reversed bird's heads may have been intended to illustrate the nocturnal phase of the course of the sun and denote a night ship of the Otherworld, a world that is the opposite of this one.

Other pairings may hold a similar message. It may be reflected in the iconography on the pair of anthropoid plaques from the Tal-y-llyn hoard, Merioneth, Wales (fig. 3.5), where both display a strange arrangement of two human heads joined together by a long straight bar and separated along a median line marked by horizontal leaf shapes. One head is flanked by reversed bird's heads while the other is framed by recurved tendrils that are highly stylized bird's heads. However these plaques were originally mounted, whether side-by-side or, as seems more likely, one above and one below a shield boss, in any of these combinations one head was always going to appear inverted.

35 S. Needham & S. Bowman, 'Flesh-hooks', *European Journal of Archaeology* 8 (2005), 120; S. Bowman & S. Needham, 'The Dunaverney and Little Thetford flesh-hooks', *Antiquaries Journal* 87 (2007), 94.   36 M. Tymoczko, 'The semantic fields of early Irish terms for black birds' in A.T.E. Matonis & D.F. Melia (eds), *Celtic language, Celtic culture*

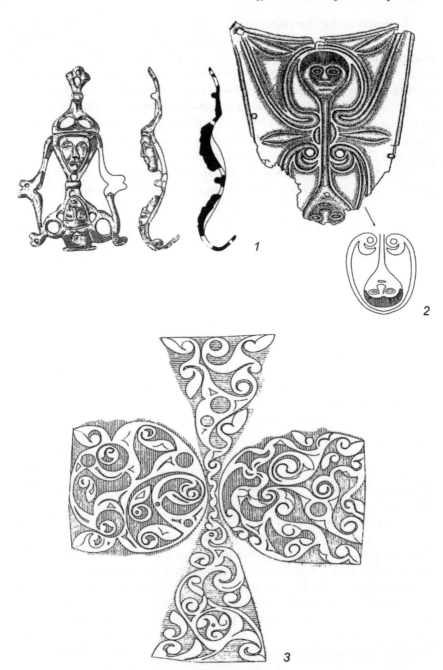

3.5, Binary opposition. 1. A small bronze mount with opposed human heads on a wine flagon from Brno-Maloměřice. 2. One of the pair of bronze plaques from Tal-y-llyn with opposed human heads; the lower image has an inverted human head and reversed bird's heads. 3. Design on the Turoe stone: a pair of triangular panels, one with a bird's head and a solar symbol, the other with a two small and one larger empty roundels, both flanked by D-shaped panels replete with vegetal motifs. Various scales.

Cú Chulainn by J.C. Leyendecker: a dramatic illustration of the mythical warrior and hero of the epic *Táin Bó Cúailnge* (The Cattle Raid of Cooley) commissioned by *The Century Magazine* for an article on the ancient Irish sagas by President Theodore Roosevelt in 1907.

2 (*above*) The River Boyne with Newgrange on the horizon in the distance and a prehistoric burial mound in the foreground.

3 (*below*) The solstice phenomenon in the tomb at Newgrange.

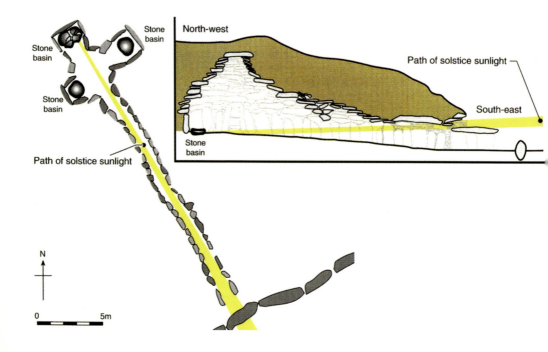

4 The large enclosure at Navan (*above*) with a view of the great mound as restored after excavation (*below*).

5 'Macha curses the men of Ulster' by Stephen Reid from Eleanor Hull's *Cuchulain* (1909).

6 Queen Maeve by J.C. Leyendecker: an imaginative illustration of the mythical queen commissioned by *The Century Magazine* for an article on the ancient Irish sagas by President Theodore Roosevelt in 1907.

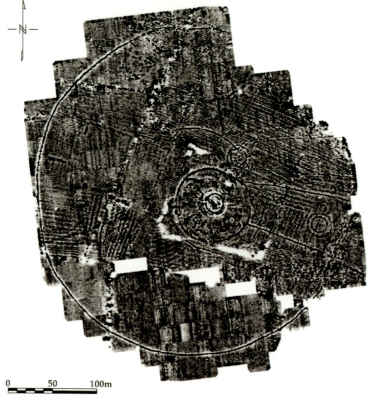

7 Rathcroghan Mound: geophysical survey has disclosed a remarkable number of sub-surface features in its immediate vicinity. Magnetic gradiometry has revealed some well-defined magnetic signatures reflecting the presence of pits, ditches or palisade trenches. The great mound is clearly defined in the centre of the image and has various structures entombed within it. On the east it is approached by a trapezoidal avenue in which two burial mounds are visible. Immediately to the north a northern enclosure has its own eastern avenue. All these features are encircled by a very large ditched enclosure 360m in diameter.

0   50   100m

8 (*above*) Left: life-sized stone statue of a warrior found at the Glauberg. Right: stone figure from Hirschlanden.

9 (*below*) A simplified reconstruction of the Vix burial as presented in Le Musée du Pays Châtillonnais, Châtillon-sur-Seine. The lady of Vix lies on the superstructure of a four-wheeled wagon, its wheels placed along one wall of the timber chamber. One of the pair of Greek ceramic cups placed on the rim of the giant bronze krater is shown. The wine flagon, on the ground, was considered by the excavator to have originally stood on the krater too.

10 The Hill of Tara viewed from the north. The Banqueting Hall and the large ring-barrow called Ráth Ghráinne are in the foreground with the Claoinfhearta (Sloping Trenches) partly obscured by vegetation on the west. The large enclosure Ráth na Rí, containing the Mound of the Hostages, the Forrad and Teach Cormaic, dominates the picture. Part of the curving bank of Ráth Laoghaire is just visible further to the south.

The recurved bird's heads suggest that here we have a representation of the solar boat of the Otherworld while the recurved tendrils form a concealed solar design, in both cases roundels being replaced by human heads. The connecting bar with its associated leaf motifs seems, like the Tree of Life, to connect one world with the other. More intriguingly still, each individual plaque presents an image – if bisected horizontally – of one head and its associated elements viewed as if above ground, the other appearing as a distorted reflection below.[37] Given that aquatic birds like ducks and swans are associated with air, earth and water, and that the Otherworld in Irish tradition can lie beneath land or water, a connection between birds and this sort of mirror imagery of the two worlds is probable. Remembering O'Rahilly's claim that the head might be a sun symbol, then its association with a pair of bird's heads might be unsurprising and, as he pointed out, the severed head sometimes played an important part in the Otherworld feast.[38]

Birds have both Otherworldly and kingly connotations. Those birds linked by silver chains who led the warriors of Emain Macha southwards in *Compert Conculainn* (The Birth-tale of Cú Chulainn) are just one of many instances of supernatural birds in early texts. Time and again birds appear as inter-mediaries between the two worlds, as Anne Ross has shown.[39] A particularly unusual linkage is depicted in *Togail Bruidne Dá Derga* (The Destruction of Dá Derga's Hostel), a story that recounts the life of the ill-fated king of Tara, Conaire Mór. His conception is the result of the impregnation of his divine mother by an Otherworldly figure who appears in the guise of a bird:

> she saw a bird on the skylight coming to her, and he leaves his birdskin on the floor of the house, and went to her and captured her and said '… you will be pregnant by me, and bear a son and that son must not kill birds'.[40]

However, Conaire does pursue a flock of great white-speckled birds of unusual size and beauty. The birds turn on him and shed their birdskins, appearing as warriors with spears and swords, but one of them protects him, saying: 'I am Némglan, king of your father's birds; and you have been forbidden to cast at birds'. He lays a series of injunctions or taboos on Conaire for whom the 'bird-reign' is prosperous as long as this contract with the Otherworld holds. But he breaks his taboos one by one on his doomed journey to his three-fold death in a murderous confrontation in the hostel of Dá Derga.

(1990), pp 151–71. 37 J. Waddell, 'The Tal-y-llyn plaques and the nocturnal voyage of the sun' in W.J. Britnell & R.J. Silvester (eds), *Reflections on the past* (2012), pp 337–50. 38 T.F. O'Rahilly, *Early Irish history and mythology*, p. 283. 39 A. Ross, 'Chain symbolism in pagan Celtic religion', *Speculum* 34 (1959), 39–59; *Pagan Celtic Britain* (1967), pp 234–96. 40 Translation in Koch & Carey, *The Celtic heroic age*, p. 157; summary in M. Ní Bhrolcháin, *An introduction to early Irish literature* (2009), p. 99.

In the ninth- or tenth-century text *Airne Fíngein* (Fingein's Night-watch), the wonders that mark the birth of Conn Cétchathach and the benefits his reign will bring are told. Conn 'of the Hundred Battles' is the legendary ancestor of various historical dynasties including the Uí Néill so closely associated with Tara. His future renown is foretold by a supernatural woman named Rothniamh, whose name has been translated 'wheel radiance' and may have solar associations. The wondrous events she relates include the bursting of the Boyne from the well of Nechtan, the appearance of one of the great sacred trees of Ireland, the creation of the five great roads of Ireland, and the discovery of the three treasures of Ireland that included the helmet or crown of Brión hidden in an Otherworld well at Crúachain, and the diadem of Laegaire mac Luchta. The tree is called the Éo Mugna, a great oak that once stood in Co. Kildare. In the tale, it is described as 'an offshoot of the tree in Paradise', implying that it sprang from the Tree of Life in the Garden of Eden.[41]

Magical birds foreshadow the greatness of Conn's kingship too:

> Trí noí én find i ronnaib dergóir dodechatar, coro sephainset céol n-ingnad for múraib Temrach, conná bía brón ná sním ná cuma ná éolchaire ná esbaid airpheitid ná frítha fri a ré i Temraig ...

> Three times nine white birds in chains of red gold have come tonight and have sung wonderful music on the walls of Tara, so that there shall not be either grief, or distress or sorrow or longing or absence of entertainment in Erin during the time [of Conn of the Hundred Battles] ...[42]

It is possible that the connection between birds and the Otherworld is depicted in the designs on two of the panels on the celebrated Turoe stone, Co. Galway, a pillar stone profusely decorated with superbly executed La Tène designs (fig. 3.5). It is a glacial erratic of fine-grained granite dressed to a cylindrical shape with a rounded top. The upper part of the stone is decorated with a finely carved curvilinear pattern delimited below by a rather irregularly executed step pattern. The decorative scheme comprises four compositions in two broad D-shaped and two narrower triangular panels, a quadripartite arrangement appropriate to a panelled or four-sided pillar. Some motifs are readily recognizable and include roundels, a symmetrical triskele, a bird's head, trumpet curves and comma leaves. Comma leaf shapes and trumpet curves are placed at the bottom corners of each panel. Curving-sided triangular shapes are a component of the background or negative pattern; in two prominent

41 D.M. Wiley, 'The politics of myth in *Airne Fíngein*' in J.F. Eska (ed.), *Narrative in Celtic tradition* (2011), p. 284. On the Éo Mugna and other sacred trees, see A.T. Lucas, 'The sacred trees of Ireland', *Journal of the Cork Historical and Archaeological Society* 68 (1963), 16–54.
42 Text: J. Vendryes, *Airne Fíngein* (1953), p. 17; modified translation from T.P. Cross & A.C.L. Brown, 'Fingen's night-watch. Airne Fingein', *Romanic Review* 9 (1918), 29–47.

cases these triangular voids contain a floating comma leaf. More complex curvilinear forms include pelta shapes with one or two spiral ends, and asymmetrical triskeles or swirling shapes whose limbs sometimes terminate in other motifs such as pelta shapes or comma leaves and trumpet curves. Its sculptor was familiar with late insular styles of La Tène art on decorated metalwork such as several engraved bronze mirrors in southern England dating to about the first centuries BC and AD and a plaque and a shield boss from the votive deposit at Llyn Cerrig Bach on Anglesea in Wales.[43]

In contrast to the designs on the two D-shaped panels, which are clearly separated, the narrow triangular panels are very deliberately connected by a slender vegetal tendril that snakes across the top of the stone. This has an unambiguous bird's head at the apex of one panel that also has an equally clearly delineated triskele set in a roundel near its base. Like the swastika, the revolving three-limbed triskele is widely accepted as a solar symbol and the bird's head is a significant appendage in this context. The empty roundels on the opposing panel present a stark contrast and once again we may have a complex message portrayed in this example of binary opposition. The bird-headed tendril may portray a link between one world and another.

The study of such oppositional pairings offers one possible route to deciphering a challenging artistic phenomenon that all too often and quite understandably has simply been judged in terms of style and technique rather than a complex iconography and a symbolic language. Ian Armit has quite rightly concluded that the many examples of opposed human heads are not mere chance arrangements. The explicit contrasts that often occur do reflect different states of being, perhaps of this world and the world of the dead.[44]

Opposed human heads occur on one of the curving basal attachments that once formed a part of the applied openwork bronze decoration on a wooden or leather wine jug from a cemetery at Brno-Maloměřice in Moravia, Czech Republic. According to Venceslas Kruta, the uppermost head bears some form of triangular head gear surmounted by a palmette, while the lower is horned. However, the terminals of the horn-like appendages on the lower upturned head seem to hint at inverted bird's heads (fig. 3.5). Kruta is surely right to see this sort of binary opposition as representing deities of light and dark, of this world and the subterranean other.[45] Monstrous twin heads decorated the tubular spout of the vessel and a pair of very strange openwork plaques, each a different composition of a lattice work of limbs, eyes and beaks, were attached

43 M. Duignan, 'The Turoe Stone' in P.-M. Duval & C. Hawkes (eds), *Celtic art in ancient Europe* (1976), pp 201–17.   44 I. Armit, 'Janus in furs? Opposed human heads in the art of the European Iron Age' in G. Cooney et al., *Relics of old decency* (2009), pp 279–86; *Headhunting and the body in Iron Age Europe* (2012), p. 111.   45 V. Kruta, *La cruche celte de Brno* (2007), p. 65. Compare his plates on pp 66–7 to the line drawing of the attachment in J. Meduna et al., 'Ein latènzeitlicher Fund mit Bronzebeschlägen von Brno-Maloměřice (Kr. Brno-Stadt)', *Bericht der Römisch-Germanischen Kommission* 73 (1992), p. 193, Abb. 6.

to its globular belly, one on either side. They reminded Paul-Marie Duval of the fantastic creations of Hieronymous Bosch,[46] but Kruta has boldly and ingeniously proposed that the eyes of the tangle of creatures in each configuration correspond to prominent stars in stellar formations visible in the latitude of Brno in the third century BC. One group would depict the star pattern of Vega in the constellation Lyra, Deneb in Cygnus, and Altair in the constellation Aquila (the bright formation of the Summer Triangle) as visible in June 280BC. The other represents a cluster with the very bright star Aldebaran at its centre in the constellations of Orion and Taurus so apparent in the winter sky in November.

The discovery of the Bronze Age Nebra disc near Halle in Germany, several hundred kilometres to the north-west of Brno, is a further reminder that the mysteries of the sun, moon and stars preoccupied prehistoric minds in this part of Europe over a thousand years before. With its gold inlay representing lunar symbols, a solar boat and star clusters such as the Pleiades, this exceptional bronze artefact at the very least implies significant astronomical curiosity.[47] The wealth of solar imagery that has survived, widely distributed in time and space, is also testimony to this and, though more difficult to demonstrate convincingly, an informed interest in the enigmas of the night sky is a real probability too. Indeed, astral symbols stamped on a range of Continental La Tène swords are just one clear indication of a measure of knowledge of heavenly bodies other than the sun.[48]

In Ireland, it has been claimed that a timber avenue leading to an Iron Age circular wooden enclosure at Lismullin, near Tara, Co. Meath, was aligned on the Pleiades.[49] While it is all too easy to forget the wonder and puzzlement celestial phenomena must have generated, early Irish literature is surprisingly all but silent on the subject. The legendary Cormac mac Airt, who though renowned for his wisdom was nonetheless bested by Mug Ruith, was described in his youth as 'a listener in the woods and a gazer at the stars', and a native term *mathmarc* means astrologer or soothsayer. However, no native words are attested for the planets or constellations – though classical astronomy became a subject of study in monastic schools.[50]

We can be sure that the mystery of the sun's nocturnal journey was once a real concern. It certainly preoccupied the medieval mind, and figures, for example, in a section of a ninth-century Old Irish apocryphal text *In Tenga Bithnua* (The Evernew Tongue), in which the spirit of the apostle Philip (whose tongue was cut out nine times and nine times miraculously regenerated)

46 P.-M. Duval, *Les Celtes* (1977), p. 131.   **47** H. Meller, *Der geschmiedete Himmel* (2004). **48** A.P. Fitzpatrick, 'Night and day: the symbolism of astral signs', *Proceedings of the Prehistoric Society* 62 (1996), 373–98; A. Rapin, 'Une épée celtique damasquinée d'or', *Antiquités Nationales* 34 (2002), 155–71.   **49** A. O'Connell, *Harvesting the stars* (2013), p. 72. **50** F. Kelly, 'The beliefs and mythology of the early Irish with special reference to the cosmos' in C. Ruggles (ed.), *Astronomy, cosmology and landscape* (2001), pp 167–72.

addresses the wise men of Jerusalem to explain the creation of the world to them. Here we are told that on the fourth day of Creation, God made 'the fiery circuit of the sun, which … illuminates twelve plains beneath the edges of the world in its shining every night'. Portions of the message of St Philip, the Evernew Tongue, are as follows:

> IS*ed* em tete in g*r*ian i fescar ca*ch* aidche.
> Doaitne cetamus a sruth n-allmuirede co sceluibh airthir na llind.
> Doaitne iarumh an ardmhuir thened dadaig 7 na treathnu sroibthenedh imm na tuatha derga.
> Toidid iarsin slogu inna ma*cc*radh isnaibh meallmuigib foc*er*dat in ngair dochum nimhe ar uam*un* in mil mharb*us* inna ilm*íli* de shloguib fo thonnuib andes …
> Toaitne iarsin ircomuir a n-airbe n-uathach ilbuidnech i[m]me ro iad donaib iff*er*ndaib fothuaith.
> Toaitne isnaib dubglindib cosnaib s*r*othaib sirrechtaibh dara ngnuisi.
> Toaitne iarum airbe in mil tindnaig na ilmuiri im toibu talm*an* di ca*ch* leith, shuiges na ilmhuire aitherr*uch*, co facoib na t*r*achtu tirma di ca*ch* leith …
> Toidid iarsin a mmag ndubhach ndérach cosnaib d*r*aconaib foruir*m*idhi fon ceo.
> Toaitne iar*um* ialla na n-enlaithe *con*chanat na ilcheola i nglinnib na mbl*átha* …
> Toaitne iarsaidiu f*r*i Pard*us* n-Adhuimh co turgaib iar*um* anair m*a*dain … [51]

It is thus that the sun goes every evening.
First it shines on the stream beyond the sea, bringing it news of the waters in the east.
Then it shines at night upon the lofty sea of fire, and upon the seas of sulphurous flame which surround the red peoples.
Then it shines upon the hosts of youths in the pleasant fields, who utter a cry to heaven for fear of the beast which kills many thousands of hosts beneath the waves to the south …
Then it shines upon the terrible populous enclosure which encircles the hell-dwellers to the north.
It shines in the black valleys with melancholy streams across their faces.
Then it shines upon the enclosure of the beast who brings the many seas around the flanks of the earth on every side, who sucks the many seas back again so that he leaves the beaches dry on every side …
Then it shines upon the dark tearful plain, with the dragons who have been placed under the mist.

51 Wh. Stokes, 'The Evernew Tongue', *Ériu* 2 (1905), 124.

> Then it shines upon the flocks of birds who sing many songs together in
> the valley of the flowers ...
> Then it shines upon Adam's Paradise until it rises from the east in the
> morning ...[52]

As Carey demonstrates, the descriptions of some of these plains (as, for
instance, the place peopled with 'flocks of birds who sing many songs') are
comparable to marvels of the Otherworld in Irish tradition but others possibly
derive from gnostic writing in late antique Egypt. Whatever the source of the
idea that the night-time sun passes through the underworld, it was still current
in fourth-century Egypt and continued to be one of the mysteries of creation
in medieval times, as Carey shows.

The question was very clearly asked in the early twelfth-century text
Immram Úa Corra (The Voyage of the Huí Corra), a story of the sea voyage of
three brothers who, when looking at the setting sun on the Atlantic coast in the
west of Ireland, demanded: *Cia leth i teit an grian o thét fon fairrciu?* (Where
does the sun go when it goes under the sea?).[53] It is evident that this question
was a part of native learning at a much earlier date, judging from the insular
solar imagery that has survived. Objects like the Petrie Crown, the
Monasterevin and Armagh discs, the Battersea shield, the Turoe stone and the
Tal-y-llyn plaques all display a preoccupation not just with solar matters but
with evanescent birds as well. They present a complex symbolism that, with
variations on the themes of pairing, reversal or inversion, and concealment,
also allude to the Otherworld.

Recalling the solar associations of Conchobar of Emain Macha and the
suggestion that the kings of Tara had similar attributes, the connection of
kingship with solar imagery is particularly significant in an archaeological
context. Some of the aristocratic metalwork with solar symbolism, like the
Petrie Crown and the Battersea shield, should be considered to have been royal
paraphernalia. Otherworldly symbolism might be expected too, because sacred
kings were mediators between this world and the next. For lower levels of
society, this symbolic code may have manifested itself in less mystical, more
rudimentary ways, as simpler charms or apotropaic signs.

What is exceptionally interesting about the solar imagery on this late Iron
Age metalwork, however, is that it demonstrates the *longue durée* of a symbolic
form. The frequency and exceptional duration of representations of the
celestial voyage of the sun in the Scandinavian Bronze Age, from the period of
Trundholm before 1500BC, is widely recognized.[54] But the concept had an

---

52 J. Carey, 'The sun's night journey', *Journal of the Warburg and Courtauld Institutes* 57
(1994), 14–34.   53 Wh. Stokes, 'The voyage of the Huí Corra', *Revue celtique* 14 (1893), 36
(trans. modified).   54 K. Kristiansen & T.B. Larsson, *The rise of Bronze Age society* (2005),
p. 294.

even longer currency. Horse heads were generally replaced by bird's heads in the twelfth or thirteenth century BC, and these continued into the Iron Age. It is true that the iconographic evidence is widely scattered over time and place. This complex solar symbolism does not find visible expression in the material record in every part of prehistoric Europe. It manifests itself at different times in different places. The late Iron Age Petrie Crown and the Battersea shield, however, are just two objects that show the persistence of this cosmological model (to at least the early centuries AD) and this is a good illustration of the retention and transmission of a deeply held belief over some two millennia in pre-literate times. Whatever its inspiration, the author of *In Tenga Bithnua*, albeit in a literate Christian context, was reiterating a solar theory that in one form or another was at least as old as the Bronze Age. It may well have been current in Newgrange when the mystery of the sun's reappearance was celebrated there.

CHAPTER 4

In pursuit of the Otherworld

As already mentioned, the Otherworld had many manifestations in early Irish literature and, though often represented as a land of peace and plenty, it had a darker side. Sometimes a series of malevolent beings emerged and involved themselves in human affairs.[1] It is of course true that 'the Otherworld is impervious to archaeological exploration' as T.F. O'Rahilly once wrote, and he was very critical of archaeologists who, 'by nature, optimists', were tempted to wander into unfamiliar fields.[2] While the Otherworld, by definition a supernatural place, had no material existence, there were those for whom it was a reality and archaeology has the capability – as we have seen in the solar symbolism found on metalwork in different parts of prehistoric Europe – to identify past processes and practices that have left us some material evidence of a belief in what was undoubtedly a variable concept.

On an archaeological level, a cave popularly known today as Úaimh na gCat or Oweynagat (the cave of the cats) in the royal complex of Rathcroghan, Co. Roscommon, brings us close to this conceptual underworld. Rathcroghan, ancient Crúachain – a name that may mean 'place of burial mounds', is often referred to in early literature as both a sacred burial place and a royal settlement.[3]

In the eighth-century *Táin Bó Fraích* (The Cattle Raid of Fraoch), for example, there is a grandiose description of the house of Ailill and Medb in the rath or fort of Crúachain:

> This was the arrangement of the house: seven partitions in it, seven beds from the fire to the wall in the house all around. There was a fronting of bronze on each bed, carved red yew all covered with fair varied ornament. Three rods of bronze at the step of each bed. Seven rods of copper from the centre of the floor to the ridge-pole of the house. The house was built of pine. A roof of slates was on it outside. There were sixteen windows in it, and a shutter of copper for each of them. There was a lattice of copper across the skylight. Four pillars of copper were over the bed of Ailill and Medb which stood in the middle of the house all adorned with bronze. Two borders of gilded silver were around it. A

1 J. Carey, 'The location of the Otherworld in Irish tradition', *Éigse* 19 (1982), 39; T. Ó Cathasaigh, 'The semantics of "Síd"', *Éigse* 17 (1979), 144.   2 T.F. O'Rahilly, *Early Irish history and mythology*, pp 281, 430.   3 J. Waddell et al., *Rathcroghan, Co. Roscommon* (2009),

silver stave reached from the border to the cross-beams of the house. It
ran round the house from one door to the other ... .[4]

An equally fanciful account of the royal house occurs in *Fled Bricrenn*
(Bricriu's Feast) and, like the description of Conchobor's house at Emain
Macha (ch. 5), this seems to be an instance where a place associated with pagan
kingly ceremonial was reinvented as a splendid royal residence in medieval
times.

Today, Rathcroghan is an archaeological complex of more than sixty
monuments scattered over some nine square kilometres of elevated ground
north of Roscommon town. It comprises enclosures, burial mounds, pillar
stones and other earthworks clustered towards the eastern end of a broad
limestone plateau that slopes gently away to the east and south. Rathcroghan
Mound, the great monument that is the focal point of the complex, is a broad
flat-topped circular mound with an average basal diameter of 89m and a height
of some 5.5m. A small circular burial mound lies to the north-west with a squat
natural limestone boulder called Milleen Meva nearby. There is a fallen pillar
stone named Miosgan Meva about 100m to the north-north-east. A number of
other burial mounds, greatly reduced in height by centuries of agriculture, are
visible to the east and south.

Geophysical survey has revealed a very large circular enclosure 360m in
diameter formed by a substantial ditch surrounding the great mound (pl. 7).
Monuments within this enclosure visible in the geophysical imagery include a
pair of ring-barrows to the east, a northern enclosure with an eastern avenue,
and another avenue forming a formal eastern approach to the central mound.
These linear features probably contained timber palisades and are similar to
the smaller avenues that lead to circular enclosures at Navan and which have
been dated to the later centuries BC.

Despite Rathcroghan Mound's deceptively plain external appearance,
geophysical survey has revealed a wealth of large and complex archaeological
features on its summit and deep within its core. It is the product of an
elaborate and calculated series of constructional phases over time. Buried deep
within it are the remains of two substantial concentric stone walls, 35m and
22m in diameter respectively; they both lie 1m to 2m below its summit. This
sort of entombment recalls the burial of the 40m structure beneath the cairn of
the great mound at Navan around 95BC (see ch. 5). A double circle of pits with
an overall diameter of about 32m partly visible in the gradiometry may
represent the remains of a substantial timber structure on top of the mound
where it must have been an imposing monument, elevated as it was above the
surrounding landscape. There are traces of radial lines on the mound's summit

p. 29.   4 M.E. Byrne & M. Dillon, 'Táin Bó Fraich', *Études celtiques* 2 (1937), 3; W. Meid,
Die Romanze von Froech und Findabair (1970), p. 56.

and evidence that other timber structures may also have been built and replaced there over time.

Most of the burial mounds in the complex are low inconspicuous monuments. One, called Rathbeg, is one of the more prominent examples because it is placed on one of the low north–south glacial hillocks that are a quite visible part of the landscape. With two encircling banks, each with internal ditch, and a low central mound, this is an elaborate ring-barrow. A monument called Dath-í's Mound (named after the supposed last pagan king of Ireland) is another ring-barrow with typical enclosing bank and internal ditch and with a tall pillar stone at its centre. The continued importance of Rathcroghan into historic times is attested by a number of ringfort-type enclosures.

A series of puzzling earthen embankments called the Mucklaghs lie to the south-west. They were so named because they were once believed to be the result of the rootings of a magical boar. They are two very large linear earthworks each formed by a curving set of parallel banks running downslope from north-east to south-west into the broad valley that forms the southern limit of the Rathcroghan complex. The northern earthwork is an enormous, closely set pair of earthen banks about 100m in length, while its southern counterpart comprises three banks with a maximum length of about 285m. They must have had some ceremonial function in the royal site.

PORTAL TO THE OTHERWORLD

Rathcroghan stands apart from other royal sites, however, in possessing an entrance to the Otherworld: *dorus iffiirn na Hérend* – Ireland's gate to Hell, as one medieval writer called it in the early ninth-century tale *Cath Maige Mucrama* (The Battle of Mag Mucrama). In great part, this is the story of Lugaid mac Con, the predecessor of Cormac mac Airt as king of Tara, but it explains the name of the battle site. This is the plain of the counting of the pigs near Athenry, Co. Galway. The tale records one of several legends associated with the celebrated Roscommon cave. A numberless band of supernatural wild pigs emerges from the cave of Crúachain and wreaks havoc and destruction on the surrounding land:

> Mag Mucrima did*iu* .i. mucca gentliuchta do-dechatar a hÚaim Ch*r*úachna. Dorus iffi*i*rn na Hér*end* sin. Is esti da*n*o tánic in tellén trechend ro fásaig Hérind, conidro marb Amairgene athair Conaill Chern*aig* ar galaib óenfir ar bélaib Ulad [n-]uili.
>
> Is esti da*n*o do-dechatar ind énlathi chrúan coro chrínsat i nHér*ind* nach ní taidlitís a n-anála, condaro marbsat Ulaid dano […] asa táblib.
>
> Is esti íarum do-dechatar na mucca-sa. Nach ní immathégtís co cend

secht mbl*íadna* ní ássad arbur na fér na duille trít. Bale i rrímtis ní antaís and acht no thégtís hi túaith [n-]aile. Dia n-irmastá a rrím, ní rímtís fo chomlín .i. 'ataat a trí and', ar in fer. 'Is mó, a secht', ar araile. 'Atát a noí and', ol araile. 'Óen muc déc'. 'Trí mucca déc'. Att-róithe a rrím fónd inna[s]-sain. Far-fémditís da*n*o a nguin, ar dia ndíbairgtís ní arthraigtís.

Fecht and di*diu* luid Medb Chrúachan 7 Ailill dia rím .i. i mMag Mucríma. Ro rímthea leo íarum. Ro buí Medb inna carput. Ro lebla[i]ng mucc díb tarsin carpat. 'Is immarcraid in mucc-sain, a Medb', or cách. 'Niba hí-seo', ol Medb, la gabáil a colpthae na muicce co rróemid a croccend fora étan conda farggaib dano in croccand inna láim cossin cholpdu 7 nocon fess cía deochatar ónd úair-sin. Is de-sin atá Mag Mucríma.

Now Mag Mucríma [was so called from] magic pigs that had come out of the cave of Crúachain. That is Ireland's gate to Hell. Out of it too came the swarm of three-headed creatures that laid Ireland waste until Amairgene father of Conall Cernach, fighting alone (?), destroyed it in the presence of all the Ulaid.

Out of it also had come the saffron-coloured(?) bird-flock and they withered up everything in Ireland that their breath touched until the Ulaid killed them with their slings.

Out of it then had come these pigs. Whatever [land] they traversed no corn or grass or leaf grew on it until the end of seven years. Wherever they were being counted they would not stay there but would go into another territory. If the attempt to count them succeeded the counts did not agree, for example: 'There are three of them', said one man. 'There are more, seven of them', said another. 'There are nine of them', said another. 'Eleven pigs', 'thirteen pigs'. Thus it was impossible to count them. Nor were they able to slay them for when cast at they disappeared.

On one occasion Medb of Crúachu and Ailill went to Mag Mucríma to reckon them. They were counted by them then. Medb was in her chariot. One of the pigs jumped across the chariot. 'That pig is an extra one, Medb', said everyone. 'It won't be this one', said Medb, seizing the pig's shank so that its skin split on its forehead and it left the skin in her hand along with the shank and it is not known where they went from that time onwards. It is from that Mag Mucríma is [named].[5]

The war-goddess, the Morrígan, is another fearsome entity associated with this famous cave. According to the metrical *Dindshenchas*:

5 M. O Daly, *Cath Maige Mucrama* (1975), p. 48.

Luid co Crúachain cróda
iarsind úath-blaid ágda
in Mórrígan mórda,
ba slóg-dírmach sámda.

Luid Odras 'na h-iarn-gait,
iarmairt nárbu ada,
's a gilla dúr dorthain,
torchair i Cúil Chada.

Cada ainm a gilla
rofinna mór fíche:
ruc Odras, úair áithe,
for lurg a búair bíthe.

Iarsin, d' éis a gilla,
luid in ben gléis glanda
co Síd Crúachan cumma,
co fríth úath-blad alla.

Roléic cotlud chuicce
in groc-dub cen glicce
i nDaire úar Fálgud
dia fúair sárgud sicce.

Dosruacht ina tathum,
trúag tachur for tulaig,
in Mórrígan úathmar
a h-úaim Chrúachan cubaid.

Rochan fuirre ind agda
tria luinde cen logda
cach bricht dían, ba dalbda,
fri Slíab mBadbgna mbrogda.

There came to blood-stained Cruachu, according to the weird and terrible tale, the mighty Morrigan, whose pleasure was in mustered hosts.

Odras came to despoil her by arms, to an issue that was not lawful, with her stark ill-fated henchman, who fell at Cuil Cada.

Cada was her gillie's name – many a fight he knew; Odras brought him, in a bitter hour, on the track of her herd of heifers.

> Afterward, when her henchman was gone, the lady came, in shining trim, to Sid Cruachan likewise, and a weird event befell yonder.
>
> Imprudently the dark-wrinkled one let sleep come over her in cold Daire Falgud, where she met mortal outrage.
>
> The horrid Morrigan out of the cave of Cruachu, her fit abode, came upon her slumbering: alas, the combat on the hill!
>
> The owner of kine chanted over her, with fierceness unabating, toward huge Sliab Bodbgna every spell of power: she was full of guile.[6]

In the complex and surreal story known as *Echtra Nerai* (The Adventure of Nera), when the royal couple Ailill and Medb and their household were celebrating the festival of Samhain (the night of 31 October) at Crúachain, the well-armed warrior Nera goes outside and cuts down a captive who had been hanged the day before and who complained of thirst. He gives him a drink and carries him back to his torture. On returning to the fort he finds that the Otherworld people of the *síd* have burnt the court and left a heap of heads. Nera follows them into the cave of Crúachain and finds a home and a wife there.

His wife eventually explains to him that the destruction he witnessed was a vision and that Crúachain will really be destroyed the following Samhain unless its inhabitants are warned. She also tells him that the *barr Briúin*, that crown of Brión, is to be found in a well near the fort of Crúachain. When he asks how he will convince the court at Crúachain that he has been in the *síd*, she tells him, in an important allusion to the inverted nature of the Otherworld, to bring the fruits of summer to the winter world outside:

> 'Beir toirthe sam*r*uid latt', ol in u*h*en. Dobe*r*t iarum crem leis oc*us* sobairche oc*us* buiderath …
>
> 'Bring the fruits of summer with you', said the woman. So he brought wild garlic with him, and primroses and buttercups …

He leaves the Otherworld to warn Ailill and Medb, who eventually destroy the *síd* and acquire the crown of Brión, but 'Nera was left in the *síd* together with his people, and has not come out yet, and he will not come out until the end of the world'.[7] Tales such as these reflect the chaos of the Otherworld and the terrors of the eve of Samhain, when supernatural beings invade the profane world; they find echoes in more recent times in the folklore of Hallowe'en when spirits walk abroad.

---

6 E. Gwynn, *The Metrical Dindshenchas Part 4* (1924), p. 198.   7 Text and trans.: K. Meyer, 'The adventures of Nera', *Revue celtique* 10 (1889), 212–28; trans.: Cross & Slover, *Ancient Irish tales*, p. 248; Koch & Carey, *The Celtic heroic age*, p. 117, for a modern translation.

4.1. An entrance to the Otherworld. The present entrance to the souterrain and cave at Oweynagat (Úaimh na gCat), Rathcroghan. The stones to the left are the roof-stones of another unexplored souterrain.

Today, Oweynagat is one of the more dilapidated and unimpressive monuments in the Rathcroghan complex (fig. 4.1).[8] The inconspicuous nature of the site, a small natural cave with a souterrain attached, stands in stark contrast to other large earthworks in the area and to its literary status with a remarkable wealth of associated legend. Indeed, its ruinous archaeological state inspires little awe today. Samuel Ferguson visited the site in 1864 and provided an invaluable account of the surface features of this monument that have suffered considerable damage since then. His sketch plan clearly depicts the cave entrance and groups of scattered stones set within a low circular earthwork.[9] A small roadway, built during the earlier part of the twentieth century, crosses the monument and is responsible for erasing most of the northern half of the earthwork visible in Ferguson's time. The field to the south of the road, from which the cave is now entered, has suffered extensive damage in more recent years, largely through poaching by cattle.

Fortunately, the sub-surface features, both the souterrain and cave, appear to have changed little since Ferguson's visit. The enclosure is no longer visible but appears to have had a maximum internal and external diameter of about 17m and 21m respectively and to have been defined by a low bank, very roughly

8 J. Waddell et al., *Rathcroghan, Co. Roscommon* (2009), p. 79.   9 S. Ferguson, 'Account of ogham inscriptions in the cave at Rathcroghan', *Proceedings of the Royal Irish Academy* 9

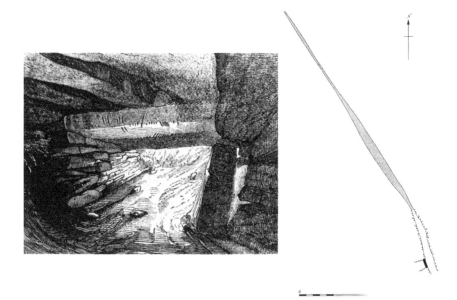

4.2. Samuel Ferguson's illustration of the entrance to Oweynagat in 1864 (left) shows the ogam inscription on the lintel at the junction of two passages. The position of this lintel in the souterrain is marked in black on the plan of the monument (right) and the long narrow natural cave to which the souterrain is attached is shown in grey.

2m wide, without an accompanying ditch, internal or external. Then, as now, the cave was entered via a hole in the roof of a partly collapsed souterrain.

The same low gap beneath a broad limestone lintel permits access to a 3m-stretch of souterrain and it is clear that this entrance is not original. It seems to be a point at which the roof has collapsed or lintels have been removed and a number of lintel-sized slabs lie nearby. The second lintel of this short passage bears an ogam inscription read as *VRAICCI MAQI MEDVVI*, '[the stone] of Fraoch, son of Medb' (fig. 4.2).[10] This short section of souterrain joins at right angles to a second passage that in turn joins a natural narrow fissure in the limestone bedrock to the north-west. How far this second passage extends to the south-east (the right-hand side on entering) is unknown, as it is blocked with collapsed debris. The last capstone visible in this collapsed section also bears ogam letters, the remains of a second fragmentary inscription (read by Macalister as *QREGAS MU …*).

The position of a number of large earth-fast stones and lintel-like slabs in the field south of the road suggest this souterrain passage may have continued for some distance to the south-east and there may be quite a complex of souterrains awaiting discovery here. There are traces of another souterrain just

(1864), 162.   **10** R.A.S. Macalister, *Corpus Inscriptionum*, 1 (1945), pp 16–7, no. 12. No. 13 is a second fragmentary inscription.

3m to the north-west of the current entrance and it is possible to peer through a small gap below a stone lintel into a rubble-filled chamber.

The main passage continues to the north-west (to the left on entering) and descends fairly steeply to join a long, narrow natural cave (fig. 4.2). The passage is largely of artificial construction for about 10m before joining the limestone cave to continue for a further 37m. In this initial section, the natural fissure appears to have been widened in places and dry-stone walling built on a footing of natural rock on either side supports large slabs that span the roof. This modified section of passage increases in height and widens considerably before joining the natural cave where the ceiling descends, coinciding with an abrupt drop in floor level. Here, a level plinth of bedrock on either side of a constricted passage (40cm wide) leads, in a series of at least five rough flagstone steps, to the natural unmodified cave below. It is conceivable that this junction between souterrain and cave proper once accommodated a trapdoor laid horizontally on the plinth when shut and leaning against the vertical wall when open.

The natural cave broadens to a narrow elongated chamber, 2.85m in maximum width at its lowest level. Its walls incline from the cave floor to a narrow apex spanned by naturally deposited rocks and boulders about 5m above. The floor of the cave is boulder strewn and muddy and displays no evidence of a paved or metalled surface. The cave ascends and narrows again from this chamber to terminate relatively close to ground level almost 50m from the present souterrain entrance. It is possible that a number of lintel stones were positioned to span the cave roof at the point where the cave narrows towards its existing end.

Even though the full extent and number of souterrains here are unknown, it is still possible to identify some very significant features at Oweynagat. Since no trace of an external ditch has been found, the small embanked enclosure was not a normal ringfort. The presence of ogam inscriptions – rare in Connacht – is exceptional and the attachment of a man-made souterrain to a natural cave is also unusual. It seems that the junction between the two with its downward steps and narrowness was of some significance. All these and the wealth of associated legend all set Oweynagat apart.

Souterrains built of unmortared stone are a relatively common monument often associated with settlements of ringfort type or with ecclesiastical sites. They are generally believed to have served as either storage places or refuges or both and the great majority are dated to the early medieval period, AD500–1000. Between 3,000 and 3,500 have been identified in every part of the island and these are certainly minimum figures. Ogam stones have been discovered in about 113 examples, mainly in the south and south-west. These inscribed stones are often used as lintel or roof stones and it has been generally believed that they were appropriated to serve as convenient building material.[11] The souterrain at Oweynagat may be firmly dated to this general early medieval timespan and its ogam stones may have been taken from somewhere else when it was decided to attach a souterrain to a natural cave that probably already had some cultic importance.

The use of the ogam stone as a roofing slab was not a casual constructional device however. The lintel bearing the Fraoch inscription was deliberately placed at a junction, presumably to mark a key point in the structure, a recurring feature in several other souterrains as well. Unfortunately, the precise position of many ogam stones in these monuments has not been documented, but in a majority of the very few that have some information recorded, the ogam stones appear to have been placed at a significant location in the monument and, it seems, deliberately positioned to expose the inscription. For example, at Dunalis, Co. Antrim, a junction and a change in floor and roof level were marked by an ogam-inscribed lintel and in a very large souterrain at Ballybarrack, Co. Louth (one of three in an oval enclosure), an ogam-inscribed lintel also occurred at a junction between two chambers.[12] Thus, they are unlikely to have been selected for building purposes alone and in all probability their purpose was to serve as talismans with a protective function.

While these underground chambers are generally considered to have been refuge places or storage places, the practice of subterranean storage, where it occurred, probably had a ritual dimension too. This was a feature of grain storage pits in the Iron Age hillfort of Danebury, Hampshire, for instance, where propitiatory offerings (including animal and human remains) were apparently made to chthonic powers to protect the grain placed in their underground domain.[13]

Underground deposition in early medieval Ireland may have been associated with a belief in the protective powers of the Otherworld, powers that might be invoked or enhanced with inscribed stones. These special stones may even have been seen as some protection against the netherworld powers let loose by the digging of the pit for the souterrain. As we have seen, the souterrains attached to the passage tombs at Dowth and Knowth were a very deliberate connection to an older monument with supernatural qualities.

11 M. Clinton, *The souterrains of Ireland* (2001), p. 68.   12 Dunalis: A.W. Lindsey, 'The Dunalis souterrain and ogham stone', *Proceedings of the Belfast Natural History and Philosophical Society* (1934–5), 61–70; Ballybarrack, Co. Louth: V.M. Buckley & P.D. Sweetman, *Archaeological survey of County Louth* (1991), p. 103; J. Waddell, 'The Cave of Crúachain and the Otherworld' in J. Borsje et al. (eds), *Celtic cosmology* (2014), pp 77–92. 13 B. Cunliffe, 'Pits, preconceptions and propitiation in the British Iron Age', *Oxford Journal of Archaeology* 11 (1992), 69–83; *Danebury*, 6 (1995), p. 85.

RITES OF TERROR

The ogam inscriptions in souterrains, where translatable, seem to provide no further clues as to the role of these stones – with the possible exception of that dedication to Fraoch in Oweynagat. If this is an allusion to the hero of the eighth-century *Táin Bó Fraích* (The Cattle Raid of Fraoch), then here we have a reference to the foremost legendary warrior of Connacht whose name is literally petrified in the roof stones of the souterrain. He is not the only warrior associated with this cave, Nera who brought those out-of-season fruits from the Otherworld and Amairgene who defeated those three-headed monsters in *Cath Maige Mucrama* (The Battle of Mag Mucrama) have already been noted. We may add to this list three heroes in *Fled Bricrenn* (Bricriu's Feast) who are tested by terrifying nocturnal cats:

> Dobretha a cuit dóib ind aidchi sin, ocus dolléicthe tre-caittini a húaim Crúachan dia saigid, i. tri bíasta druidechta. Techit iarom Conall ocus Loeg*aire* for sparrib na tigi ocus fácbait a m-biad oc na bíastaib, ocus feoit fón samail sin cusarnabárach. Nirtheig Cuculainn assa inud frissin m-bíasta rosiacht chuci, acht in tan dosíned in beist a bragit cosin n-esair, dounsi Cuchulainn béim din claid*iub* na cend doscirred di mar bad do charraic. Nothairned si sís di sudi. Nirthomail ocus nírsúan Cuchulainn fon cruth sin co matain. Rothinsat na cait, o robo maten, ocus atcessa iat-som fon cruth sin arabarach.[14]

> One night as their portion was assigned to them, three cats from the Cave of Cruachan were let loose to attack them, i.e., three beasts of magic. Conall and Lóegaire made for the rafters, having left their food with the beasts. In that way they slept until the next day. Cú Chulainn did not flee from his place from the beast which was attacked him. But when it stretched its neck out for eating, Cú Chulainn gave a blow with a sword on the beast's head, but [the blade] glided off as it were striking stone. Then the cat set itself down. In the circumstances Cú Chulainn neither ate nor slept. As soon as it was early morning the cats were gone. The three heroes were seen in such a condition the next day.[15]

These tales of monstrous cats, destructive pigs and some of the other bizarre creatures are echoes of the cave's links with the powers of chaos. The antagonistic juxtapositioning of a hazardous entrance to the Otherworld with a nearby kingly settlement might appear at first glance to be remarkably poor planning. However, it should be seen as an expression of the sacred and the

14 G. Henderson, *Fled Bricrend. The Feast of Bricriu* (1899), p. 72.   15 Trans.: Koch & Carey, *The Celtic heroic age*, p. 82.

social aspects of the community, the Otherworld signifying disorder, the king representing cosmic order and well-being.

As Jacqueline Borsje has pointed out, those supernatural and destructive pigs in *Cath Maige Mucrama* (The Battle of Mag Mucrama) cannot be killed but counting them would make them depart. This, however, turns out to be impossible, but when Medb and Ailill attempt this, one pig jumps over their chariot, the queen grabs a leg and the pig leaves it in her hand together with his skin. As a result, the swine disappear forever and here Medb and Ailill are portrayed in their sacral function of protecting the land.[16] Though placed in a non-Christian past, this aspect of myth and its depiction of righteous rule would have had a very pertinent meaning in the real world of early medieval Ireland.

Of course, the Otherworld was also a place of refuge and protection. In *Táin Bó Fraích*, for example, the wounded hero is carried therein by 'three times fifty women' to come out 'quite healed without defect or blemish' the following day.[17] The cave may well have had ambivalent functions. In *Echtra Nerai*, that warning given to the nearby royal settlement about its impending destruction might mean that prophetic rites once took place here, something well documented in the Greek and Roman world where caves were often instrumental in producing altered states of consciousness.[18]

The numerous warrior associations hint at yet another related purpose for the famous souterrain and cave. If, as Dumézil has claimed, a hero's combat with a triple-headed monster is a transformation into myth of an ancient warrior initiation rite (which once might have involved a mock combat with a tricephalic wooden image), then the tale of the triple-headed creatures killed in single combat by Amairgene may imply that the cave was once the location of initiation practices. Such rites of passage may involve other forms of testing besides combat such as deprivation and isolation, and anthropological studies have documented the potent effectiveness of such 'rites of terror'.[19]

The number of legendary heroic warriors linked to the site raises the interesting possibility that such activities were once part of the cults performed here. A part of the ritual could have involved the introduction of the initiate to the spirits of the warrior dead and the Fraoch inscription may have had a role in this.

The subterranean testing of a warrior inevitably recalls that other entrance to a hellish Otherworld at St Patrick's Purgatory in Lough Derg, Co. Donegal, and the trials of the Knight Owein that were so popular and so widely

16 J. Borsje, 'Druids, deer and "Words of Power": coming to terms with evil in medieval Ireland' in K. Ritari & A. Bergholm (eds), *Approaches to religion and mythology in Celtic Studies* (2008), p. 207; 'Supernatural threats to kings' in Ó hUiginn & Ó Catháin, *Ulidia 2*, p. 182. 17 M.E. Byrne & M. Dillon, 'Táin Bó Fraich', *Études celtiques* 2 (1937), 8. 18 Y. Ustinova, *Caves and the ancient Greek mind* (2009). 19 G. Dumézil, *Horace et les Curiaces* (1942), pp 126, 131ff; H. Whitehouse, 'Rites of terror', *Journal of the Royal Anthropological*

translated in medieval Europe. Given the scanty and conflicting descriptions, we cannot be sure if the original 'cave' here was a souterrain. Whether medieval usage, first recorded in the twelfth century, had pre-Christian roots is also uncertain, but St Patrick's Purgatory may be a Christianized version of the kind of rituals proposed at Oweynagat.[20]

It seems likely that Oweynagat was a focus for cult practices in pre-Christian times that included sensory deprivation and altered states of consciousness associated with divination, oracular activity and warrior initiation. The tales that hint at this sort of usage may be echoes of ancient prehistoric customs, but of course they could also be an indication that some or all of them were practised in early medieval times too. Even in early Christian Ireland aspects of a mythical past were relevant to the present, the Otherworld continued to have power over the living, and martial heroism was as highly prized as in earlier periods.

There are interesting analogies in Scotland. Anna Ritchie was one of the first to draw attention to the impractical nature of some of the so-called wells or cellars in the brochs and round houses of the west and north. In particular, the complexity of the stone-built subterranean structure in the broch of Gurness on Orkney with its steps and chambers seemed to indicate that it was not just a well or a storage place. Ritchie suggested some ritual usage, perhaps a place associated with a water-cult and oracular performance.[21]

The noteworthy discoveries at Mine Howe lend weight to this possibility. Here, a glacial mound some 95m in diameter and 4m in height was surrounded by a substantial ditch with an impressive entrance on the west. There was little or no evidence of domestic activity, but a 7m-deep pit had been dug in the natural hillock and a subterranean stone-built shaft constructed within it. With steps and lateral chambers, the very bottom of the structure is a relatively narrow 90cm deep and roughly circular basin-like feature that could have held water. Nonetheless, its complex architecture and situation once again imply this was other, or more, than just a water container. Mine Howe seems to have been a site of religious importance and its chamber should be considered, in the words of Nick Card and Jane Downes, 'in the context of the Iron Age religious interest in water cults and the underworld'.[22]

These sites appear to indicate that the prehistoric Otherworld is not as obscure and archaeologically elusive as one might think. We have seen the iconographic evidence for the nocturnal sun's connection with it in chapter 3.

Institute 2 (1996), 703–15. **20** Y. de Pontfarcy, 'The historical background to the pilgrimage to Lough Derg' in M. Haren & Y. de Pontfarcy (eds), *The medieval pilgrimage to St Patrick's Purgatory Lough Derg and the European tradition* (1988), 7–34; A. & B. Rees, *Celtic heritage* (1961), p. 304. **21** A. Ritchie, *Prehistoric Orkney* (1995), p. 113; 'Paganism among the Picts' in J. Downes & A. Ritchie (eds), *Sea change* (2003), p. 7. **22** N. Card & J. Downes, 'Mine Howe' in J. Downes & A. Ritchie (eds), *Sea change* (2003), p. 17. Also I.

There is abundant evidence for prehistoric cult practices with a subterranean focus at different times not just in Ireland, Scotland and England but across a wide area of northern and western Continental Europe. It seems that some shafts were primarily wells filled with later debris, but even excluding those sites where usage as a ritual shaft or a well is debated, there are many cases where a ritual purpose seems undeniable.

To cite just a few examples: a subterranean shrine at Mill Hill in Kent decommissioned some time in the second century AD was found to contain a small chalk carving of a human figure that may once have stood in a wall niche (ch. 7). A large 1.1m-deep central pit in a rectangular sanctuary of the early Iron Age at Vix 'les Herbues' in eastern France was plausibly interpreted as a portal to another world.[23] Some centuries later in date, a 7.6m-deep and carefully cut shaft in a rectangular timber shrine at Acy-Romance in the Ardennes, whose base was well above the water table over 50m below, clearly had a cultic purpose. The discovery of a group of male burials in peculiarly contorted positions (cross-legged and bent double) prompted the intriguing argument that these sacrifical victims had been placed in a timber box in the shaft in a process of dessication before their dried corpses were interred nearby.[24]

GIFTS TO THE OTHERWORLD

There are numerous other indications that the digging of a pit or a ditch was one way of engaging with this underworld. The extraordinarily widespread custom of depositing hoards of metal objects or other materials in them has deep prehistoric roots and reflects an extensive preoccupation with the powers of a netherworld.[25] 'Votive offerings', 'ritual deposits', 'structured deposition', 'gifts to the Gods', are all terms used by archaeologists to describe a variety of practices on dry land, in rivers, lakes and bogs, that reached their height in late prehistoric times.

Inevitably, it is difficult, if not impossible, to reconstruct what detailed form these took and it is obviously even more difficult to establish what perception of the netherworld these ancient peoples may have had. We may never know whether it was thought to be a parallel world, a mirror world or a land of the dead, or what sort of powers were thought to reside there, but the enormous amount of ritually deposited material suggests this world below was a major preoccupation in many prehistoric lives.

Armit, *Towers in the north* (2003), p. 110.   **23** B. Chaume & W. Reinhard, 'Les dépôts de l'enclos cultuel hallstattien de Vix "les Herbues"', *Bulletin de la Société préhistorique française* 104 (2007), 347.   **24** B. Lambot & P. Méniel, 'Le centre communautaire et culturel du village gaulois d'Acy-Romance' in S. Verger (ed.), *Rites et espaces en pays celte et méditerranéen* (2000), p. 53.   **25** R. Bradley, *The passage of arms* (1990).

Just to name some Irish instances, a pair of hoards of gold bracelets carefully placed in small pits in the earth on Cathedral Hill, Downpatrick, Co. Down, or the great deposit of bronze objects found in a watery context at Dowris, near Birr, in Co. Offaly, are just two examples of many that demonstrate this island shared in wider European cult practices.[26]

The two Downpatrick hoards are rare Irish examples of well-documented discoveries – most finds of this sort are old and poorly recorded. One, found in the course of grave-digging in 1954, had been carefully deposited in a very small pit, 20cm in greatest diameter, covered by some stones. It consisted of eleven bracelets and part of a neck ring which had been carefully stacked one upon the other, the smaller ones at the bottom, the three largest at the top and separated from the rest by an inch of clay filling. One bracelet was represented by just one half and it had evidently been cut by a chisel-like implement. Only about half the neck ring had been deposited and it too had been partly cut with a chisel. The peculiar clay filling and the destruction of some pieces imply that this was not just a cluster of personal ornaments buried for safe-keeping.

The second hoard was discovered in similar circumstances two years later some 20m from the site of the first. This time, four bracelets had been stacked in a very small pit and three small stones had been placed in the pit on top of them. Both hoards were found within some 20m of the site of limited excavations undertaken on the south-western side of the hill in the 1950s. These excavations had revealed extensive traces of late prehistoric occupation mainly in the form of coarse pottery. Whether hoards and settlement are contemporary is uncertain and the site was not a hillfort as was once thought.

The Dowris deposit, found in the early nineteenth century, is the largest collection of bronze objects ever found in Ireland (fig. 4.3). Originally it may have comprised over two hundred items including tools, swords, spears and cauldrons, sometimes fragmentary, and it included that exotic bucket of central European type (fig. 4.3, 1). It was discovered in reclaimed bogland near the site of a former lake that in the early nineteenth century formed a large area of deep open water. In prehistoric times it would probably have been a much more extensive body of water located at the foot of several low glacial ridges and encompassed by bog. It was certainly situated on the edge of a vast expanse of midland bog.

This immense and inhospitable area stretched northwards to the horizon and was broadly demarcated to the south and east by the higher, undulating good agricultural land that formed a broad arc at the foot of the Slieve Bloom mountains. The lake's liminal location – on the interface between the wild and the tamed – must have invested it with special meaning, and the area of still water may have been perceived as an opening in the earth giving access to an

26 J. Waddell, *The prehistoric archaeology of Ireland* (2010), pp 206, 232.

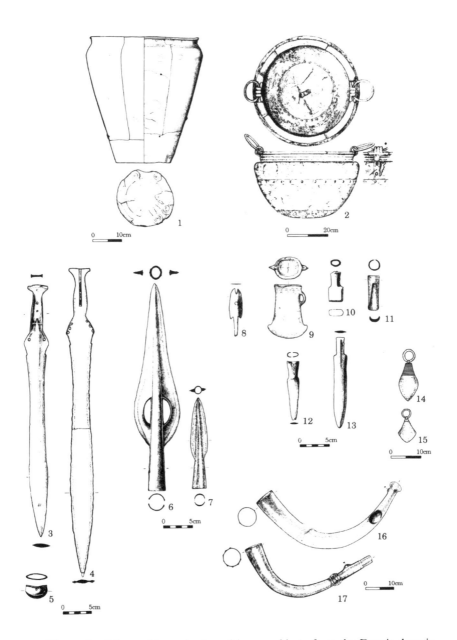

4.3. Gifts to the Otherworld: a selection of bronze objects from the Dowris deposit.
1. Bucket of central European type. 2. Cauldron. 3–4. Swords. 5. Scabbard chape.
6–7. Spearheads. 8. Razor. 9. Socketed axehead. 10. Socketed hammer. 11. Socketed gouge.
12–13. Knives. 14–15. Pendants. 16–17. Horns.

other- or under-world. The bog would have been a place shaped by non-human forces, and both water and bog may have demanded a votive offering from time to time to placate whatever supernatural creatures lived there.

The term 'hoard' was applied to the Dowris find because it was assumed that it represented a collection of objects all deposited at the one time, but the range of material suggests that it was a diverse set of objects deposited over a period of time, possibly several centuries, around 1000BC. To dispose of a complete bronze bucket or cauldron, even an old one that had seen some use as the centrepiece of a long series of elite feasts, must have been an act of particular significance. Its submergence in the lake may have been a part of a public ceremony celebrated by someone of religious or political importance. The deposition of a broken spear or sword, on the other hand, might conceivably have been a more private commemorative event coinciding with its use in a victorious combat or with the death of its warrior owner. A woodworker's axe or gouge may have been a craftsman's tribute, and scrap bronze or a polishing stone the gift of a metalworker. Some poorly finished axeheads may even have been specially made or selected for formal discarding. In fact, the diverse range of objects could denote a hierarchy of participants. There was probably a protracted series of different sorts of performance, some communal in the hope of benefiting a social group, some perhaps of a more individual nature.

The gold objects found at Downpatrick may once have been personal ornaments, but their very careful deposition in a dry-land context may hint at yet another purpose. If contemporary with that nearby settlement, the gold may have been an offering to the land, marking a reciprocal relationship between people and environment. If, however, the land was perceived as female, and if – as is sometimes said – such goldwork was female adornment, then there is another deeper dimension to these precious gifts. This may have been a more directed deposit than an all-purpose 'gift to the gods'. They may have been specific offerings to a goddess of the land, a figure well attested in Irish tradition (ch. 6).

While lakes, wells, groves, hills, burial mounds and royal sites all had supernatural associations and were points of access to the Otherworld, the great oval earthwork known as Ráth na Rí on the Hill of Tara (fig. 7.1) may be a good archaeological example of another form of engagement with the subterranean supernatural. Limited excavation has demonstrated that this huge monument was enclosed by a large earthen bank with an internal ditch and with a timber palisade on the inner edge of the ditch. It was a laborious undertaking, dating to sometime in the first century BC. The ditch alone was rock-cut to a maximum depth of 2.7m with a width of about 7m at ground level. As at Navan Fort, this reversal of the natural order, placing a ditch inside rather than outside a rampart, has long been recognized as a means of demarcating a sacred space, perhaps for containing supernatural forces and even protecting the outside world (ch. 5). This reversal, bank outside ditch, is also a feature of burial mounds such as ring-barrows.

Aside from its internal configuration, the enormous ditch cutting into Tara may have had a potent magical significance of its own, intruding as it did into the world beneath.[27] The earthen bank outside and the timber palisade within may not just have delimited the consecrated space of the interior but may have offered some protection from the forces emanating from the ditch. The idea that the ditch itself had a special significance is reinforced by the large amount and the composition of material recovered from it in two relatively small excavation trenches. Disarticulated human bone, the skeleton of an infant and quantities of animal bone were the principal finds and the remains of butchered dogs and horses may have had particular cultic associations.[28] In one instance, a horse bone showed evidence of roasting and, as we shall see (ch. 7), the horse remains may be the residue of equine rites associated with kingly inauguration.

Like the extraordinary discoveries in pits and ditches in some late prehistoric Continental cult sites – such as the great pit at Vertault (Côte d'Or, France) that contained the carcasses of ten pole-axed stallions[29] – these bones at Tara could have been consigned to the ditch as offerings to supernatural powers. As a Greek writer said nearly two thousand years ago, 'The chthonic gods welcome trenches and ceremonies done in the hollow earth'.[30]

THE FRUITS OF SUMMER

That burial places, whether tomb, mound or pit grave, should be special places that were seen to interface with the Otherworld is not surprising. However, this raises the interesting question: 'does inversion or reversal of grave contents signify a relationship with a world sometimes seen as the opposite of this one?' The inversion of pottery vessels in burials, either as urns containing bones or as covering vessels, is a practice found at different times in various parts of Europe. It is particularly common in the British and Irish Bronze Age burial record, for example. Large cinerary urns containing cremated bone are often placed mouth downwards and sometimes empty vessels are also inverted in a grave (fig. 4.4). It has been proposed that the larger urns might, in some cases, represent a house of the dead.[31] It is true to say, however, that plausible house-

---

27 G. Dowling, 'The liminal boundary: an analysis of the sacral potency of the ditch at Ráith na Ríg, Tara, Co. Meath', *Journal of Irish Archaeology* 15 (2006), 15–37.   28 E. Bhreathnach, 'Observations on the occurrence of dog and horse bones at Tara', *Discovery Programme Reports* 6 (2002), 117–22.   29 P. Méniel, *Les sacrifices d'animaux chez les Gaulois* (1992), p. 71.   30 Philostratos in his Life of Apollonius: J.E. Harrison, *Prolegomena to the study of Greek religion* (1903), p. 125.   31 C.J. Lynn, 'House-urns in Ireland?', *Ulster Journal of Archaeology* 56 (1993), 70–7.

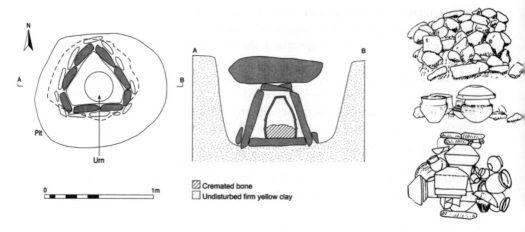

4.4. Inverted pottery in Bronze Age burials. Left: a large urn found inverted and containing cremated bones in a polygonal cist at Ballyvool, Co. Kilkenny. Right: Urnfield burials from Saxony, eastern Germany.

like ceramic forms are not to be found, and even what might be imprecise copies do not occur. It is likely that some other symbolism is intended here and inversion at times does seem to be a reference to the Otherworld, as we shall see (below).

Ethnographic evidence reminds us just how notoriously difficult the interpretation of burial activity can be and that there may be no associated belief in a journey to an afterworld. As Peter Ucko once memorably pointed out, one west African tradition neatly illustrates the sort of difficulties sometimes confronting the archaeologist. Among the Ashanti, custom once ordained that the buried corpse should not face the village but a minority believed that the dead turned over in the grave and consequently, to compensate for this post-mortem revolution, they buried them facing the settlement.[32]

As noted before, the Otherworld was often seen as a land of peace and plenty; it was also a timeless region and, sometimes, the mirror image of the human world. In *Echtra Nerai*, much of the action occurs at the feast of Samhain, the beginning of winter, and emerging from the *síd*, Nera brings 'the fruits of summer' with him. It is evident that when it is summer in one world, it is winter in the other.

This particular sort of Otherworldy inversion is rarely mentioned, but it is alluded to in the early thirteenth-century *History of the Danes* of Saxo Grammaticus. The king Hadingus is approached at supper by a woman bearing hemlock and, in inviting him to see what part of the world such fresh plants might grow in winter, she enveloped him in her cloak and 'vanished

32 P.J. Ucko, 'Ethnography and archaeological interpretation of funerary remains', *World Archaeology* 1 (1969), 273.

away with him beneath the earth'. They both found themselves eventually in a sunny Otherworld region where such herbs grew.[33] Here, influence from Irish tradition cannot be ruled out,[34] but Jens Peter Schjødt has drawn attention to the significance of another feature of the Hadingus story. His journey to the Otherworld ends when he and the woman who had taken him there come to a wall. She cuts the head off a cock and throws it over the wall. The cock crows and lives and Hadingus abruptly finds himself in the real world again. There is a striking inverted parallel between this myth and the ritual to be found in the celebrated tenth-century description of a Viking ship burial by the Arab traveller Ibn Fadlan. This complex funeral of a chieftain of the Rus people involved the bringing of the corpse and grave goods to the ship along with the sacrifice of a slave girl who is eventually burnt with chieftain and ship. Part of the ritual included the decapitation of a hen by the girl who threw away the head; some men then threw its body into the ship. Schjødt emphasizes the contrasts here. In Ibn Fadlan's account of the funeral ceremony, a woman is about to join the dead, the body of a hen is thrown by men into the ship, the world of the dead. In the Hadingus myth, a man is about to leave that world and a cock's head is thrown by a woman into the land of the living.[35]

It is a distinct possibility that this notion of reversal or inversion between two worlds was a widespread belief and one occasionally reflected not just in solar symbolism (ch. 3) but in other ways in the archaeological record. In the famous Iron Age burial at Hochdorf (Baden-Württemberg, Germany), the dead man was laid on a bronze couch and accompanied by all the status symbols of the Hallstatt period elite – namely a drinking set, a wagon and rich personal ornaments (fig. 7.2). Craftsmen were summoned to the burial site to make some of the ornaments, including strips of decorated sheet gold for the dead man's shoes (fig. 4.5). Golden shoes were a symbolic attribute of kingship in Irish and Welsh tradition and Calvert Watkins noted some etymological evidence in Old and Middle Irish that suggests shoes 'with uppers of gold' may have been marks of distinction (ch. 7).[36]

The Hochdorf individual's shoes had perished, but the decorative golden attachments indicated that the right shoe had been placed on the left foot and vice versa. Ulrich Veit noted how the inversion of grave goods may represent the passing of a person from this world to the next, to a '*verkehrten Welt*' or upside-down world.[37] Eugène Warmenbol too has remarked that it was unlikely this was a simple mistake in this highly ritualized context.[38] He drew attention

33 H.E. Davidson & P. Fisher, *Saxo Grammaticus* (1996), p. 30; H.R. Ellis, *The road to Hel* (1943), p. 172.   34 E. Ól. Sveinson, 'Celtic elements in Icelandic tradition', *Béaloideas* 25 (1957), 3–24.   35 J.P. Schjødt, 'Ibn Fadlan's account of a Rus funeral' in P. Hermann et al. (eds), *Reflections on Old Norse myths* (2007), p. 143.   36 C. Watkins, 'Language, culture or history?' in C.S. Masek et al. (eds), *Papers from the parasession on language and behavior* (1981), p. 243.   37 U. Veit, 'Des Fürsten neue Schuhe', *Germania* 66 (1988), 162–9.   38 E. Warmenbol, 'Miroirs et mantique à l'âge du Bronze', in C. Burgess et al. (eds), *Beyond*

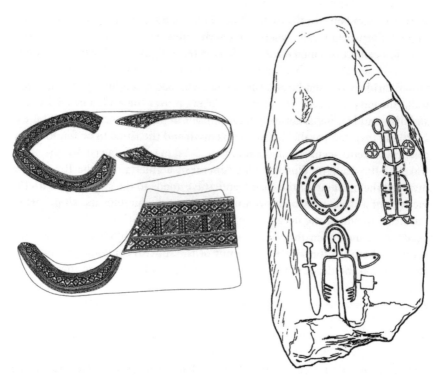

4.5. *Left*: a reconstruction of one of the shoes bearing gold decoration from Hochdorf, Baden-Württemberg. *Right*: an engraved slab from Cabeza de Buey, Badajoz, depicting a helmeted warrior with sword, spear, shield and chariot; the shield is shown reversed with the grip rather than the frontal boss visible.

to Hittite mythology where the god of fertility and agriculture Telipinu disappears in winter having put his sandals on the wrong feet. He undergoes a symbolic death and spends a time in the land of the dead with predictable effects on nature until he is located and brought back to this world.

There seems to be an echo of this notion of reversed footwear in Slavonic folklore, where the *leshy* or *leshii* are malevolent demon-gods, spirits of the forest, who are particularly active in the spring after dying in autumn like the leaves on the trees among which they lived. Their style of dress included clothing worn back to front and shoes worn on the wrong feet.[39] It must be confessed there is a great distance, in every sense of the word, between an ancient Anatolian myth and more recent eastern European folk beliefs, but it is possible that this idea of reversed footwear associated with an Otherworldly journey was once a commoner motif now all but lost in the welter of myth and

Stonehenge (2007), p. 392. **39** M. Dixon-Kennedy, *Encyclopedia of Russian and Slavic myth and legend* (1998), p. 166; G. Alexinsky, 'Slavonic mythology' in R. Aldington & D. Ames (trans.), *New Larousse encyclopedia of mythology* (1968), p. 290.

folklore about shoes. This ranges from widespread tokens of good luck to the 'hel-shoes' of the dead worn on their way to Valhalla in Nordic mythology.[40]

There is an obvious difference between the wearing of shoes on the wrong feet and the wearing of just one shoe with the other foot unshod, but it is possible that the rite of the single shoe or sandal, like reversed footwear, is another form of reversal or inversion. There are early Irish references to Otherworld figures associated with a single piece of footwear. It was said of Ábartach mac Ildathaig, one of the supernatural Tuatha Dé Danann, 'It was you who, in seeking to escape to Doireann, alternated the golden sandal so that each of your feet had the turn of it'. Another Otherworld figure also wore one golden sandal, which, as he walked, was on whichever foot touched the ground; another wore a silver sandal in a similar fashion and yet another wore a silver sandal on his left foot and a golden one on his right. As Mac Cana suggested, this may be a motif in some way related to the Indian taboo that prohibited a king treading the ground unshod lest his potency be drained away into the earth but in early Irish tradition its supernatural associations are not in doubt.[41]

There are some references in classical literature and art to what has been called *monosandalisme*. Some cases seem to have magical significance denoting a critical transition from one state of being to another. Among them is a bronze statuette of Mercury from Saint-Révérien, Nièvre, in central France, with left foot shod and right foot bare. If, as has been pointed out, this is a representation of Mercury in his capacity as psychopomp or Guide of Souls escorting the dead to the afterlife, then there is an evident Otherworldy connection.[42] The rite of the single shoe emerged as an element in lordly inauguration ceremonies in Gaelic Ireland in the fifteenth and sixteenth centuries. A shoe was placed on the foot of the chief-elect or in one recorded instance cast over his head.[43]

There is now an appreciation in archaeological studies that prehistoric burials may be more than just events for social display and that grave goods may bear some relationship not just to a past life but also to who the deceased might become in an afterlife. His shoes seem to mean that the Hochdorf body was deliberately prepared for an Otherworld journey. This voyage is alluded to in the panel of decoration on the back of the bronze couch on which the body rested; its ends are decorated with pairs of stylized bird's heads, a reference to the solar boat that travels to this destination. This was a mirror realm where all

40 P. Sartori, 'Der Schuh im Volksglauben', *Zeitschrift des Vereins für Volkskunde* 4 (1894), 41ff.   **41** P. Mac Cana, 'The *topos* of the single sandal in Irish tradition', *Celtica* 10 (1973), 162.   **42** J.F. Killeen, 'Fear an énais', *Celtica* 9 (1971), 202–4. Classical examples: E.P. de Loos-Dietz, 'Le *monosandalos* dans l'Antiquité', *Babesch* 69 (1994), 175–97; P. Bruneau, 'L'impair de chaussures' in P. L. de Bellefonds (ed.), *Mythes et cultes* (2000), pp 63–72. Illustrations of a cast of the Mercury statuette: S. Reinach, *Bronzes figurés de la Gaule romaine* (1894), p. 65, fig. 48 and *Catalogue illustré du Musée des antiquités nationales*, 2 (1921), p. 168, fig. 82.   **43** E. FitzPatrick, *Royal inauguration in Gaelic Ireland* (2004), p. 122.

might be inverted. As we saw, the bronze mounts on the Vix wagon with their pairs of bird's heads above and below the solar symbol (fig. 3.4) are another allusion to this in a funerary context.

Half a millennium earlier, a series of funerary or commemorative stelae in south-western Iberia were engraved with schematic motifs including stylized figures of warriors, swords, spears, chariots and circular shields. It is clear that the shields are frequently shown not with their central frontal boss but with the rectangular handle or grip on the back of the object clearly depicted (fig. 4.5).[44] Marion Uckelmann, in her splendid study of European shields, sees this back-to-front view as one from a shield-bearer's perspective and a means of expressing the protective purpose of these objects rather than their offensive role. Thus the stone itself could have been a territorial marker presenting an offer of safety and protection.[45] But there may be another and related meaning; it is possible that the shield is reversed because the dead warrior denoted by the weaponry belongs to the Otherworld, his supernatural status giving him even greater power.

The occasional depiction of a sword on the warrior's right (rather than on the left as might be expected in a right-handed person) may be another expression of this reversal. Some Hallstatt swords in male graves in France and Germany have been found inverted on the body – the point towards the head, the hilt towards the feet.[46] Such 'rites of reversal' have been noted in several English Iron Age burials as well. The iron spines of some shields have been found placed face downwards in the grave suggesting inversion and a coat of chain mail placed on the body in a Yorkshire chariot burial at Kirkburn (K5) had been laid upside-down and back to front.[47] Careful scrutiny of other funerary evidence may provide some more clues for a deeply rooted concept of an inverted Otherworld, a belief conceivably widely distributed in time and space and, as pointed out, even reflected in the inversion of pottery vessels.

Reversed or inverted grave goods may not be the only funerary indication of this preoccupation with the passage of the dead between two very different worlds. The stone packing above a series of pre-Christian Migration period graves at Sylta, north of Stockholm, was carefully laid in a counter-clockwise direction and once again this reversal of the normal order, like reversed footware, seems to be a symbolic allusion to the inverted world of the dead.

In a discussion of the Sylta phenomenon, Andreas Nordberg has drawn attention to the connection between some funerary practices and the necessity to perform some actions backwards, upside-down or contrary to the course of the sun. He instances, for example, a scene on the eighth-century picture-

44 R.J. Harrison, *Symbols and warriors* (2004), passim.   45 M. Uckelmann, *Die Schilde der Bronzezeit* (2012), p. 136.   46 L. Olivier, 'The Hochdorf "princely grave" and the question of the nature of archaeological funerary assemblages' in T. Murray (ed.), *Time and archaeology* (1999), p. 125.   47 M. Giles, *A forged glamour* (2012), p. 210.

stone at Tängelgårda in Gotland that depicts a funeral procession in which a horse with eight legs, Odin's horse Sleipnir, is carrying a fallen warrior to the Otherworld. Behind the horse, the three men in the procession are walking backwards and carrying their swords upside-down.[48] It is beyond the scope of this enquiry, but could it be that some of the footprints or some of the processional scenes found in Bronze Age Scandinavian rock art also represent people walking backwards?[49]

The sort of anti-clockwise construction noted at Sylta may occur elsewhere. To cite one possibility, it may be a feature of some Bronze Age cists in these islands where it is always feasible that the side-stones were erected in this type of sequence. It has been claimed that the stones of a cist at Corroy, Co. Roscommon, where one end of each slab extended beyond its neighbour, were arranged 'in cyclic order' and this rare overlapping detail has been noted in Scotland too.[50] There could, of course, be a simple functional explanation for this. It could just have been a means of stabilizing the sides of the grave and it does not necessarily imply counter-clockwise behaviour. However, the Sylta evidence reminds us that we should be alert to the possibility that Otherworldly references might sometimes be reflected not just in burial deposits like reversed swords or shoes or inverted pottery but also in grave architecture.

Whether in burials, in rock engravings, on the Trundholm sun chariot, on the designs on some Bronze Age and Iron Age metalwork, or in the custom of hoard deposition, archaeological allusions to this supernatural underworld are widely scattered in prehistoric Europe. A belief in an Otherworld is not surprising, but what precisely this belief entailed is difficult, almost impossible, to determine. There are some clues, however, in Irish and other traditions. There was probably a complex cosmology attached to it and it was much more than just 'a land of the dead'.

This Otherworld was also a place of prosperity and harmony. In *Echtra Laegairi* (The Adventure of Laegaire), Laegaire, the son of Crimhthann Cass, king of Connacht, journeys to Magh Mell, the plain of delights, a name found in other tales and denoting the pagan Otherworld.[51] His journey takes him beneath a lake, Loch na nÉn, 'the lake of the birds', to a place of 'fine plaintive fairy music ... drinking mead from bright vessels, talking with the one you love' where, perhaps understandably, he decides to stay and 'has not come out

---

48 A. Nordberg, 'The grave as a doorway to the Other World', *Temenos* 45 (2009), 51. The Tängelgårda, Lärbro, stone is illustrated in G. Jones, *A history of the Vikings* (1984), pl. 13. **49** R. Bradley, 'Death by water: boats and footprints in the rock art of western Sweden', *Oxford Journal of Archaeology* 16 (1997), 315–24; *An archaeology of natural places* (2000), p. 141; J. Coles, 'And on they went ... processions in Scandinavian Bronze Age rock carvings', *Acta Archaeologica* 74 (2003), 211–50. **50** H. Morris, 'Ancient graves in Sligo and Roscommon', *Journal of the Royal Society of Antiquaries of Ireland* 59 (1929), 99; J. Waddell, 'Irish Bronze Age cists', *Journal of the Royal Society of Antiquaries of Ireland* 100 (1970), 94. **51** D. Dumville, 'Echtrae and immram', *Ériu* 27 (1976), 79.

4.6. Bronze chain-link object, perhaps insignia of high status worn on the shoulder, found in Loughnaneane near Roscommon town.

yet'.[52] Assuming that the identification of this lake with a former lake in Loughnaneane townland near Roscommon town is correct, it cannot be just a coincidence that marshy ground around this body of water has produced one of the most exceptional pieces of prehistoric metalwork from the west of Ireland.

Discovered around 1840, this object essentially consists of two broad bands composed of multiple chains of linked bronze rings forming an oval piece with each end connected by a large circular ring containing a wheel-shaped design (fig. 4.6). Though incomplete, its slightly arched rectangular central pieces indicated to George Eogan that it may have been an insignia of high rank worn over both shoulders. He suggests its closest parallels are to be found among late Bronze Age chain-link objects in central Europe, some of them clearly ceremonial items with bird and wheel sun symbols.[53] Like that bronze bucket of central European type from Dowris, this is a good illustration how various forms and fashions might be transmitted over great distances in late prehistoric Europe to eventually become a singular and exotic offering to the netherworld.

The peaceful and fruitful Otherworld was accessed in various ways. In Loch na nÉn, it was entered via a lake but mounds, certainly, were common portals. One tale that represents it entered in this manner is *De Gabáil int Sída* (The Taking of the Otherworld Mound), where we are told that in the *síd* of Newgrange, there is a wonderful land: 'There are three trees there perpetually bearing fruit and an everliving pig on the hoof and a cooked pig, and a vessel with excellent liquour, and all of this never grows less'.[54] When the legendary king, Conn of the Hundred Battles, is transported to the Otherworld (ch. 7),

52 K.H. Jackson, 'The adventure of Laeghaire Mac Crimhthainn', *Speculum* 17 (1942), 384.
53 G. Eogan, 'A composite late Bronze Age object from Roscommon, Ireland' in W.H. Metz et al. (eds), *Patina* (2001), pp 231–40.   54 Koch & Carey, *The Celtic heroic age*, p. 145.

he is offered a portion of meat over-sized by any standard: '... ox-rib and the rib of a boar ... the ox-rib was twenty-four feet long, and there were eight feet between its flank and the ground'.

This world was also a land of the dead. Though the subject of extensive folklore, there are but a few references to an Otherworldly figure named Donn in early literature. In *Togail Bruidne Dá Derga* (The Destruction of Dá Derga's Hostel), Conaire Mór encounters three horsemen with red tunics and mantles, with red weaponry and riding red horses, one of whom ominously declares 'We ride the steeds of Donn Desscorrach from the *síd*-mounds. Though we are alive we are dead ...'

This Donn, the dark one, ruled over the world of the dead and was associated in particular with an island named Tech Duinn, the house of Donn, off the Beara Peninsula in the south-west.[55] Various writers have believed this figure to be the insular counterpart of the Gaulish god that Caesar equated with Dis Pater, the Roman god of the dead. There are hints that Donn represents a primordial forebear of mankind and is a reflection of a primeval ancestor and lord of the dead found in Indo-European myth.[56] His former significance may explain the scanty references to him in early Irish literature. Once again, the censorious hand of monastic redactors may have been at work.[57]

This darker aspect of the Otherworld is very evident in Irish tradition in the remarkable series of malevolent creatures associated with Oweynagat for instance. It is a feature of Homer's description of Hades, Old Norse accounts of Hel, or in the picture presented in Iranian legend as Bruce Lincoln has shown. There was an Indo-European image of the world of the dead as a fearful, dark and sorrowful place, sometimes filled with serpents and other terrifying creatures. There was also an Indo-European belief in a very different Otherworld where we find reference to a paradisal realm reserved for specially favoured souls, a place of radical otherness, 'the endless, deathless world' of one Vedic verse.[58]

55 K. Müller-Lisowski, 'Contributions to a study in Irish folklore', *Bealoideas* 18 (1948), 142–99. For *Togail Bruidne da Derga* (The Destruction of Da Derga's Hostel), see Koch & Carey, *The Celtic heroic age*, p. 162.   **56** J. Carey, 'Donn, Amairgen, Íth and the prehistory of Irish pseudohistory', *Journal of Indo-European Studies* 38 (2010), 319–41.   **57** P. Mac Cana, *The cult of the sacred centre* (2011), p. 222.   **58** B. Lincoln, 'On the imagery of paradise', *Indogermanische Forschungen* 85 (1980), 151–64.

CHAPTER 5

The horse goddess

The name 'the Navan complex' has been given to a concentration of over forty archaeological monuments in an area of much late prehistoric activity stretching for just over a kilometre around Navan Fort, Co. Armagh. This great enclosure is considered to be Emain Macha, the capital of Ulster in early Irish literature. To the west of Navan Fort lie Haughey's Fort with the King's Stables nearby. The major ecclesiastical centre at Armagh is situated just over 2km to the east. Haughey's Fort is a large multivallate hillfort constructed in or about the twelfth century BC. Limited excavation has revealed it was a high-status site and its importance is confirmed by the discovery of the exceptional Tamlaght hoard about 700m to the south-west. Found in marshy ground, this comprised a leaf-shaped sword, a small bronze bowl, parts of a decorated bronze cup and a small bronze ring. The sword is of native manufacture but the bowl and cup were prestigious imports from central Europe where they are types dated to approximately 1000BC. No doubt part of a drinking set, they are testimony to the great distances covered by some fashionable bronze objects.

The monument traditionally known as the King's Stables was popularly thought to be the site where the ancient kings of Ulster stabled and watered their horses, but excavation has shown that it was an artificially constructed flat-bottomed pond. Fragments of clay moulds for bronze swords, pottery sherds, animal bones and a part of a human skull were deposited in it at the time Haughey's Fort was occupied. To the north of Navan Fort are the sites of two possible passage tombs, while to the north-east is a small natural lake called Loughnashade that was the focus of Iron Age ritual offerings that included a well-known decorated bronze trumpet.[1]

Excavations were undertaken at Navan Fort by Dudley Waterman between 1963 and 1972 with exceptional results. This large earthwork encloses the summit of a drumlin ridge and, though only about 60m above sea level, has commanding views in all directions, especially to the north-west. The enclosure is six hectares and is a large circle surrounded by a wide deep ditch and a very substantial external earthen bank with an overall diameter of approximately 286m (pl. 4). One of two oak timbers recovered from excavation of the lowest fill of the ditch has provided a dendrochronological estimated felling date of about 95BC. Thus, the enclosure presumably dates to the last

---

1 C.J. Lynn, *Excavations at Navan Fort* (1997), p. 3. Tamlaght hoard: R.B. Warner, 'The Tamlaght hoard', *Emania* 20 (2006), 20–8.

century BC and is broadly contemporary with the similar internally ditched Ráth na Rí on the Hill of Tara.

Waterman's excavations were conducted at two visible monuments in the interior. One, which had the appearance of a small ditched enclosure, was partially excavated in 1961 and has been the subject of more recent geophysical survey and limited excavation. The other, excavated between 1963 and 1971, was a large circular flat-topped mound 50m in diameter and 6m high. Prominently sited on the centre of the hilltop, it lies about 55m west-north-west of the centre of the large enclosure. Both revealed evidence of protracted prehistoric usage and the construction of complex circular timber structures in which ritual rather than domestic activity was to the fore.

On present evidence, the belief of medieval storytellers that the great enclosure was a royal settlement would appear to be a literary fiction invented to obscure its association with pagan ceremonial. The heroic realm and the royal house are described in terms of extravagant splendour in *Tochmarc Emire* (The Wooing of Emer):

> There lived once upon a time a great and famous king in Emain Macha, whose name was Conchobar, son of Fachtna Fathach. In his reign there was much store of good things enjoyed by the men of Ulster. Peace there was, and quiet, and pleasant greeting; there were fruits and fatness and harvest of the sea; there was power and law and good lordship during his time among the men of Erin. In the king's house at Emain was great state and rank and plenty. On this wise was that house, the Red Branch of Conchobar, namely, after the likeness of the Tech Midchuarta of Tara. Nine compartments were in it from the fire to the wall. Thirty feet was the height of each bronze partition in the house. Carvings of red yew therein. A wooden floor beneath, and a roofing of tiles above. The compartment of Conchobar was in the front of the house, with a ceiling of silver with pillars of bronze. Their headpieces glittered with gold and were set with carbuncles, so that day and night were equally light therein ...[2]

Like the description of the royal house of Ailill and Medb at Rathcroghan, this seems to be a literary stereotype applied to any royal residence.[3] While the Heroic or Ulster Cycle celebrates the exploits of the warriors of the Ulaid, especially those of Cú Chulainn, and is centred here where Conchobor, king of Ulster, has his court, not all is a literary construct. As we have seen in that account of the birth of Cú Chulainn, for example, some elements take us to a more archaic mythical realm and themes such as the sovereignty goddess, solar myth and the Otherworld are certainly a large part of the story of Emain Macha.

According to the prose *Dindshenchas* of Ard Macha (Armagh), various manifestations of a deity are reflected in the place-names Emain Macha and Ard Macha:[4]

Macha ben Nemedh m*ei*c Agnomoin atbath and 7 rohadnacht, 7 ba hé indara magh .x. roslecht la Nemedh, 7 dobretha dia mnoi co mbeith a ainm asa. Un*de* M*ag* M*acha*.

Ailit*er*: Macha ing*en* Aedha Ruaidh m*ai*c Bad*uirn*, is le rothornedh Emoin. Is ann ro hadnacht dia r*us*-marb Re*ch*t*ai*dh Rigd*er*g, 7 is dia guba rognith Oenach Macha. Un*de* M*ag* M*acha*.

Ailit*er*: Machae da*no* ben Chru[i]nd m*ei*c Agnom*an* doriacht and do comrith f*ri* heacha C*on*cobai*r*, ar atb*er*t an fer ba luaithiu a bean. Aml*ai*d da*no* bói in ben, is hi inbadhach, cor' chuinnigh cairde coro thoed a brú, 7 ni tuc*ad* di, 7 dognith in comrith iar*um*, 7 ba luaithem si, 7 o ro siacht [cenn] in céiti b*er*idh mac 7 ingen – Fir 7 Fial a n-anmand – 7 atb*er*t co mbedis Ul*ai*d fo ceis óited in ca*ch* uair d*us*-ficfad eicin. C*on*id de bái in cess f*or* Ullt*ai*b f*ri* re *noma*ide o fl*aith* C*on*cobair co flaith Mail m*ei*c Ro*ch*raidhe, 7 atb*er*at ba hí sin Grian Banch*ur*e ing*en* Mid*ir* Brí L*éith*, 7 atbeb iar suidhiu, 7 focresa a fert i nArd Machae 7 focer a guba 7 roclan[n]udh a líae. Un*de* Ard M*acha*.

Macha wife of Nemed son of Agnoman died there (on Mag Macha) and was buried, and it is the twelfth plain which was cleared by Nemed, and he bestowed it on his wife so that it might bear her name. Whence *Mag Macha* 'Macha's Plain'.

Otherwise: Macha daughter of Aed the Red, son of Badurn – 'tis by her Emain was marked out – was buried there when Rechtaid of the red fore-arm killed her. To lament her, *Oenach Macha* 'Macha's Fair' was established. Whence *Mag Macha*.

Otherwise: Macha wife of Crund, son of Agnoman went thither to race against king Conchobar's horses, for her husband had said that his wife was swifter (than they). Thus then was the wife, big with child: so she asked a respite till her womb should have fallen, and this was not granted to her. So then the race was run, and she was the swiftest. And when she reached the end of the green she brings forth a boy and a girl – Fír and Fíal 'True and Modest' their names – and she said that the Ulaid would abide under feebleness of childbed whensoever need should befall them. Wherefore the Ulaid suffered feebleness for the space of a *nomad* from the reign of Conchobar to the reign of Mál son of Rochraide 'Great

Emania 5 (1988), 27.   4 Wh. Stokes, 'The prose tales of the Rennes Dindsenchas', *Revue celtique* 16 (1895), 44; M.B. Ó Mainnín, "'*Co mBeith a Ainm Asa*'': the eponymous Macha in the place-names *Mag Macha*, *Emain Macha* and *Óenach Macha*' in R. Ó hUiginn & B. Ó

heart'. And men say that she was Grían Banchure 'the Sun of Womanfolk', daughter of Mider of Brí Léith. And after this she died, and her tomb was raised on Ard Macha, and her lamentation was made, and her gravestone was planted. Whence *Ard Machae* 'Macha's Height'.

While etymological invention is common in the *dindshenchas* tradition, there is more than just creative story telling and wordplay here. As Marie-Louise Sjoestedt noted in her pioneering book *Dieux et Héros des Celtes* published in 1940,[5] there is reference to no fewer than three different women named Macha. Here we should remember Mac Cana's observation about variants like this in myth where different versions serve to confirm and complement rather than contradict one another.

The first of this trio is the wife of Nemed, the leader of the third of the mythical invasions of Ireland that form a part of the *Lebor Gabála* (The Book of Invasions). She is specifically associated with the plain of Macha, *Mag Macha*, and this is one of many instances in which a goddess is linked to a feminized land. In another version of the *dindshenchas* of Ard Macha, this first Macha is credited with prophetic powers and has a vision of the slaughter that will occur when the *Táin Bó Cúailnge* is undertaken: 'in her sleep was shown to her all the evil that was suffered therein, and the hardships and the wicked quarrels: so that her heart broke in her'.[6] In another manifestation (which some would see as a fourth Macha), this Macha is also identified as one of the great war goddesses along with Badb and the fearsome Morrígan, 'the guides of savage battle, the splendid daughters of Ernmas'.[7]

The second is Macha, the daughter of Áed Rúad, who is described at greater length in the metrical *Dindshenchas* description of Emain Macha:[8]

Emain Macha, whence the name? Not hard to say. Macha Redmane, daughter of Aed *ruad* son of Badurn, laid on the sons of Dithorba the task of trenching the rath. When they were in outlawry in the wilds of Boirenn, she came to them disguised as a leper, while they were roasting a wild boar in the wood. Each of them in turn carried her off to mate with her, and then she bound each fast. After that she carried the five sons of Dithorba with her in this plight to Emain; Baeth, Brass, Betach, Uallach and Borbchass were their names. And she ordered them to trench the rath, for she preferred to make slaves of them rather than kill them. She traced afterwards for them the rath round about her with her brooch-pin, and they trenched it. Whence men say 'Emain', that is

Catháin (eds), *Ulidia* 2, 195–207. **5** M.-L. Sjoestedt, *Gods and heroes of the Celts, translated by Myles Dillon* (1949), p. 26. **6** Wh. Stokes, 'The Edinburgh Dinnshenchas', *Folklore* 4 (1893), 481. **7** Koch & Carey, *The Celtic heroic age*, p. 247. **8** E. Gwynn, *The Metrical Dindshenchas Part 4*, p. 308.

eó-muin, that is 'the brooch at Macha's throat', that is 'the pin at her
throat'. But see further the Succession of Kings, if thou desirest to learn
the full story, which for brevity's sake I here omit.

This red-headed Macha, credited with creating the enclosure at Emain Macha
and in whose memory the *óenach* (modern Irish *aonach*) at Emain Macha
was established, is also described as the wife of Cimbáeth in the prose
Dindshenchas. As the daughter of a king, she seized the kingdom from
Cimbáeth (whom she later wed) and Díthorba in turn and routed the latter's
sons. She appears as a martial figure, ruling Ireland for a time and repelling by
force those who oppose her sovereignty.

The third Macha gave her name to Emain Macha when she gave birth to
twins (*emain*). The second recension of *Noínden Ulad* (The Debility of the
Ulstermen) gives the fullest account of this explanation for the name:[9]

> Whence the affliction of the Ulaid? It is not difficult. Crunniuc mac
> Agnomain of the Ulaid was a hosteller of one hundred cows. He lived in
> the wilderness and mountains and he had many sons. Moreover, his wife
> was dead. One day he was in his house on his own when he saw a woman
> coming towards him in the house. He deemed her appearance shapely.
> The woman immediately began to prepare food as if she were in a house
> she had always been in. When night came, she served the family without
> question. She slept with Crunniuc that night. She remained with them
> for a long time afterwards and they lacked no produce with her, neither
> food nor clothing nor wealth.
>
> It was not long after that that an assembly was held by the Ulaid. The
> Ulaid used to go to the assembly, both men and women, boys and girls.
> Moreover, Crunniuc went to the assembly along with everyone else. He
> was wearing good clothes and looking very prosperous. 'You are advised,
> then', said the woman to him, 'not to say anything indiscreet'. 'That is
> unlikely', he said.
>
> The assembly was gathered. The king's chariot was brought onto the
> green at the end of the day. The chariot and horses won. The crowd said,
> 'there is nothing faster than these horses'. Crunniuc said, 'my wife is
> faster'. He was immediately seized by the king. That is told to the
> woman. 'I am prevented from going to help him, however', she said, 'for
> I am pregnant'. 'Although you may be hindered', said the messenger, 'he
> will be killed unless you come'.
>
> She went to the assembly then and they got her a spancel. 'Help me',
> she said to the crowd, 'for it was a mother who gave birth to each of you.
> Wait until I give birth'. They refused. 'Well then', she said, 'there will be
> a greater evil because of it, and it will be upon the Ulaid for a long time'.

9 As translated by G. Toner, 'Emain Macha in the literature', *Emania* 4 (1988), 32.

'What is your name?' said the king. She replied, 'my name and the name of my offspring will be given to this assembly forever. Macha daughter of Sainreth son of Imbath is my name. She raced against the chariot then and when the chariot reached the end of the green her childbirth began in front of it. So that she gave birth to twins, a boy and a girl. It is from this that Emain Macha was named then. She cried out in her childbirth. Anyone who heard her fell ill for five days and four nights. That pain used to come perpetually to every Ulsterman who was there, for nine generations of each man who was there. Five days and four nights, or five nights and four days. That was the affliction of the Ulaid. Each of the Ulstermen had the strength of a woman in childbirth for nine generations during the affliction. Three people among the Ulaid who did not suffer the affliction: boys, the women of the Ulaid, and Cú Chulainn. This is the period it remained on the Ulstermen: from the time of Crunniuc mac Agnomain meic Curir Ulad meic Fiatach meic Urmi to the time of Forc mac Dallain meic Mainich meic Lugdach etc. The Ulaid are named after Curir Ulad.

This, then, is the cause of the affliction of the Ulaid and the origin of the name Emain Macha.

This third Macha appears as the supernatural wife of a wealthy mortal husband 'of one hundred cows' and their union evidently increased his wealth. His boastful utterance at the assembly or *óenach*, however, broke his pledge of silence and discretion. His pregnant wife is forced to race, like a mare, against the horses of the king. She gives birth to twins and curses the Ulstermen (pl. 5) who for nine generations must suffer the same debility as she, a weakness that means that only Cú Chulainn can defend Ulster when Medb and the men of Connacht attack as recounted in the *Táin Bó Cúailnge*.

While on one level we have an explanation for the name of Emain Macha, there are multiple allusions here. The cultural meaning attached to a myth may change and this tale may also be seen as exemplary myth especially expressed in the names of the twins Fír and Fíal, 'True' and 'Modest'. Bernard Martin has argued that Macha's plight and her exposure to the gaze of spectators was an affront to certain societal ideals that held that the unjust denial of women of modesty risked depriving men of true manliness. The 'truth' of men and kings and the 'modesty' of women were indispensable complements to one another. As Martin has said the appropriate traditional tales must be told and re-told – both the positive ones, like the triumphs of Cú Chulainn, and the negative ones, like that of the debility of the Ulstermen, which mark the opposite of what was held to be just and right.[10] In addition, it is possible, as Máirín Ní

10 B.K. Martin, '"Truth" and "Modesty": a reading of the Irish Noinden Ulad', *Leeds Studies in English* 20 (1989), 99–117.

Dhonnchadha has indicated, to read this as an illustration of the importance of preserving the separation of the domestic and public spheres: Macha, the perfect wife is best kept at home well away from the royal assembly.[11]

It would appear that the three manifestations of Macha are all goddesses associated with land and fertility. As Dumézil wrote, Macha wife of Nemed was also a prophetess, Macha daughter of Aed Rúad was a warrior and the third Macha signified wealth and sexuality, the trio representing his tripartite Indo-European ideology of the sacral, the martial and the fertile.[12] He remarked that both Macha the wife of Nemed and Macha wife of Crunniuc (or Crund) each had a husband described as a son of one Agnomain and he thought that this might mean that there was once a more ancient goddess with a single identity.

While Mac Cana was happy to accept the notion of a trio of Machas, Carey notes that the legendary Nemed is virtually unknown outside the inventive *Lebor Gabála* (The Book of Invasions). This particular Macha (Nemed's wife) might be simply considered as a representative of the widespread theme of a prophetess who appears before a battle to predict what will happen and who is in fact often a war goddess. The other two Machas would then reflect the commoner theme in Irish mythology of the essential dual character of female deities, a twofold partition as goddess of war and aggression and goddess of land and prosperity.[13] In a detailed study of this complex figure and in particular her variants in the three recensions of *Noínden Ulad* Gregory Toner prefers to believe that the horse-like fertility goddess probably owes more to medieval scholasticism than residual pagan belief.[14]

Of course not every legendary female was a goddess of sovereignty and 'the lure of the sovereignty goddess' may mean this goddess designation was sometimes applied too liberally,[15] but local reference is important and the clear connection between each Macha and the territory of Emain Macha and the third Macha's actions in Crunniuc's dwelling leave little doubt in this case. Her ritualized actions there, clearest in the first recension of *Noínden Ulad*, present a picture of an Otherworld woman taking control of the domestic sphere and include her entering the house three times and twice turning *deiseal* or sunwise to enter the kitchen and to go to Crunniuc's bed.[16]

---

11 M. Ní Dhonnchadha, 'Gormlaith and her sisters, *c.*750–1800 (Noínden Ulad: The Debility of the Ulidians)' in A. Bourke et al., *The Field Day anthology of Irish writing*, 4 (2002), pp 173–4. 12 G. Dumézil, 'Le trio des Macha', *Revue de l'histoire des religions* 146 (1954), 5–17; *Mythe et épopée*, 1 (1968), p. 602. 13 P. Mac Cana, *Celtic mythology*, p. 90; J. Carey, 'Notes on the Irish war-goddess', *Éigse* 19 (1983), 263–75. 14 G. Toner, 'Macha and the invention of myth', *Ériu* 60 (2010), 81–109. 15 M. Ní Dhonnchadha, 'On Gormfhlaith daughter of Flann Sinna and the lure of the sovereignty goddess' in A.P. Smyth (ed.), *Seanchas* (2000), p. 230. 16 The ritualized aspect of this episode in Crunniuc's dwelling is examined by P. Mac Cana, 'The Irish analogues of Mélusine' in P. Lysaght et al. (eds), *Islanders and water-dwellers* (1999), pp 154–7 and in *The cult of the*

MACHA – RHIANNON – EPONA

The association with horses is of great importance and there are deeper and older layers of meaning here. One of Cú Chulainn's two chariot horses was called the Liath Macha, 'the grey of Macha', and these two horses may have been the twin foals born at his birth. The Liath Macha was a powerful animal that shed tears of blood before the hero's death and then, though mortally wounded, came to protect him 'so that fifty were slain by his teeth and thirty by each of his hooves'.[17]

This link between Macha and horses, including her association with racing horses at Emain Macha, may be an allusion to ancient equine rituals at Navan linked to the goddess and to sacral kingship. True, not every woman who races horses and curses the men of Ulster necessarily has equine associations, and this hippomorphic quality is rejected by Françoise Le Roux and Christian-J. Guyonvarc'h. Behind the trifunctional figure they see one Macha representing the war-like aspect of the sovereignty goddess whose very name links her to land and fertility.[18]

Many writers, however, have considered Macha to be an Irish equivalent of the Welsh Rhiannon and the Continental horse-goddess Epona. Rhiannon, whose name derives from *Rigantona*, 'Great Queen', figures in the series of prose tales known as *Pedair Cainc y Mabinogi* (The Four Branches of the Mabinogi) written between the late eleventh and early fourteenth century.[19]

In the first branch of the Mabinogi she appears as an Otherworld figure riding a great white horse and is pursued by Pwyll, lord of Dyfed in south-west Wales, who has won the title *Pen Annwfn*, 'Lord of the Otherworld'. He follows her on horseback. Even though she appears to ride at an even, slow pace, her horse is magical and he is never able to catch up with her. The horse-woman, as he calls her, eventually halts. She indicates that she wishes to be his bride but, tricked into keeping a careless promise, Pwyll is obliged to permit her betrothal to a certain Gwawl who in turn is eventually outwitted and induced to relinquish his claim. After some time, the union of Pwyll and Rhiannon produces a male child but on the night of his birth the boy disappears.

Accused of infanticide, Rhiannon is sentenced to spend seven years at the mounting block outside the gate of the court and to offer to carry strangers to the court on her back like a horse. Teyrnon Twrf Liant (*Tigernonos*, 'Great Lord'), lord of Gwent, 'the best man in the world', has a mare that foaled with

---

sacred centre (2011), p. 126. This text is reproduced in M. Ní Dhonnchadha, 'Gormlaith and her sisters', p. 173.   **17** Koch & Carey, *The Celtic heroic age*, p. 124, in 'The Death of Cú Chulainn as related in the Book of Leinster'.   **18** F. Le Roux & C.-J. Guyonvarc'h, *Mórrígan – Bodb – Macha* (1983), pp 45, 135.   **19** P.K. Ford, *The Mabinogi and other medieval Welsh tales* (2008), p. 35. M. Green, *Celtic goddesses* (1995), p. 47.

great regularity every May Day and each foal would promptly disappear. On this occasion, coinciding with the boy's birth, he prevented a fine newly-born colt from being stolen and simultaneously found a child at the door. After four years, the colt is given to the child who has grown prodigiously. Teyrnon then recognizes the boy as the son of Pwyll and takes him to the court where Rhiannon is released from her punishment and *pryder* (anxiety) and the child is named Pryderi, the word his mother uttered when she got the good news about him.

While the Mabinogi is a complicated narrative cycle combining aristocratic lore and international folk tale motifs, there are many traces of mythic themes notably referring to the Otherworld and supernatural beings. Like Macha, Rhiannon is seen as a goddess of sovereignty. While her literary character is not in doubt, besides her magical and equine qualities she possesses the principal features of this deity who seeks and promotes an acceptable male candidate for kingship. She deliberately chooses Pwyll as her mate, offers him a feast, he achieves wisdom, consummates his marriage and after the various difficulties described, he has a son and secures dynastic succession.[20]

In addition to this sort of supernatural content, the other threads of evidence that connect the stories of Macha, wife of Crunniuc, and Rhiannon are slender but persuasive. In each there is a horse race with supernatural qualities. There is a contest between a goddess and a king. A birth follows: twins in the case of Macha; the simultaneous birth of Pryderi and a colt in the case of Rhiannon. Both are compromised by the careless comments of their respective mates and both undergo a humiliation that blurs the distinction between horse and woman.[21]

This equine dimension has suggested a connection with the horse goddess Epona well known in carvings and inscriptions in the Gallo-Roman world notably in eastern Gaul and in the Rhineland. Her Celtic origin is clear and the features associated with Macha and Rhiannon are the remnants of a mythology that once linked Epona with equine and kingship rituals. Her name derives from Indo-European *ekwos* (horse) like the Old Irish *ech* and she is invariably depicted with one or more horses, sometimes with a mare and a foal. She seems to have been venerated as a protector of horses and guarantor of prosperity and fertility. In Britain, the four or five dedications or representations include fragments of a stone statuette from Colchester and an inscription on a Roman altar on the Antonine Wall in Scotland.[22]

20 C.A. McKenna, 'The theme of sovereignty in *Pwyll*', *Bulletin of the Board of Celtic Studies* 29 (1980), 35–52; J.T. Koch, 'A Welsh window on the Iron Age: Manawydan, Mandubracios', *Cambridge Medieval Celtic Studies* 14 (1987), 33.   21 S. O'Brien, 'Dioscuric elements in Celtic and Germanic mythology', *Journal of Indo-European Studies* 10 (1982), 121; J. Gricourt, 'Epona – Rhiannon – Macha', *Ogam* 6 (1954), 26.   22 M. Euskirchen, 'Epona', *Bericht der Römisch-Germanischen Kommission* 74 (1993), nos 143, 226(?), 256–8; M. Green, *Symbol and image in Celtic religious art* (1989), p. 16; K.M.

There are further clues, however, to Macha's equine nature. The Ulster hero Fergus mac Róich is a prominent figure in the *Táin Bó Cúailnge*. A former Ulster king, he is an ally of Medb and renowned for his remarkable sexual prowess. Próinséas Ní Chatháin points out that while the shadowy figure Roach/Róch is generally taken as being the virile Fergus' father from whom he inherits the strength of 'the great horse' (Ro-ech), the twelfth-century text *Cóir Anmann* (The Fitness of Names) records two traditions concerning Fergus' mother. In one, Róich daughter of Eochaid son of Daire is named, in the other a certain Róch daughter of Ruadh son of Derg Dathfhola from the *síd* is cited. To be brief, the Roach/Róch figure is unequivocally female and Ní Chatháin proposes that Ro-ech is better understood as 'the great mare', the Irish equivalent of Epona.[23]

Garrett Olmsted has independently argued that Roech (gen. Roich) might have been another name for Macha. According to him, the name Macha itself may have been a secondary development meaning 'field' or perhaps 'plain' and related to *macha*, an enclosure for milking cows and *machaire*, a large field or plain.[24]

If 'great mare' or 'great horse' was an epithet for the insular horse goddess, this may be an intriguing clue to another manifestation of this elusive female. In a study of the iconography of the famous Gundestrup cauldron, Olmsted has argued, not very convincingly, that the motifs on the panels of this object represented scenes from a Gaulish version of the *Táin Bó Cúailnge*. In particular, he has suggested that the motifs on one panel (showing a female bust flanked by stylized inward-facing elephants with two wheel-shaped symbols and several other fantastic animals below) portrayed an event at the beginning of the epic in which Queen Medb made a circuit of her camp in her chariot accompanied by eight others. The wheels represented her chariot; the elephants (associated with the military power of Rome) her warlike nature.[25]

The fact that this female figure is flanked by elephants, however, permits another and more plausible interpretation. Rather than a representation of a Medb-like person, the presence of a pair of elephants plus three other fantastic

Linduff, 'Epona: a Celt among the Romans', *Latomus* 38 (1979), 817–37; A. Ross, *Pagan Celtic Britain*, p. 224. **23** P. Ní Chatháin, 'Traces of the cult of the horse in early Irish sources', *Journal of Indo-European Studies* 19 (1991), 124–31. R. Ó hUiginn stresses the tenuousness of a tradition of a female Roach: 'Fergus, Russ and Rudraige', *Emania* 11 (1993), 33. **24** G.S. Olmsted, *The gods of the Celts*, pp 43, 169, 378. Máirín Ní Dhonnchadha tells me that Olmsted is mistaken in part when he argues that 'Aed Abaid Essa Ruaid' can be linked with 'ro-fhessa'. On place-names, see J.B. Arthurs, 'Macha and Armagh', *Bulletin of the Ulster Place-name Society* 1 (1953), 25–9; K. Muhr, 'The early place-names of County Armagh', *Seanchas Ardmhacha* 19 (2002), 1–54. **25** G.S. Olmsted, 'The Gundestrup version of *Táin Bó Cuailnge*', *Antiquity* 50 (1976), 95–103; *The Gundestrup cauldron* (1979), p. 211; his argument that renderings of horses with curving or tendril-like muzzles comparable to elephant trunks on some Gaulish coins and on the Marlborough bucket, might be 'elephant-horses' with a blend of features of horse and elephant is quite

animals might indicate that we have here the relatively common theme of 'the mistress of beasts',[26] but the prominent arrangement of a female with animals on either side is also reminiscent of a series of sculptures of Epona.

She is commonly depicted riding side-saddle on a horse, but in a number of cases, notably in Germany, she appears as a standing or seated figure with a horse on either side.[27] The horses may face inwards like the Gundestrup elephants, but outward-facing horses are also associated with images of the goddess. Horses facing this way occur on a portion of the Marlborough bucket, a wooden vessel with very fragmentary sheet bronze decoration possibly from a burial in Wiltshire. Here they flank a head that might be that of a female.[28] Since it is very possible that a huge and exotic elephant was taken to be a giant horse in Celtic Europe and was a means of portraying the exceptionally powerful attributes of a 'great horse',[29] it is conceivable that both the Gundestrup and the Marlborough images are representations of the horse goddess.

In any event, Macha's association with Navan seems to imply that horse rituals were especially important here. Such activities were probably a part of the *óenach* often alluded to, an assembly in which horse-racing, an encampment and an ale-house were essential elements.[30] Where this took place is uncertain, the townland of Enagh to the south of Navan Fort has had its claimants[31] and other locations such as Drumconwell (the find-spot of an ogam stone) to the south-east have been proposed.[32]

But other equine activities may have taken place at Navan Fort itself and these may have been a part of the *hieros gamos*. The Irish sacred marriage or *banais rígi* (from *ban*+*feis* 'woman-marriage', + *rígi* 'kingship') was a ritual mating in which a mythic sovereignty goddess granted the right to rule to a king who symbolically slept (*feis*) with her. It was a contract with the supernatural. There is a brief reference to a *feis* at Emain Macha in one recension of *Cath Maige Rath* (The Battle of Moira): *ite teora feisa hErenn .i. feis Eamna feis Temra fes Chruachna* (these are three feasts of Ireland: the feast of Emain, the feast of Tara and the feast of Crúachain).[33] However, *feis* usually denotes 'feast' so we cannot be certain that this is an allusion to a sacred marriage.

problematic given the degree of stylization.   26 M. Green, *Symbol and image* (1989), p. 24.
27 M. Euskirchen, 'Epona', *Bericht der Römisch-Germanischen Kommission* 74 (1993), types
VI and VII.   28 See E.M. Jope, *Early Celtic art in the British Isles* (2000), p. 98 and pl. 148d.
29 L.S. Oaks, 'The goddess Epona' in M. Henig & A. King (eds), *Pagan gods and shrines of
the Roman Empire* (1986), pp 77–83.   30 E. Bhreathnach, *Tara: a select bibliography* (1995),
p. 78.   31 J.P. Mallory, 'The literary topography of Emain Macha', *Emania* 2 (1987), 15.
32 R.B. Warner, 'The Drumconwell Ogham', *Emania* 8 (1991), 43–50; 'Emania varia 1',
Emania 12 (1994), 69.   33 C. Marstrander, 'A new version of the Battle of Mag Rath', *Ériu*
5 (1911), 232.

NAVAN MOUND

When excavations commenced at the great Navan Mound in 1963, it was probably a widespread assumption that it would prove to contain a passage tomb like Newgrange. After all, Seán P. Ó Ríordáin's excavation at the smaller Mound of the Hostages on the Hill of Tara a decade before had revealed that it covered a small megalithic tomb of this sort. The Navan mound (pl. 4) proved to be something very different. About two-thirds of it was excavated and approximately one third of the lowest part of the mound, on the north, was left undisturbed for future investigation.[34] After excavation the mound was restored to its original form.

Removal of the uppermost levels demonstrated that a mantling of carefully deposited layers of turves and clay 2.5m deep at the centre had been laid on top of a great cairn of stones, a sequence found at the Mound of the Hostages too. Any similarity ended there, however, because the cairn, which measured 37.5m in diameter with a maximum height of 2.8m high at the centre, did not contain a tomb. Its surface was divided into fairly well-defined but somewhat irregular radial segments by the use of different sizes of stones, by slight variations in height, by various arrangements of stones and by varying admixtures of soil, clay or turf in the sectors. The radial divisions, of which there were at least a dozen, did not seem to extend downwards through the mass of stones.

The cairn had entombed some sort of timber structure because the voids left by some decayed upright wooden posts were encountered within it as excavation proceeded. The void left by a great central timber extended almost 1.5m into this stony material and the radial lines had this central post as their focus. The voids of other timbers extended some 1.7m and all the vertical cavities were once even longer, their upper parts having been closed by movement in the upper cairn. The bases of these timbers were set in deep post-holes in the ground beneath. With the removal of the mass of stones, the nature of this wooden structure that had been enveloped by the cairn became clearer.

This construction proved to be a huge circular building almost 40m in diameter formed by five rings of spaced timber posts with a large central post. The outer ring comprised an estimated thirty-four large post-pits, 1.25m in diameter and depth and widely spaced about 3.5m apart (fig. 5.1). Each pit originally contained a single post (in every case supplemented later by the insertion of a second, identical, contiguous post). It has been suggested that these posts were linked by horizontal split timbers set in a shallow trench and effectively formed an outer wall. This may have been so, but clear traces of

34 C.J. Lynn, *Excavations at Navan Fort* (1997); *Navan Fort: archaeology and myth* (2003).

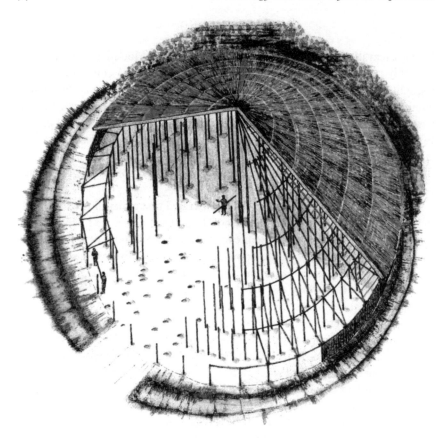

5.1. An artist's reconstruction of the 40m structure at Navan as a roofed building.

horizontal planking, surviving as charcoal, were only found in one segment of the trench between two pits on the east. Outside this possible wall was a narrow, deeper, discontinuous trench 40.5m in diameter. This narrow trench and the light walling it contained were quickly abandoned, being cut away by the sloping pits dug to insert the secondary posts in the outer ring, indicating that it may have served as a fence slot during the construction phase or even as some sort of external lean-to against the main wall.

The four internal rings had post-pits that measured about 36–46cm in diameter and were dug to an average depth of about 91cm through the underlying soil into the subsoil. The oak butts of many of these large posts were preserved in the damp ground and these were about 30cm in diameter. The entrance was on the west and here the internal post-ring system was interrupted by four roughly parallel rows of posts forming three aisles, each about 3m wide, leading to the centre of the structure. Apart from the posts of these aisles, the posts in the four rings were usually set fairly regularly 50–75cm apart. At the centre was a timber post so large that it had to be dragged at an angle into its pit on a sloping ramp 6m long cut into subsoil. The axe-dressed stump of this great post, about 50cm in diameter, was found in the central pit, which was 2.3m deep. About 1.4m of this post survived because of the damp conditions in the pit dug for it and because of a rise in the water table after the cairn was built. This immense central post (perhaps a carved pillar) could have been 13m or more in height and, as already emphasized, it was the focus of the radial lines in the cairn surface.

Large patches of the area inside this structure were covered with spreads of relatively clean clay, material that could not be packed back into the post-pits. This often sealed the packing around individual posts and was directly covered by cairn material. There were no hearths or other evidence for occupation. Furthermore, surplus clay spread out from the very large central post-pit sealed the clay spreads and packing of neighbouring posts showing that the central post was inserted later than these and perhaps last of all. This huge monument was carefully built to a pre-determined radial plan. A number of posts (and all of the paired examples on the perimeter outer ring) were pushed 10–15cm into the soil below the bases of the sockets dug for them, implying they were load-bearing. For this reason, it has been argued that the structure was temporarily roofed.

Dendrochronological analysis has determined that the large central post was felled in late 95BC or early 94BC and this dates the completion of the great timber structure. Whether roofed or not, it is not at all unreasonable to describe it as a temple or shrine with a great oak pillar as its focus. But it was a shrine that appears to have had a remarkably short life. No contemporary material was found within it to indicate what it might have been used for and its interior seems to have been relatively quickly filled with cairn stones deposited inside the outer ring. This possible wall was then burnt and some burnt twigs and fine straw-like material were thought to be kindling used to set fire to it, although the straw-like material might also have been the remains of roof thatch. However, no significant traces of burning were found on the summit of the cairn.

The construction of the superimposed clay and turf mound sealing the wheel-like pattern of radial lines in the upper cairn was the final act in this extraordinary sequence of events. Limited excavation in the ditch of the great enclosure in 1998 produced two heavily charred oak timbers, both roughly squared. One was dendrochronologically dated to about 95BC, as we have seen, and could be contemporary with the circular shrine. It is even possible that they were roof timbers.[35]

35 J.P. Mallory et al., 'Dating Navan Fort', *Antiquity* 73 (1999), 427–31; J.P. Mallory, 'Excavations of the Navan ditch', *Emania* 18 (2000), 21–35.

The interpretation of this monument presents great challenges. It is evident that the aisles lead towards the huge central oak post. Waterman referred to this feature as the ambulatory, and the three aisles were probably broad 17m-long ceremonial pathways to the centre of the shrine and to the huge post that was its focal element. The timbers used in these pathways were slightly larger than those in the concentric circles, and Chris Lynn, in his careful analysis of the structural evidence, indicated that this could be due to the fact that their wider spacing meant they had to support a greater weight of superstructure – whatever form this may have taken. Elsewhere, in the circles, the posts were of a consistent size and depth and what variations in size did occur suggested that the rings were built in simultaneously constructed radial sets rather than one complete circle after the other. As Lynn pointed out, a conical-roofed building should ideally have taller and larger timber roof supports near the centre and he does allude to the possibility that the roof could have been a circular pergola-like structure with the tops of some of its posts connected by horizontal concentric and radial timbers.

Even though reconstructions of a conical-roofed 40m structure have been well publicized,[36] an alternative un-roofed possibility should not be forgotten. If this was a more open-plan structure, with little or no outer walling, the great central post would have been visible from without, surrounded by a veritable forest of vertical timbers, like a transplanted oak grove. Perhaps, in this creation of a *nemeton* or sanctified stand of wood, we see an archaeological expression of the cult of the goddess. This may have been a sacred offering to the eponymous Macha, just as at Vaison-la-Romaine in south-eastern France, where a Gaulish inscription records that one Segomaros established a consecrated area, a *nemeton*, in honour of the goddess Belisama.[37] The fearsome war goddess Nemain, who appears at various times in the *Táin Bó Cúailnge* and wreaks havoc among the opponents of Ulster, may be another aspect of Macha. She may derive her name from a sacred grove at Emain Macha just like the name of the Gaulish goddess Nemetona stems from *nemeton* in that part of the Celtic world.[38] Images of shrines or temples associated with or even containing a horse are known on a number of Gaulish coins,[39] so to see the Navan structure as a shrine of some description to the horse goddess is not at all unreasonable. It may even have been a shrine with a flat stage-like superstructure for some ceremonial purpose.

---

36 For instance, in J.P. Mallory & T.E. McNeill, *The archaeology of Ulster* (1991), p. 147; N.B. Aitchison, *Armagh and the royal centres in early medieval Ireland* (1994), p. 82; B. Raftery, *Pagan Celtic Ireland* (1994), p. 77; C.J. Lynn, *Navan Fort: archaeology and myth* (2003), p. 31; J.T. Koch (ed.), *Celtic culture*, 2 (2006), p. 694; J. Waddell, *The prehistoric archaeology of Ireland* (2010), p. 356.   37 C.-J. Guyonvarc'h, 'Nemos, Nemetos, Nemeton', *Ogam* 12 (1960), 189; P.P. Coe, 'Belisama' in J.T. Koch (ed.), *Celtic culture*, 1 (2006), p. 201. 38 T. Ó Broin, '"Craebruad": a spurious tradition', *Éigse* 15 (1974), 112. For Nemain, see C. O'Rahilly, *Táin Bó Cúailnge* (1967), pp 58, 197.   39 D.F. Allen, 'Temples or shrines on

Lynn has speculated on the possible cosmological significance of this composite monument in a series of studies.[40] Taking note of Dumézil's belief that the three Machas were another expression of an Indo-European tri-functional ideology, and well aware of the inherent interpretative difficulties, he has raised the interesting possibility that the mound's three-fold hierarchical nature, of timber, stone and earth, might be a monumental expression of Dumézil's tripartite system. The timber shrine would be associated with the priestly first function, the cairn with the second martial function and the earthen mantle with third-function cultivators. While Dumézil's work has produced important insights into correspondences between the myths and religious traditions of Indo-European peoples and his tripartite conception has found wide acceptance as a satisfactory explanation for similarities between them, it has its critics too not least because a degree of imprecision and various inconsistencies give it a highly flexible character that permits its widespread deployment.[41]

Whatever about its application in this instance, the notion that the various components of a monument might carry different symbolic connotations is uncontroversial. Like the stones of Newgrange, the stones of Navan Mound could well have been selected from a particular and special location for a specific reason. Waterman was struck by the fact that they appeared to be weathered and not freshly quarried and Lynn has advanced the possibility that they might have come from an older prehistoric cairn in the vicinity. He has speculated that the huge central pillar was a representation of the *axis mundi* and that the radial lines creating a wheel shape in the summit of the cairn were intended to be visible from the domain of a sky-god who might have been an insular counterpart to the Gaulish Taranis. He has also argued that the ultimate objective in the building of a great mound like Navan was to create one that contained an Otherworld hall or *brug*. In addition, given the well-documented use of mounds for kingly inauguration in medieval Ireland, Navan Mound, with its flat summit, was an appropriate location for this sort of royal ceremonial in pre-Christian times.

REPLICATING THE SACRED CIRCLE

The large Navan Fort with its rampart and internal ditch, the timber shrine and the great mound of the first century BC were just the culmination of a protracted phase of activity on this drumlin ridge in the Navan complex. The

Gaulish coins', *Antiquaries Journal* 53 (1973), 71–4. **40** C.J. Lynn, 'The Iron Age mound in Navan Fort', *Emania* 10 (1992), 32–57; 'Hostel, heroes and tales', *Emania* 12 (1994), 5–20; 'That mound again', *Emania* 15 (1996), 5–9; 'Suggested archaeological and architectural examples of tripartite structures', *Journal of Indo-European Studies* 34 (2006), 111–41; C.J. Lynn and D. Miller, 'Crossing boundaries', *Studia Indo-Europaea* 2 (2005), 161–75. **41** W.W. Belier, *Decayed gods* (1991); D.A. Miller, 'Georges Dumézil', *Religion* 30 (2000), 27–40.

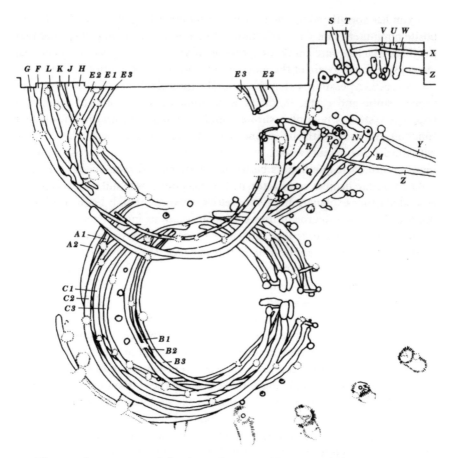

5.2. The complex sequence of circular enclosures at Navan pre-dating the 40m shrine. Some of the large pits of the earlier timber circle are visible on the lower right.

earliest significant development on the site of the mound is thought to have begun with the digging of a circular ditch about 5m wide and 1m deep enclosing a space approximately 45m in diameter. About 3m inside this ditch, and apparently contemporary with it, was a ring of large pits a little over 4m apart, centre to centre. The pits ranged in maximum diameter from 1.8 to 3.3m and may have held a large circle of twenty-eight timber posts standing concentrically within the ditch that was interrupted by a cobbled causeway 4.4m wide on the east. Animal bones and charcoal were found throughout the filling of the ditch. Although the timber circle and the ditch seem to have been contemporary, the radiocarbon dating evidence was inconclusive. The ditch of this circle may have begun to silt up before the middle of the last millennium BC but it was still an important and visible feature in the first century BC because the shrine and mound were carefully situated within it.

An exceptionally complex sequence of round timber structures was then constructed within the line of this circular enclosure from the fourth to the second century BC (fig. 5.2). A series of narrow foundation trenches overlay the line of the timber circle on the south, so it had probably been dismantled when this new phase began. A layer of dark soil *c*.30cm deep, which would normally be interpreted as an occupation layer (called 'fossil soil' in the excavation report), accumulated during the period represented by the construction and use of these trenches (called ring-slots in the report).

The circular trenches formed two contemporary groups: the southern enclosures and the northern enclosures. There was a later third group named the middle enclosures, whose circles cut through the earlier southern and northern groups. Some trenches may have been robbed of their wooden contents and were filled with material identical to that into which they were cut. Many were disturbed and partly destroyed by later trenches and by the post-holes of the 40m shrine. Lynn and Waterman's unravelling of the construction sequence represented by this maze of features was an outstandingly skilful piece of work.

While a few trenches could not be fitted into any sequence, the southern enclosures more or less occurred in three groups of two or three concentric circles (labelled A–C) and the sequence in each group was the same: the middle ring represented the earliest structure, the outer was the next replacement and the inner trench was the last to be dug. Their diameters ranged from 10 to 13.5m and gaps on the east, 1–2m wide, sometimes inturned and flanked by post-pits, were presumably entrances. A later group, the middle enclosures (E) with diameters ranging from 11.3 to 13.6m, partly overlapped the position of the A–C circles and also consisted of three concentric ring-slots dug in the same sequence. They had two opposed entrances on the east and the west and the latest ring-slot, the inner one, was narrower than the others and retained clear traces at intervals of the sockets of small elongated timbers (stakes with timbering between them?).

In general, little evidence of timber walling survived but where this occurred it seems that the wall was formed of stakes or posts set about 80cm apart in the slots and linked by a seam of soft fill denoting the earlier presence of wood. Small burnt areas and groups of flat stones indicated the former presence of hearths at the centres of the A–C and E structures.

Attached to or touching the northern side of the southern A–C enclosures was a series of six further ring-slots of greater diameter, *c*.20–25m. Their full extent was not revealed, so it was not possible to demonstrate exactly which of the five or six slots on the east (S–W) were linked with which of the six on the west (F–H, J–L) but there clearly had been a sequence of large circular enclosures here. It seems possible that in at least two cases the individual elements of these northern and the southern ring-slot groups were attached and formed conjoined units that communicated by means of narrow gaps on the northern sides of the southern ring-slots.

It is likely that the rebuilding of the northern structures did not follow the same sequence as those on the south and the construction sequences of the two groups were to some extent independent. It is possible that some circles were not conjoined. Chris Lynn has suggested that one reason for the consistent repositioning of the southern ring-slots could be that each structure, or group of three structures, had to be placed so that it could be joined to a northern structure already in existence, which was not renewed at the same time.

The northern ring-slots had wide gaps on the east, approached by parallel entrance palisade slots 5.5m apart, later replaced by a second pair 7.8m apart. Some of the slots retained impressions of the sockets for stout upright posts *c*.50cm apart. These appear to have been imposing access routeways. If the middle enclosures (E) were attached to larger enclosures, these lie in the unexcavated area to the north.

It is an astonishingly complicated picture of successive circular structures. The two- or three-fold sequencing in wall construction identified in ring-slots A–C and E is equally remarkable. It was cleverly explained by Lynn in the excavation report as a mechanism for replacing a wall with the roof still in position. It was argued that these southern enclosures represented the wall trenches of eight or nine successive round houses with doors on the east, most of them communicating with open-air enclosures on the north, these in turn being approached by fenced avenues.

With the presence of hearths and what seemed to be occupation debris including animal bone, it was reasonable to consider them to have been domestic dwellings with attached stockyards approached by droveways. However, the connection between southern ring-slots and northern enclosures could only be demonstrated as a possibility in two instances: A1 and A2, with northern slots K, H and N, M and C1–3 with F, G, L and Q, P. Nonetheless, these two twinnings are significant because, of course, it is fair to say that it may have been the case with other circles as well.

Though Lynn was aware of the possibility that these conjoined enclosures could have been ceremonial, the idea that they represented houses and attached cattle enclosures has been popularized in a number of published reconstructions.[42] A relatively small amount of fragmentary coarse pottery was associated with this phase of activity, as were a few bronze and iron items. Some of these, such as a decorated ring-headed pin, were perhaps high-status items.

42 Reconstructed as house and attached stockade in J.P. Mallory & T. McNeill, *Archaeology of Ulster*, p. 117; N.B. Aitchison, *Armagh and the royal centres in early medieval Ireland*, p. 82; J. Waddell, *The prehistoric archaeology of Ireland* (2000), p. 338; for version with a ceremonial enclosure, see M. Parker Pearson, *Bronze Age Britain* (1993), p. 123.

A relatively large quantity of animal bones was recovered, with plenty of evidence of butchery. There were twice as many pigs as cattle and nine times as many pigs as sheep or goat. These unusual proportions and the high incidence of pig in particular have prompted the suggestion that the bones represent a ritual rather than a domestic assemblage. A few horse bones were found, some displaying signs of butchery, implying the occasional consumption of horse flesh or horse sacrifice. The discovery of a skull and jaw of a Barbary Ape (*Macaca sylvanus*) was most unusual. This animal must have been a prestigious import from north Africa and is a valuable indication that far-flung contacts existed and included perishable objects such as apes. The skull, which was found in ring-slot C2, has been radiocarbon dated to the period 390–20BC.

It seems very likely that these were ceremonial enclosures. This probablity has been strengthened by the identification of another set of twin enclosures nearby. A combination of geophysical survey and limited excavation to the east of the great mound has shown that three ring-slots found by Waterman beneath what appeared to be a small ditched enclosure are a part of a large pair of conjoined circles with general diameters of approximately 20 and 30m respectively with probable entrances on the east. Unlike the structures under the mound, it is evident that even the smaller of these two could not have been roofed and they were also burnt. The inner and outer slots contained burnt material including burnt animal bone; the middle slot – the first to be dug – contained a clean fill with no trace of timber posts. The other two, however, did contain traces of successive timber structures that were burnt down in a process that involved the cremation of pig, cattle and sheep or goat.[43]

The repetitive constructional pattern seen in the southern A–C ring-slots beneath the mound indicates, at the very least, an obsessive concern with the positioning of trenches in relation to one another and a desire to locate on the same spot time and time again. This compulsion is also apparent in the middle enclosure (E) slots. It represents a prolonged period of ritual observance possibly spanning several centuries after the timber circle phase and just before the construction of the great timber shrine and its covering mound. Other than the animal bones that might be the residue of feasting episodes or sacrificial performance, there is no direct evidence of what acts might have been performed here but they were clearly repetitive and highly significant.

HIEROGAMY AND EQUINE RITUAL

It is very possible that cyclical equine rites associated with kingly ceremonial were a feature of the activities that took place within these Navan structures.

43 C.J. Lynn, 'Navan Fort site C excavations', *Emania* 18 (2000), 5–16; 'Navan Fort site C excavations', *Emania* 19 (2002), 5–18.

Support for this possibility lies in the fact that this activity clearly foreshadowed the building of the great mound where, as we shall see, kingship ritual is a likely explanation. The rites associated with these earlier timber circles must have taken place in an atmosphere permeated with the supernatural. The presence of the Otherworldly Macha, horse goddess and goddess of sovereignty, was never far away. As Richard Warner has observed, the internal ditch and external rampart of the great enclosure is the reversal of the normal defensive order to repel external attack; it was configured to contain the forces of the Otherworld within the sacred precincts.[44]

Charles Doherty has considered the rituals that may have been performed here. Like many scholars who have written on Indo-European characteristics preserved in Irish tradition and lost or attenuated almost beyond recognition elsewhere in the west, he cites the remarkable parallel between the Indian and Irish kingship ceremonial.

This is the oft-quoted twelfth-century account of the inauguration practices of the Cenél Conaill, one of the northern septs of the Uí Néill in Donegal. This was recorded by Giraldus Cambrensis in his *Topography of Ireland*:

> When the whole people of that land has been gathered together in one place, a white mare is brought forward into the middle of the assembly. He who is to be inaugurated, not as a chief, but as a beast, not as a king, but as an outlaw, embraces the animal before all, professing himself to be a beast also. The mare is then killed immediately, cut up in pieces, and boiled in water. A bath is prepared for the man afterwards in the same water. He sits in the bath surrounded by all his people, and all, he and they, eat of the meat of the mare which is brought to them. He quaffs and drinks of the broth in which he is bathed, not in any cup, or using his hand, but just dipping his mouth into it about him. When this unrighteous rite has been carried out, his kingship and dominion has been conferred.[45]

As Giraldus admitted in his later work *The Conquest of Ireland*, he was recording a story of days of old in his *Topography*, these were 'events and scenes of time past'.[46] Many writers have pointed out that this rite has parallels with the Hindu *asva-medha* or horse sacrifice, in which the principal spouse of the king submits to a symbolic union with a dead stallion.

The major historical source for this is the religious narrative the *Satapatha Brahmana*, compiled around 800BC, but elements are evidently much older,

44 R.B. Warner, 'Keeping out the Otherworld', *Emania* 18 (2000), 39–44.   45 C. Doherty, 'Kingship in early Ireland' in E. Bhreathnach (ed.), *The kingship and landscape of Tara* (2005), pp 3–31; translation from Latin by J.J. O'Meara, *The first version of the Topography of Ireland by Giraldus Cambrensis* (1951), p. 94.   46 A.B. Scott & F.X. Martin, *Expugnatio Hibernica* (1978), p. 3.

going back to the second millennium BC. The preparatory ritual began with the selection of a stallion that was purified and released in a north-easterly direction. Allowed to wander for a year, escorted by a hundred princes and others, the return of the horse marked the beginning of the elaborate consecration ritual. It was bound to a central stake and various other animals including goats and cows were tied to it. When the stallion saw mares penned in the sacrificial area, its neighing was interpreted as the recitation of Vedic chanted verse. It was then attached to a chariot and driven about before being unharnessed and laid on a gold cloth and suffocated, no blood being shed. At the moment of death, there was the invocation 'You do not die of this, indeed you come to no harm; You go to the gods on easy paths'. The chief wife or queen lay with the dead animal and imitated copulation while priests and other women present engaged in scabrous dialogue. Finally, the horse was dissected, portions were roasted and offered to the god Prajapati, the lord of creation, and then to those present.[47]

Myles Dillon was one who noted the obvious inversion. In India, the ritual involved a stallion and a woman, while the Irish ceremony concerned a king and a mare, but both included a symbolic union and the killing and dismemberment of a horse to ensure fertility and prosperity.[48] It is worth observing, too, that both rites of kingship culminated in the consumption of parts of the animal.

This concept of kingship has been considered by Doherty in an examination of the cosmogony of sacral kingship of early India and Ireland. Only the greatest of ancient Indian kings could perform this supreme rite, which, as late as the eighth century AD, was the only touchstone to test the might of kings. He deserved to govern the world. A paramount king would, in performing a version of this equine ritual, effectively become *cakravartin* or 'world king'.

Doherty maintains that Navan was not just the inauguration place of a local king but was a location associated with universal kingship. He agrees that the great central post was an *axis mundi* because, as in Vedic India, the world king could only reside in the middle, the zone of the sacred. Here, the greatest of kings was a wheel-turner, a *cakravartin* (*cakra-* meaning 'wheel') who behaves like the sun protecting and destroying all creatures with its rays, and who promotes the welfare of his people and governs the world (fig. 5.3). The final structure at Navan, the clay mound that formed the king's seat or *forad*, was the equivalent of the Indian *prasada*, a seat of divinity and home of gods and kings.

---

47 M. Stutley, 'The asvamedha or Indian horse sacrifice', *Folklore* 80 (1969), 256; W. Doniger O'Flaherty, *Textual sources for the study of Hinduism* (1990), p. 16; R. Zaroff, 'Asvamedha: a Vedic horse sacrifice', *Studia Mythologica Slavica* 8 (2005), 75–86; J. Puhvel, 'Aspects of equine functionality' in J. Puhvel (ed.), *Myth and law among the Indo-Europeans* (1970), pp 159–72. The liturgical mantras are cited by C. Watkins, *How to kill a dragon*

5.3. A *cakrævartin* or world king with various symbols of kingship including the *cakrastambha* or wheel-pillar (on upper left) depicted on a relief from Jaggaiahpeta, Andhra Pradesh, *c.* first century BC.

We can be sure that in the act of mimicking copulation with a mare that was the equine avatar of the goddess of sovereignty, a king at Emain Macha would present an especially powerful expression of the significance of the sacred marriage. It has been contended as well that in so publicly professing himself to be a beast (... *se quoque bestiam profitetur*) the Cenél Conaill inaugurant might have voiced an actual ritual utterance such as 'I am *ekwos*, thou art *ekwā*', recalling the Vedic marriage formula 'I am he, thou art she'.[49] This too could have been a part of the rites at Emain Macha.

This raises an intriguing archaeological point, because images of horses with human features are known in various parts of Europe. There is an unusual statuette of a horse with a human head on the lid of an early La Tène gilt-bronze spouted flagon from a rich grave at Reinheim (Saarland, Germany); the bearded male head bears a leaf-crown, a mark of high status or divinity (fig. 5.4, 1). This figure is not a hybrid creature like a centaur with arms and human torso, it is probably much more than a mythical beast. Pairs of human-headed winged horses flank a standing goddess figure in a scene on a

(1995), p. 267.   48 M. Dillon, *Celts and Aryans*, p. 107.   49 J. Puhvel, *Comparative mythology* (1987), p. 275.

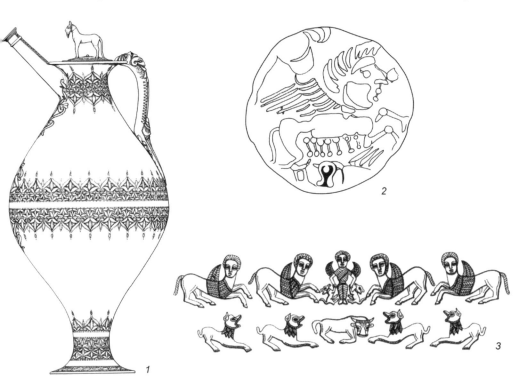

5.4. Human-headed horses – images of equine rituals. 1. Statuette of a horse with a human head on the lid of an early La Tène gilt-bronze spouted flagon from a rich grave at Reinheim (Saarland, Germany). 2. A gold coin, possibly from Brittany, bears an unusual image of a winged human-headed mare and a winged foal. The wings express both animal's supernatural nature while the mare with seven distended udders may also be a symbol of fecundity. 3. Pairs of human-headed winged horses flank a goddess figure in a scene on a silver flagon from a fourth-century hoard from Rogozen (Bulgaria).

silver flagon from a great fourth-century hoard of vessels from Rogozen in north-western Bulgaria (fig. 5.4, 3).[50] This arrangement recalls those depictions of Epona with horses on either side. Horses with human heads occur on some Continental coinage and on one, a gold coin possibly from Brittany, there is an unusual image of a winged mare and foal. Along with its wings and human head, the mare has no less than seven distended udders (fig. 5.4, 2). Paul-Marie Duval saw the wings on both mare and foal as an attempt to express the animals' supernatural nature, with the udders denoting exceptional fecundity.[51]

50 I. Marazov, *The Rogozen treasure* (1989), p. 128. Marazov has also suggested that some depictions of riders and severed horse's heads on Thracian metalwork may be allusions to horse sacrifices akin to the *asva-medha*: 'Philomele's tongue' in L. Bonfante (ed.), *The barbarians of ancient Europe* (2011), p. 134.   **51** P.-M. Duval, *Monnaies Gauloises* (1987), p. 39.

Green has proposed that disconcerting images like human-headed horses, as on the Reinheim vessel and on these Gaulish coins, are expressions of the chaos and violence associated with transgressing boundaries.[52] An alternative possibility is that such a very unusual combination of horse and human head was meant to be a compelling representation of equine invocations that were a momentous part of kingship rites once performed over a wide area of ancient Europe.

Doherty points out the concept of the 'world king' is to be found in early Ireland in poetry associated with Leinster. In one seventh-century poem, a king named Bressual is said to have 'ruled the boastful world' and in another he is identified with both the whole world and the sun:

> Án grēn grīssach
> goires brēo: Bressual –
> bress Elce, aue Luirc,
> lāthras bith – Bēolïach

> A brilliant burning sun
> that heats is the flame: Bressual –
> fair one of Elg [Ireland], descendant of Lorcc
> who lays waste the world – Beolïach.[53]

The association of kingship with solar imagery is noteworthy but unsurprising because, as we have seen, there is a body of archaeological evidence to support the thesis of a widespread solar cult of some description in late prehistoric Ireland. If rituals of kingship were one of the motivations for the creation of Navan Mound, then those who carefully built the clay mound to make the king's seat would have been well aware of sacred precedents, of the purpose of the timber shrine and of the solar symbolism of the wheel-like device etched in the surface of the cairn. Indeed, the insertion of the great pillar and the creation of that wheel-shaped design above it was an act of profound significance.

At Navan, we find a crucial link between solar symbolism and the concept of an *axis mundi*. In many cultures, the link between heaven and earth was conceived as a tree, a mountain or a pillar and in the earliest Indian cosmogony, reflected in the *Rig Veda*, the cosmic pillar is the mythical axis of the world both separating and uniting heaven and earth.

Founded in the waters below the earth, this pillar was the channel through which cosmic order was imposed on the world. When the sun unites with its

52 M. Green, 'Images in opposition', *Antiquity* 71 (1997), 906; 'Cosmovision and metaphor', *European Journal of Archaeology* 4 (2001), 207.   53 Text and trans. by J.T. Koch in Koch & Carey, *The Celtic heroic age*, p. 42. On Bressual, see J. Carey, 'Bresal/Bressual Beolïach' in

5.5. The *axis mundi* and the solar wheel. A. The radial divisions in the surface of the cairn at Navan. B. An artist's reconstruction of the building of the cairn in the 40m structure with the central pillar emphasized. C. A *cakrastambha* from Amaravati in the Government Museum Chennai, Madras.

summit, sun and pillar become a metaphysical unity represented by a wheel above the pillar. This is the *cakrastambha* or 'wheel-pillar', a carved pillar surmounted by a solar wheel, a relatively common early Buddhist symbol (fig. 5.5).[54] This configuration of pillar and wheel finds an exceptionally interesting and powerful parallel in the Navan timber post, with its super-imposed wheel image in the upper cairn. The wet foundations of the Navan pillar may be an important detail, for the Vedic evidence indicates that the presence of water was a necessary element in the foundation of votive pillars.

While Lynn's argument that the radial lines forming a wheel shape in the summit of the cairn were intended to be visible from the domain of an insular counterpart to the Gaulish Taranis is not implausible, there is another possibility. Bearing in mind the possibility of horse rituals at Navan, this combination of wheel and pillar symbolism is more likely to be another illustration of the survival of Indo-European beliefs and practices. On a level with the sun and at the axis of the world, the flat clay-capped summit of the great mound was an exalted stage for royal ceremonial and those who stood here would have been acutely conscious of its cosmic import.

There are a few other hints of equine concerns in Ireland and elsewhere. Among these, Doherty notes the story of St Moling, who rejected the eating of horseflesh, and tales of 'horse-eared' kings in literature. In contrast to horse sacrifice, of course, it is debatable as to whether these are echos of ancient customs.

The *asva-medha*, it will be remembered, demanded that the chosen stallion be set loose to roam without hindrance for a time. Claude Sterckx has suggested that a Scottish legend retains an echo of this practice. In the fourteenth century, William, thane of Cawdor, dreamt that he should place a coffer of gold on the back of a donkey and let it roam freely for a day. Wherever it came to rest after one day was the place to build a castle to ensure his family's prosperity. The animal lay down under a holly tree that is preserved in the castle dungeon. A nineteenth-century account is as follows: 'the Thane resolved to build a tower of fence, but hesitating as to its site, was admonished in a dream to bind the coffer containing the treasure he had collected for the purpose on an ass; to set the animal free, and to build his tower wherever it stopped'. The treasure-laden ass stopped exactly at 'the third hawthorn tree' and there the castle was built.[55] The long-dead tree has been dendrochronologically dated to AD1372, presumably the year it died for lack of sunlight. Sterckx thought this might be a confused memory of an ancient equine ritual.

He also alludes to the possibility that the Roman legend recorded by Plutarch that one Fulvius Stellus consorted with a mare and fathered the goddess Epona might be an echo of the horse ritual.[56] It has been suggested, too, that the horse sacrifice in the Roman *October Equus* is yet another reflection of this rite, even though the element of a symbolic mating is absent. In this ceremony, a horse (the right-hand animal in a chariot pair) was dedicated to Mars, killed with a spear thrust and then dismembered.[57] Tacitus, in his *Germania*, records the practice of the keeping of pure white wild horses that were allowed to roam in sacred groves. Their neighs and snorts were interpreted as divine omens by priests and kings. They were sometimes yoked to a sacred cart or chariot, an act that Newman has compared to the

---

55 J.V.F. Campbell, *The Book of the Thanes of Cawdor* (1859), p. 18; C. Sterckx, *Mythes et dieux celtes* (2010), p. 45.   56 C. Sterckx, *Mythes et dieux celtes* (2010), p. 127.   57 J. Puhvel, 'Aspects of equine functionality' (1970), p. 162; R. Zaroff (2005), '*Asvamedha*', 80.

description of Conaire Mór's inauguration at Tara, where two unbroken steeds were yoked to his chariot.[58]

Navan was not merely a place concerned with kingly inauguration. As Doherty concluded, Emain Macha, like Tara and Rathcroghan, was a point where the creation of the world was re-enacted and was the physical expression of a sophisticated philosophical reflection on the cosmos. Even though much of the interior and all of the immediate exterior of Navan Fort remain unexplored, on present evidence the creation of the great mound was the last major monumental act there.

As Emain Macha, the fort became a focal point in the topographical and literary landscape. Its prehistoric kingly associations captured the imagination of medieval storytellers and literati in a series of tales of which the *Táin Bó Cúailnge* is only the best known. It achieved a mythic status of another sort as a royal residence and the epicentre of heroic exploits. It became an emblem of immemorial royal authority, with Ulster kings employing such titles as *rí Eamna acus Ulad* ('the king of Emain and the Ulaid').[59] In a twelfth-century poem on its Christian kings, parallels are sought with Homeric Troy:

> Cosmail gach áen-fher d'iath Emna
> d'fhir ar Tróe muirnig na máer...
>
> Each single man of Emain's territory
> has a counterpart in tumultuous lordly Troy ...[60]

The great prehistoric ritual centre was in time superseded by nearby Armagh with its new and more powerful Christian magic. In recreating Emain Macha as a royal settlement and the dwelling place of heroes, medieval scribes left us just fleeting glimpses of its horse goddess and other older myths.

---

58 H. Mattingly, *Tacitus*, p. 109. C. Newman, 'The sacral landscape of Tara' in R. Schot et al. (eds), *Landscapes of cult and kingship* (2011), p. 25.   59 M. Dillon, *Lebor na Cert* (1962), p. 93.   60 F.J. Byrne, 'Clann Ollaman Uaisle Emna', *Studia Hibernica* 4 (1964), 62, 76.

CHAPTER 6

The goddess of sovereignty

The great Queen Medb is the foremost figure associated with ancient Crúachain, but the evidence is more literary than archaeological. In Rathcroghan, the name does figure in that ogam inscription in Oweynagat (albeit in a masculine form *MEDVVI*),[1] but surprisingly her name is attached to no major monument. She is merely linked to two stones in just two brief folkloric references recorded in the nineteenth century.

In the course of the pioneering work of the Ordnance Survey in 1837, John O'Donovan noted the name Miosgan Meva (Medb's heap) for what seems to be a prostrate pillar stone lying about 100m north-north-east of Rathcroghan Mound. A squat natural boulder for which O'Donovan recorded the name Milleen Meva (Medb's lump), some 105m to the north-north-west of the great mound, was noted in 1852 by the antiquarian Richard Brash, who simply recorded the name 'the Milleen' and a local tradition that the stone was brought from Elphin by Oisin, the warrior son of Finn mac Cumaill.[2] The latter stone, like the cave at Oweynagat, is a reminder that natural features were also reference points in the ritual topography of the complex.

Medb of Crúachain (pl. 6) is a prominent figure in medieval literature, notably in the *Táin Bó Cúailnge*. In fact, she is best known as the protagonist in this famous cattle raid. Here, her character is a complex and mainly medieval creation: at once warrior queen and headstrong female. She is sometimes depicted in an unflattering light, a picture inspired by contemporary Christian misogyny and concerns about female lust and waywardness. The author of the pillow talk between her and her husband Ailill that begins the epic in the second recension clearly demonstrates a knowledge of medieval law concerning women.[3]

This argument in the royal bed in Crúachain as to who had the most wealth prompts Medb's quest for the Donn Cúailnge, the brown bull of Cooley. As the instigator of the raid, however, she has arrogated power, status and a male role to herself. In usurping a man's function, she effectively doomed the expedition from its inception. She is the dominating partner in a marriage in which Ailill is presented as a compliant spouse tolerant of her promiscuity,

---

1 S. Ziegler, *Die Sprache der altirischen Ogam-Inschriften* (1994), p. 206.   2 Ordnance Survey letters: M. Herity, *Ordnance Survey letters Roscommon* (2010), p. 55; R.R. Brash, *The ogam inscribed monuments of the Gaedhil* (1879), p. 300.   3 D. Ó Córráin, 'Early medieval law, *c.*700–1200' in A. Bourke et al., *The Field Day anthology of Irish writing*, 4 (2002), p. 38; P. Kelly, 'The Táin as literature' in J. Mallory (ed.), *Aspects of the Táin*, p. 77.

especially evident in her alliance with the virile Fergus. Her sexual capacity is apparent in other tales as well, in her declaration that 'I never was without one man in the shadow of another', and in the fact that she had at least four husbands, Ailill being the last.[4]

In the early twentieth century, Medb's behaviour was seen as an illustration of the licentiousness and moral laxity of pre-Christian Ireland but as Mac Cana memorably put it 'this is one of the not infrequent instances where bad morals make good mythology'.[5] This Medb of medieval times was not, in all probability, a historical person for while there were powerful and influential women, they did not inherit political power and the annals record no example of a female political or military leader. Her promiscuity is an echo of an older and much more significant mythic figure. As Máire Herbert has said, 'in early Ireland women were not sovereigns, but sovereignty was conceived of as female'.[6]

The original Medb was a goddess and her name is cognate with words in Irish and other languages signifying drunkenness (like the English word 'mead'), it means 'the drunken one' or 'she who intoxicates'. Since Medb herself is never understood as intoxicated, Heinrich Wagner thought 'she who is (of the nature) of mead' or 'she who belongs to the mead' were more likely meanings for this divine dispenser of liquor.[7] Her name may have had the added attraction of ambiguity because, while the association with drink and mead (*medhw-o-*) is generally acknowledged, there may also be an allusion to one who rules or commands (*med-wo-*).[8]

Interestingly, there is an Indo-European dimension to this motif of an intoxicating goddess associated with fertility and human kingship. Dumézil saw a connection in both name and function between this Medb and the beautiful Mādhavī of the great Indian epic the Mahabharata. She was gifted with the ability to become a virgin after childbirth and provided sons for a succession of world kings ensuring the continuation of their royal lineage. Her name is a derivative of the Indo-European *medhu-* (mead), and Dumézil argued that it could mean 'the intoxicating one'. One of her sons, named Ashtaka, gained fame as a king who performed grand *asva-medha* or horse sacrifices.[9]

Just as a horse sacrifice at Emain Macha may have been an element in the wedding of king and goddess in that *hieros gamos* or *banais rígi*, Medb's links with mead are a reflection of the importance of drinking ceremonial in the affirmation of kingship. Her multiple liaisons are an echo of this kingship

---

4 T. Ó Máille, 'Medb Chruachna', *Zeitschrift für celtische Philologie* 17 (1928), 129–46.   5 P. Mac Cana, *Celtic mythology*, p. 85.   6 M. Herbert, 'Goddess and king: the sacred marriage in early Ireland', *Cosmos* 7 (1992), 264.   7 H. Wagner, 'Studies in the origins of early Celtic traditions', *Ériu* 26 (1975), 12.   8 G.-J. Pinault, 'Gaulois *Epomeduos*' in P.-Y. Lambert and G.-J. Pinault (eds), *Gaulois et celtique continental* (2007), p. 301; P.-Y. Lambert, 'Deux mots Gaulois', *Comptes-rendus des séances de l'Académie des Inscriptions et Belles-Lettres* (2006), p. 1522.   9 G. Dumézil, *The destiny of a king* (1973), p. 81.

marriage. Ailill was king of Connacht because of his marriage to Medb and her several matings are a reflection of her role as sovereignty figure with whom the reign of each pagan king was inaugurated in a mystic union.

To gain possession of Medb of Crúachain was to gain possession of the kingship, a fact that explains the unusual number of her husbands. She had a Leinster counterpart in Medb Lethderg of Tara, of whom it was said she would have no one as king in Tara unless she was his wife and who, according to a genealogical miscellany in the Book of Lecan, compiled in the fifteenth century, 'slept with nine kings of the kings of Ireland'.[10] The epithet Lethderg, red-sided or half-red, may be an allusion to the fact that the sovereignty of Ireland was always half red or bloody.[11] The various husbands of the several manifestations of Macha are presumably another expression of a multiplicity of sacred pairings.

In addition to symbolic intercourse with the goddess, the associated symbolism of alcoholic drink indicates that kingship rituals may have included a form of drinking session that induced a 'divine' intoxication of the new king. Time and again, the offering of a drink by a woman to a prospective ruler is a highly significant act. For instance, in *Baile in Scáil* (The Vision of the Spectre) that legendary king of Tara, Conn of the Hundred Battles, is transported to the Otherworld and granted foreknowledge of his future kingship and that of his successors. He sees a man of wondrous appearance seated on a throne, beside him a woman in a crystal chair and wearing a golden diadem. Beside her is a silver vat, a golden ladle and a golden cup. The man declares he is no mere spectral apparition but the god Lug:

> My name is Lug, son of Ethliu, son of Tigernmas. For this reason I have come, to tell you the duration of your own rule, and that of every future ruler in Tara …

Lug's consort, the young woman, is described as the 'eternal Sovereignty of Ireland' and:

> It was she who gave this repast to Conn, an ox-rib and the rib of a boar. The ox-rib was twenty-four feet long, and there were eight feet between its flank and the ground. When the girl went to distribute the drink, she asked: 'To whom is this cup to be given?' The Spectre answered her. He named every ruler in turn from Conn's time until Doomsday …[12]

---

10 J. Carey, 'Tara and the supernatural' in Bhreathnach (ed.), *The kingship and landscape of Tara* (2005), p. 46.   11 T. Ó Máille, 'Medb Chruachna', *Zeitschrift für celtische Philologie* 17 (1928), 142.   12 Text: K. Meyer, 'Baile in Scáil', *Zeitschrift für celtische Philologie* 3 (1901), 457–66; trans. M. Herbert, 'Society and myth, *c*.700–1300' in A. Bourke et al. (eds), *The Field Day anthology of Irish writing*, 4 (2002), p. 260.

Then all disappear but Conn retains the vat, ladle and cup.

Sometimes the goddess has a loathsome aspect. In *Echtra mac nEchach Muigmedóin* (The Adventure of the Sons of Eochaid Muigmedón), we are told how Níall Noígíallach (Niall of the Nine Hostages), ancestor of the Uí Néill dynasties, wins the kingship of Tara.[13] He and his brothers are thirsty and one after another they come across a well that is guarded by a hideous female who demands a kiss in exchange for a drink of water. All except one of the brothers refuse. One does offer a kiss but Níall not only kisses her but also has intercourse with her:

> Niall went then to seek water, and reached the same well. 'Give me water, woman', said he. 'Give me a kiss, and I will give it', she answered. 'As well as giving you a kiss I will lie with you', said he. Then he bent down over her and kissed her. Afterwards, however, when he looked at her, there was not in the world a girl fairer than her in appearance and form …
>
> 'Who are you?' asked the lad.
> 'I am Sovereignty', said she.

Here myth is co-opted to serve the purpose of projecting the Uí Néill claim to the sovereignty of Ireland back to primordial time.[14] The transformation of the ugly woman into a beautiful girl when she gains a fitting partner is an indication of the benefits that the land will gain from a rightful and just ruler.

That medieval tales such as these contain allusions to older practices in which kingship ceremonial included a sacred marriage with a goddess is not in doubt. This has been identified in Mesopotamia and elsewhere in the deification of kings where the goddess in the form of a priestess chooses a ruler to act as her bridegroom.[15] Whether it is represented in scenes of coupling figures in Scandinavian rock art[16] is debatable, but it is widely accepted that this custom, and practices such as horse sacrifice recorded in Ireland and India, represent a common Indo-European inheritance.

As with equine rites, only fleeting traces of sacred marriages or sovereignty goddesses survive elsewhere in Europe. There may be a clue in the well-known tribal name Brigantes. It is found in Ireland and northern Britain and is represented in some Continental place-names. The tribal goddess was *Brigantī*, 'the exalted one', a name that corresponds to the Irish goddess (subsequently saint) Brigit, and their leaders may have dubbed themselves

13 Text: Wh. Stokes, 'Echtra mac Echach Muigmedóin', *Revue celtique* 24 (1903), 190–203; trans. M. Herbert, 'Society and myth, *c.*700–1300' in A. Bourke et al. (eds), *The Field Day anthology of Irish writing*, 4 (2002), p. 261.   14 M. Herbert, 'Goddess and king', *Cosmos* 7 (1992), 270.   15 E.O. James, 'The sacred kingship and the priesthood' in *La regalità sacra* (1959), p. 66.   16 K. Kristiansen & T.B. Larsson, *The rise of Bronze Age society* (2005), p. 344.

consort of the goddess. D.A. Binchy has argued that the Welsh word for king, *brenin*, derives from the kingly title **Brigantīnos*, meaning spouse of 'the exalted one'.[17]

THE CUP-BEARER

There may be another allusion to this marriage rite in one version of the foundation myth of the Greek colony of Massalia (Marseille). Several writers have drawn attention to the account preserved by Aristotle of the wedding of Petta, daughter of the local king. The Greek Euxenus of Phocaea was an invited guest, and the bride, instead of offering a bowl of wine to whoever was to marry her, gave it to Euxenus. Her father concluded she had acted according to divine will and Euxenus took her as his wife (fig. 6.1). He founded the colony and their descendants lived in Massalia thereafter. Again, we should be aware that not every cup-bearing woman is necessarily a goddess of sovereignty, but the Celtic name of the bride Petta is probably important in this context, as *pett* or *pitt* may mean a holding of land.[18] In recording this story, Aristotle may have inadvertently recorded one of the earliest surviving Celtic myths.[19]

Ian Armit, in his fine study of headhunting and head imagery in Iron Age Europe, has drawn attention to the women of Entremont, neglected by modern commentators. This famous third-century BC sanctuary near Aix-en-Provence, north of Marseille, is renowned for its stone carvings of seated warriors with associated severed heads. All are fragmentary, having been deliberately destroyed. A series of torso parts and detached heads of warriors have been found, each torso representing a distinct individual with either chain-mail armour, leather cuirasse or clothing depicted. As Armit suggests, these may be representations of the elite of the local tribe, the Saluvii, perhaps a heroic lineage of war-leaders or kings.

Fragments of carvings of seated female figures have been found too, and at least three female heads have been identified, their hair covered by a veil. These statues could have faced or flanked the male warriors as an image of a family group, but the presence of a number of stone carvings of metal vessels found in their vicinity is significant. Just as the severed heads were emblems of male heroism, these vessels may have been female attributes and an expression of the women's role in the rituals of serving and drinking wine.[20] Of course,

---

17 D.A. Binchy, *Celtic and Anglo-Saxon kingship* (1970), p. 12.   18 Koch & Carey, *The Celtic heroic age*, p. 32; B. Jaski, *Early Irish kingship and succession* (2000), p. 66.   19 P. Freeman, *The philosopher and the druids* (2006), p. 84. For variants of this sort of marriage tale, see D. Pralon, 'La légende de la fondation de Marseille', *Études Massaliètes* 3 (1992), 51–6.   20 I. Armit, *Headhunting and the body* (2012), pp 173–87. Illustrations in M. Py, *La sculpture Gauloise méridionale* (2011), pp 119–68.

6.1. The cup-bearer. A nineteenth-century illustration by Alphonse de Neuville of the foundation myth of Marseille in which Petta daughter of the local king offers a cup of wine to the Greek Euxenus from F. Guizot's *L'histoire de France* (1872).

there may have been even more potent symbolism intended here. Given what we know of the sovereignty goddess of Irish tradition and that foundation myth of Massalia, it is surely possible that Entremont was once the location of a striking display of sculpted imagery of sacral kingship.

A much later allusion to the sovereignty concept is to be found in the Breton legend of St Judicael. Even though Brittany has no surviving written vernacular literature, the Latin lives of some saints contain elements from earlier sources. The eleventh-century tale of the warrior-saint Judicael, who reigned in the seventh century, narrates the youthful vision of his father Iudael. It begins:

> One night, Iud-hael, most noble king, then yet of but youthful years, weary after hunting, slept in the house of his subject Ausoc, in Trefles, which is at the end of the long coastline on the west, within the limits of Bra Leon and Kemenet Ili. In a dream he saw a most lofty mountain standing in the middle of his kingdom, i.e. in its very centre. It was difficult to reach by way of a stony track. And there, at the summit of that mountain, he saw himself seated in an ivory chair. And within his view there was a wondrous huge post in the form of a round column, founded by its roots in the ground, its mighty branches reaching the sky, and its straight shaft reaching from the earth up to the heavens ... And just then, he saw next to him the daughter of his subject Ausoc. She was named Pritell, a lovely girl, as yet unknown by man, whom he had seen the previous day and had desired in his mind. Immediately, she saluted him in the manner of a subordinate, saying, 'Hail, lord Iud-hael!' Then, turning to look at her, he said, 'Girl, what are you doing here?' She answered him: 'My king Iud-hael, in some manner it has been fore-ordained by our maker that you and I should come to this place, and that the custody of this ornamental pillar should be handed on for a time from no man in the world but yourself to no woman but myself and that after that it be passed on from no woman other than myself to no man but yourself' ...[21]

Iudael dreams that he was seated on an ivory chair on the summit of a mountain in the middle of his kingdom in north-western Brittany. Nearby, a great tree richly decorated with weaponry, gold and candles, stretched from the earth to the heavens. A beautiful virgin named Pritell appears whose physical union with him brings prosperity to him and his kingdom and produces a child who will become the saint. Mac Cana has noted the significance of the conjoined core themes of *axis mundi* and sovereignty figure, echoes of that

[21] For this translation of the story 'De Sancto Iudicaelo Rege Historia', see Koch & Carey, *The Celtic heroic age*, p. 387.

marriage between king and goddess here dramatically placed at the sacred centre of the kingdom.[22]

Jan de Vries thought that the legend of Amleth, prince of Denmark, recounted in the *History of the Danes* of Saxo Grammaticus might be an allusion to this sort of regal union. Herminthrud, queen of Scotland, accepts the fortunate Amleth as king for 'whatever man she honoured with her bed was actually king, and received a realm and her caresses together'.[23] Like the story about the foundation of Cawdor Castle (ch. 5), it is a curious coincidence that there should be two legends with Scottish connections that might be much reduced memories of ancient rites of kingship.

In Old Norse court poetry, there is a portrayal of the land of Norway as a woman waiting for a mate, namely the king Hákon, who 'took possession of the only daughter of Ónarr, overgrown with trees'. In the *Skírnismál*, a terrestrial maiden representing 'the protected, enclosed earth' is won by the sword of the heavenly god Freyr.[24] It has been proposed too that the relationship between Freyr and his sister Freyja and that between Odin and his mistress Jord might be an echo of some form of sacred marriage, but it is true that this notion is the subject of some debate.[25] Some loathsome females who appear to be sovereignty goddesses are adept at sorcery and have been compared to fertility deities associated with witchcraft in Norse literature.[26]

Variants on the loathly aspect of the female sovereignty figure also surface in medieval literature and are possibly inspired by Irish tradition. In the tale told by Chaucer's wife of Bath, for example, domestic rule takes the place of royal rule: a knight is challenged on pain of death to discover what women most desire. An ugly crone provides the answer that women desire to have sovereignty and to be in mastery over their husbands. In return for this gift that saves his life, she demands marriage and offers the unhappy knight the choice of having an ugly but faithful or beautiful but faithless wife. In leaving the choice to her, however, he offers an answer that gives her mastery and, transformed, she becomes both a good and a beautiful spouse.[27]

---

22 P. Mac Cana, *The cult of the sacred centre* (2011), p. 161. It has been proposed that elements of a sovereignty figure are to be found in a story recorded by Herodotus in which the brothers Pigres and Mantyes of Paeonia, in northern Greece, introduce their sister to Darius I the Great in an obviously ritualized fashion: Y. de Pontfarcy, 'The sovereignty of Paeonia' in M. Richter & J.-M. Picard (eds), *Ogma* (2002), pp 145–50.   **23** J. de Vries, *La religion des Celtes* (1963), p. 251; Davidson & Fisher, *Saxo Grammaticus*, p. 98.   **24** R. Frank, *Old Norse court poetry* (1978), p. 64.   **25** J.P. Schjødt, 'Ideology of the ruler in pre-Christian Scandinavia', *Viking and Medieval Scandinavia* 6 (2010), 183; O. Sundqvist, 'Religious ruler ideology' in C. Raudvere & J.P. Schjødt (eds), *More than mythology* (2012), pp 225–61.   **26** M. Bhreathnach, 'The sovereignty goddess as goddess of death?', *Zeitschrift für celtische Philologie* 39 (1982), 248. The theme of the loathsome lady may be a universal one: A.K. Coomaraswamy, 'On the loathly bride', *Speculum* 20 (1945), 391–404.   **27** M. Aguirre, 'The riddle of sovereignty', *Modern Language Review* 88 (1993), 273–82; R. McTurk, *Chaucer and the Norse and Celtic worlds* (2005), p. 106.

There is no shortage of evidence for drinking rituals of one sort or another in European prehistory, but securely linking the archaeology of intoxication with goddess figures is a difficult task. According to Green, a relief of a divine couple from Pagny-la-Ville near Beaune (Burgundy), the young woman holding an offering plate and a cornucopia full of fruit, the older bearded man bearing a hammer in his left hand and a large vessel in his right, might be a representation of this ceremonial offering of drink by a goddess to a king. A fragmentary image from a Roman shrine at Nettleton (Wiltshire), showing a woman apparently handing a cup to her male partner, may depict a similar act.[28] Here, as at Entremont, iconographic representations of this sort obviously entail real interpretational difficulties, but the cumulative evidence does indicate that kingship rites should be considered as a possible explanation.

Dumézil, it will be remembered, compared Medb and Mādhavī and was impressed by this parallelism between ancient India and early Ireland and the perspective it provided on Indo-European kingship. Here, we seem to get a glimpse of a widespread prehistoric ritual in which authority such as sacral kingship was confirmed by the proffering of a drink by a woman of special status.

Michael Enright has explored this theme is his very original study of the 'lady with a mead cup'. In examining the literary evidence for the role of women in liquor service in the Germanic world from the first to the ninth centuries AD, he identified an archaic rite of the acknowledgment of lordship. In it, women had a pivotal role in a service that affirmed a man as lord of a warband or as head of a household. He instanced a wealthy female burial dated to about AD100 at Juellinge on the Danish island of Lolland. She was a high-status woman who died in her thirties. The accompanying grave goods included Roman imports and personal ornaments; drinking utensils were a major feature of the contents and comprised a bronze cauldron, a ladle, a wine-strainer (placed in her right hand), two glass beakers and two drinking horns. He considered her to have been someone who had a respected position as a distributor of drink.[29]

There may have been other women who had such responsibilities in earlier times. Gold mounts for a pair of drinking horns were found in the rich Reinheim burial already mentioned. Though the skeleton did not survive, it is generally accepted that the exceptional quantity and quality of jewellery in this grave and the presence of a bronze mirror all indicate that a high-status woman had been interred here. Among the jewellery, stylized human faces (surmounted by birds) on a gold torc and on a bracelet are conceivably female

---

28 M. Green, *Symbol and image in Celtic religious art* (1989), p. 51; 'Pagan Celtic iconography and the concept of sacral kingship', *Zeitschrift für celtische Philologie* 52 (2000), 105.
29 M.J. Enright, *Lady with a mead cup* (1996), p. 100. A mead-offering woman is a recurring theme in the Old Norse Poetic Edda: M. Kvilhaug, *The maiden with the mead* (2009).

images.[30] The two gold-mounted drinking horns and the superbly decorated gilt-bronze flagon imply that she too may have had a role in drinking ceremonies. Indeed, she may have been a woman of superior rank who had a singular sacral function.[31]

THE LADY OF VIX

Such a wealth of drinking equipment in rich female graves inevitably recalls the celebrated burial of the so-called 'princess of Vix'. This famous grave, excavated in the 1950s near Châtillon-sur-Seine in eastern France, contained all the high-status symbols of the fifth century BC: a four-wheeled wagon, rich personal ornaments (including a gold neck-ring decorated with a pair of winged horses) and a drinking set. The body had been laid on the wagon superstructure with the wheels placed against one wall of the wooden grave chamber. The drink-related objects comprised an immense bronze wine vessel or krater capable of holding nearly 1,100 litres made in a Greek colony in southern Italy, an Etruscan bronze wine flagon, a silver libation bowl, a pair of Greek ceramic cups (one a decorated black-figure cup, the other plain but both placed together on the rim of the krater), two bronze handled basins and a third basin without handles (pl. 9).

The female imagery on some of these objects is remarkable. Amazons are depicted on the decorated cup and grotesque gorgons form the great handles of the krater. A small statue of a veiled female figure stands in the centre of the krater's lid. She has been compared to images of various Greek divinities and, by several writers, to women represented on a situla from Vače, Slovenia. Christopher Knüsel has seen these women as participants in a ritual in which serving liquid played a part and comparable to 'servants in the same sense as a Christian priest when performing a mass, who becomes a figurative servant of God'.[32]

There is abundant evidence in the funerary record of Iron Age Europe that many women achieved high social status. Many dozens of rich female graves are known and their significance debated.[33] In particular, much has been written about the role and status of the woman of Vix who was honoured with such remarkable grave goods and there is a measure of agreement that there was a religious dimension to her power (and a tendency to drop the secular title 'princess').[34]

30 J.V.S. Megaw, *Art of the European Iron Age* (1970), p. 80.   31 R. Echt, *Das Fürst-innengrab von Reinheim* (1999), p. 222, compares her high-born status and sacral role to that of a Roman Vestal Virgin.   32 C.J. Knüsel, 'More Circe than Cassandra', *European Journal of Archaeology* 5 (2002), 285.   33 C. Metzner-Nebelsick, 'Wagen- und Prunkbestattungen von Frauen der Hallstatt- und frühen Latènezeit' in J.M. Bagley et al. (eds), *Alpen, Kult und Eisenzeit* (2009), pp 237–70.   34 C. Rolley, *La tombe princière de Vix* (2003). S. Verger,

An earlier Hallstatt period female burial of the seventh century BC is worthy of note because it too contained a distinctive pair of drinking vessels. A mound, part of a largely destroyed tumulus cemetery, was the subject of a rescue excavation in the 1980s at Mitterkirchen, Upper Austria. A wooden chamber contained the remains of a 30-year-old woman laid on the body of a wagon. Little of its four wheels survived, but they appear to have been dismantled and placed against one wall, as at Vix. Personal ornaments included an amber necklace, two bronze fibulae, ankle rings and a decorated leather belt. In addition to wagon fitments and horse harness, a large quantity of animal remains was deposited in one quadrant, along with two iron knives and a very small pottery vessel comprising three conjoined miniature cups.

Over twenty pottery vessels were found in various other parts of the grave and included several dishes beneath the wagon and a very large pottery cauldron in the north-eastern corner. Two large, handled vessels were placed on the ground beside the wagon. They were very similar but not identical ornate pieces. While most of the ceramic assemblage was typical of Upper Austrian and southern Bavarian traditions of the time, the handled pair (and the small triple vase found with the animal bones) were different and represented more easterly fashions in the Hallstatt world.[35]

Mention should also be made of the rich burial in the Kleinaspergle near Ludwigsburg, Baden-Württemberg.[36] This huge burial mound was partly investigated in 1879 when an exploratory tunnel exposed the remains of two large timber chambers. One, near the centre, had been pillaged in the past and all its contents removed. Some human bone and, interestingly enough, some bones of horse were found. A second large timber chamber discovered several metres to the west was intact and richly furnished. Its contents included a bronze basin, a small ribbed cylindrical bucket, an Etruscan vessel, a wine flagon, two Greek ceramic cups and gold terminals for two drinking horns.

The two cups were clearly particularly valuable items. One, a piece of painted red-figure ware, had a depiction of a priestess standing before a sacrificial altar on its interior surface. The other, a simpler black cup, bore painted decoration in white around its rim, representing a wreath of myrtle (sacred to Aphrodite). Both cups had been broken and carefully repaired, the repairs being concealed by applied sheet-gold La Tène leaf motifs. This is undoubtedly an indication of their exceptional significance and ceremonial purpose. Megaw perceptively noted that 'such enrichment of exotic objects almost amounts to enshrinement'. The horn mounts differ in decoration and

'Qui était la Dame de Vix?' in M. Cébeillac-Gervasoni & L. Lamoine (eds), *Les élites et leurs facettes* (2003), pp 583–625; 'La Dame de Vix' in J. Guilaine (ed.), *Sépultures et sociétés* (2009), pp 285–309; 'Archéologie du couchant d'été' in J.-P. Le Bihan & J.-P. Guillaumet (eds), *Routes du monde et passages obligés de la Protohistoire au haut Moyen Âge* (2010), pp 293–337.   **35** M. Pertlwieser, 'Frühhallstattzeitliche Wagenbestattungen in Mitterkirchen' in *Prunkwagen und Hügelgrab* (1987), pp 55–65.   **36** W. Kimmig, *Das Kleinaspergle* (1988).

in quality and each terminal is formed by a ram's head. Megaw thought this combination indicated that one drinking horn was intended for the deceased and one for their companion in the Otherworld.[37] Some cremated bone was found, but it does not seem to have been preserved so we do not know whether a man or a woman was buried here, though the absence of any weaponry might imply the latter.

Obviously, the presence of pairs of vessels in rich burials may have various meanings. But the repeated occurrence of pairs of special or unusual vessels in female burials does seem to be an indication of some sort of cult practice. Pierre-Yves Milcent has emphasized the significance of the Vix evidence: the two cups and the wine flagon were placed on high on the krater; the two matching basins for ablution were placed on the ground. This indicated usage by two persons, the deceased and another who may have been a close relation or an equal.[38] In fact, this may have involved a formal etiquette of sharing drink with a co-celebrant, possibly male.

'La dame de Vix' was of small stature, less than 160cm (about five feet) in height and aged between 30 and 55 when she died. Knüsel has suggested that not only was she far from physically distinguished but she was marked by asymmetrical facial features and hip dysplasia that impaired her walking. He argues that her appearance and her capacity to overcome her disability may have contributed to her status as a 'ritualist'.[39] It may be more than a coincidence but the Juellinge woman was also lame, suffering a deformity of her right leg caused by an osteochondroma, a large benign tumour on her thigh bone.[40] In passing, it is worth noting that irregularity of form (being one-eyed or lame) or asymmetry of posture (standing on one leg, raising one hand) are among female ritualistic traits in early Irish literature.[41]

Like Medb and Mādhavī, the women of Juellinge, Reinheim, Vix, Mitter-kirchen – and possibly Kleinaspergle – may have been a privileged minority among the elite women of their time. They may have had a special gift: the capability to validate the authority of a ruler. Neither goddess nor wife, but invested with a supernatural power deliberately echoing if not derived from a sovereignty figure, their ritualized actions served to legitimize male rule. Their role in life (so well expressed in Enright's phrase 'lady with a mead cup') was so important that it deserved to be commemorated in death as well.

37 J.V.S. Megaw, *Art of the European Iron Age* (1980), pp 20, 61–2.   38 P.-Y. Milcent, 'Statut et fonctions d'un personnage féminin hors norme' in C. Rolley (ed.), *La tombe princière de Vix* (2003), p. 316.   39 G. Depierre and H. Duday in C. Rolley (2003), p. 46, dispute some of Knüsel's conclusions such as facial asymmetry and, while accepting the evidence of hip deformation, are uncertain as to its effects on the subject's bearing.   40 P. Bennike, *Palaeopathology of Danish skeletons* (1985), p. 205; D. Brothwell & A.T. Sandison, *Diseases in antiquity* (1967), p. 323. The claim that a high-status woman in a chariot burial at Wetwang Slack, Yorkshire, was disfigured is disputed: M. Giles, *A forged glamour* (2012), p. 248.   41 J. Borsje, *The Celtic evil eye* (2012), p. 101.

To revert to Irish tradition, we saw the supernatural woman in *Baile in Scáil* (The Vision of the Spectre) offer a golden cup to Conn of the Hundred Battles, king of Tara. The sovereignty goddess Étaín had a similar role. The serving of drink was her 'special gift' in the ninth-century *Tochmarc Étaíne* (The Wooing of Étaín). When Eochaidh, king of Tara, had to choose a wife, he chose her from among fifty Otherworld women 'of like form and raiment', declaring 'my wife is the best at serving drink in Ireland. I shall recognize her by her serving'.[42]

LAND AND SOVEREIGNTY

There is another dimension to the goddess. The connection of a female figure with the land and its sovereignty is an enduring feature of Irish tradition. In the twelfth-century *Lebor Gabála* (The Book of Invasions) when the Sons of Míl, the mythical ancestors of the Gaelic Irish, defeat the gods of the Tuatha Dé Danann, they encounter three goddesses, Banba, Fótla and Ériu. The latter, whom they meet at Uisneach in the very centre of Ireland, gives her name to the island as a whole.

Other goddesses, like Macha or Medb, have more provincial territorial associations but they all are instances of land and sovereignty conceived as a female divinity intimately linked to the institution of sacral kingship. This ancient concept and the idea that the righteous king was wedded to his territory continue as a well-known metaphor in later literature to the collapse of the Gaelic order in the seventeenth century. It is found in Jacobite poetry in the following century, where one poet called Ireland 'the daughter of Conn, and the spouse of the Stewarts'. T.F. O'Rahilly gives a list of later poetic references to Ireland as the 'wife' of one or other of her legendary or early historical kings including an early seventeenth-century allusion to Crúachain as 'the ancient wife of the kings (of Connacht)'. One medieval text refers to a king of Tara as the husband (*fer, nuachar*) of Tara (*Temair*) and of Ireland (*Banba, Inis Fáil*). Centuries later, in 1736, a poem on the death of Manus O'Donnell, a major seventeenth-century Donegal lord, begins 'Éire was never a widow until now'.[43]

If such feminine imagery should retain its force for over a millennium in historical times, then it would not be surprising to expect an even longer ancestry in the mentality of some prehistoric European peoples with animistic traditions. Obviously, archaeological evidence for these is difficult to come by. Nonetheless, the prehistoric world view probably conceptualized the earth as a

---

42 O. Bergin & R.I. Best, 'Tochmarc Étaíne', *Ériu* 12 (1938), 186–7.   43 B. Ó Buachalla, 'Irish Jacobite poetry', *Irish Review* 12 (1992), 44. T.F. O'Rahilly, 'On the origin of the names *Erainn* and *Ériu*', *Ériu* 14 (1946), 19.

female entity and saw some interactions with it in terms of a sexual encounter between a man and a woman. Land-winning, taking possession in a literal sense, ploughing a furrow, penetrating the land and inserting a standing stone, are just three actions replete with this sort of imagery. Quite alien to the modern mind, in this fundamentally different attitude to nature, landscape features might be experienced as animate entities. There are many cases where topography is anthropomorphized. They remind us of a time when nature and culture were inextricably intertwined and animated landscapes influenced cultural practice and beliefs.

Just to focus on Medb, the name of Sawel Mountain on the border of Cos Tyrone and Derry was recorded as 'Mullanesawla', that is 'Mullach na Samhla', 'Hilltop of the Likeness' in the early seventeenth century. A feature on the side of the mountain was briefly noted by the Ordnance Survey and the name 'Samhail Phite Meidhbhe' recorded; it appears as 'Sawell pit a Mew' on a seventeenth-century map. What precisely it was that was a likeness of Medb's vulva is not stated, but Kay Muhr believes it may have been a mountain stream that rises high up between the summits of Sawel and a neighbouring mountain and flows across a grassy shelf at Oughtmame, a name possibly representing 'Ucht Meidhbhe', 'Maeve's front'. She also notes a townland in Co. Antrim near Glenavy called Ballypitmave that contains the same anatomical allusion though the likely referent, a megalithic tomb, is destroyed.[44]

Even though Macha is the sovereignty figure with the greatest equine character, Medb of Crúachain had equine associations too. Her lover Fergus was known as Ro-ech, 'Big Horse', and the name of one of her several husbands Eochaid may be connected with Old Irish *ech*, 'horse'.[45] The role of untamed horses in the kingship rituals at Tara (ch. 7) and the toponymic references in that sacral environment to the sovereignty goddess in the personification of a white mare (an animal that was such an important part of the Cenél Conaill sacrifice) have led Newman to think that such a personage guaranteed the institution of kingship there as well.

The name of Tara's goddess, Medb Lethderg, is linked to Rath Maeve, a huge embanked enclosure about 1.5km south of the hill. The monument is very briefly alluded to in a poem entitled *Cnucha cnoc os cionn Life* (Cnucha a hill above the Liffey): 'The Leinstermen built Raith Meadhbha on the slope for Meadhbh Lethderg and thenceforth Raith Meadhbha was the name for one side of Temhair'.[46]

The Níth river that issued from the well of Nemnach on the Hill of Tara was, Newman suggests, a significant feature of the sacralized landscape

---

44 K. Muhr, 'Place-names and the understanding of monuments' in R. Schot et al. (eds), *Landscapes of cult and kingship* (2011), p. 247.   **45** J. Puhvel, 'Aspects of equine functionality' (1970), p. 167.   **46** M. Power, 'Cnucha cnoc os cionn Life', *Zeitschrift für celtische Philologie* 11 (1917), 48.

because its waters, flowing from Tara, came from the goddess herself, literally emanating from her divine body. The Níth joined the Gabhra river near Rath Lugh and the course of both rivers is marked by important monuments. The equine nature of the goddess is reflected in the name of the Gabhra, the river of the white mare, flowing between the hills of Tara and Skreen and a key component of the sacral landscape. The Hill of Skreen, to which a blemished king was exiled (ch. 7), was the cosmographical counterpoint of Tara and these two landmarks were united by the waters of the sovereignty goddess that flowed between them.

The name *gabor* (Old Irish: white horse or mare) is incorporated in other place-names associated with royal sites such as Sgiath Gabhra (the shield or defence of the white mare), an enclosure and mound that was a part of the inauguration landscape of the medieval Maguire lordship in Co. Fermanagh studied by Elizabeth FitzPatrick. Another noteworthy example is Lagore, the royal lake dwelling of the medieval kings of Brega some 7km from Tara, known in Irish as Loch nGabor (lake of the white mare) or Loch Da Gabor (lake of the two white mares).[47]

As the great white horse carved in the chalk on the upper slope of White Horse Hill on the Berkshire Downs at Uffington reminds us, white mares are not confined to Ireland. This large stylized figure about 100m in length was first cut in later prehistory (possibly some time between 1380 and 550BC judging from Optically Stimulated Luminescence dating of feldspar and quartz samples from the feature). It seems to have been reworked and maintained over the millennia.[48] It lies some 160m from a small hillfort known as Uffington Castle, where limited excavation has not revealed any extensive traces of occupation. The scanty settlement evidence indicates that there may have been a ritual focus to much of the activity detected there, the monument perhaps being a special place just visited periodically.

Constructed in the eighth or seventh century BC, its ramparts were modified over several centuries. An entrance occurs on the west and a second imposing eastern entrance flanked by timber posts was blocked up, possibly in the fourth century BC. Thereafter, little trace of use was found until the third and fourth centuries AD when again activity seems to have been sporadic, with no evidence of occupation as such. This is in contrast to the amount of occupation activity identified in the neighbouring hillfort of Segsbury Camp just 8km to the east.[49] Visits to Uffington Castle may have been coupled with the periodic cleaning and refurbishment of the horse. At one time, both may have been tribal symbols of the local Atrebates, but like the white mare

47 E. FitzPatrick et al., 'Evoking the white mare' in R. Schot et al. (eds), *Landscapes of cult and kingship* (2011), pp 163–91. C. Newman, 'The sacral landscape of Tara' in R. Schot et al. (eds), *Landscapes of cult and kingship* (2011), pp 22–43. 48 D. Miles et al., *Uffington White Horse and its landscape* (2003). 49 A. Payne et al., *The Wessex hillforts project* (2006), p. 89.

associated with Tara, the Cenél Conaill sacrificial rite, the Hindu horse sacrifice and those human-headed horses on the Continent (fig. 5.4), it is very possible that Uffington's White Horse once had a part to play in kingship rituals.

A belief in a divine female associated with the earth, traces of which survive in various Indo-European myths, may well have dictated past actions and archaeologists should at least be mindful of the possibility. For instance, if the land at Downpatrick was thought to be feminine in any way in prehistoric times, the very careful deposition of those two hoards of gold ornaments (ch. 4) may have been not just a generalized 'gift to the gods' but a very focused offering to a female deity. If these items were once female jewellery, then they may have been considered a particularly appropriate deposit in the circumstances.

Two exceptionally large gold torcs found near the Rath of the Synods at Tara in the early nineteenth century may have been similar offerings. As their name implies, it is generally assumed they were worn as neck ornaments, but the Tara pieces and some others are large enough to be worn around the waist if indeed they were ever worn as ornaments at all. Significantly, though the details of their discovery are unknown, they were deposited in a context associated with Medb Lethderg, the goddess of the sovereignty and land of Tara.

The finely crafted goldwork from Downpatrick and Tara are just two examples of finds of torcs, bracelets, ear rings and tress rings that are a notable feature of a phase of the Irish Bronze Age *c.*1400–1100BC and most (though not all) seem to have been found in dry-land contexts. While the custom of depositing hoards of metal objects in the ground in a dry-land as opposed to a wet-land environment is not a new departure (bronze axes and halberds were the favoured objects at an earlier date), such a range of personal ornaments and the predilection for the use of gold is a new development. The belief that these were valuable possessions buried for safekeeping in a time of danger is an old one, but why conceal just a selection of gold objects and not some prized bronzes as well? The restricted range of objects and the rarity of combined finds of gold and bronze artefacts indicate that other factors apply and a ritual explanation is now widely accepted.

Because such objects are not found in burials and because the range is so limited, it is not even possible to know if we are dealing with sets of male or of female ornaments, but there is one potentially significant comparison. The principal contemporary weapon in this period is a narrow stabbing elongated bronze blade, the so-called dirk or rapier. Many have no details of their find circumstances recorded, but, of those that do, a majority come from rivers, bogs and lakes. These objects were valuable items, not lightly discarded or lost, and their formal disposal in this fashion would appear to have been an elite activity. Since we are presumably dealing with a male weapon fashion eventually superseded by the bronze sword, the wet-land disposal of rapiers obviously contrasts in a striking way with the dry-land context of much of the gold work at this time.

There are different meanings in this picture of selective deposition of specific objects; one practice seems to be associated to a great degree with liminal watery contexts, the other with land and possibly settlement. The religious motivations were possibly different too, and speculating about such matters is undoubtedly a hazardous exercise. David Fontijn, for example, has dismissed the 'gifts to the gods' explanation for Bronze Age deposition in watery contexts as an interpretation that simply allows scholars to cope with the irrationality of metalwork deposition.[50] That said, though depositional conventions changed over time, the offering of gifts to gods – or goddesses in a feminized landscape – remains a possibility.

It should be stressed too that some of that bronze weaponry recovered in such quantity from rivers like the Shannon comes from a context with feminine connotations. Here the tutelary goddess was Sinann, whose story is very similar to that of Bóand of the Boyne. River goddesses are a widespread phenomenon but are difficult to date. We may never know if Sinann was a suitable subject for metalwork offerings in prehistory. The suggestion raises one interesting question, given that this sort of material also comes in large quantities from lakes and bogs, as the Dowris find so graphically illustrates. As various writers have argued, there seems to have been important distinctions between various sorts of water.[51] It may be that there was an important difference in the supernatural attributes of the fresh, flowing water of some rivers and springs and the still, unmoving water of lakes and bog pools. Their motionless water was a doorway to a mirror world – with which a goddess of the land was an intermediary in Irish tradition.

---

50 D.R. Fontijn, *Sacrificial landscapes* (2002), pp 18, 267.   51 D. Yates & R. Bradley, 'Still water, hidden depths', *Antiquity* 84 (2010), 405–15.

CHAPTER 7

Sacral kingship

Tara and its landscape are closely associated with kingship in myth and history. In medieval times they lay in the Uí Néill kingdom of Brega, which extended from the River Dee in Co. Louth southwards to the River Liffey, embracing the Boyne and the Blackwater to the west. From at least the fifth century, the kingship of Tara had been contested by rival dynastic groups from Leinster, Ulster (the Ulaid), the north-west (the Northern Uí Néill) and the midlands (the Southern Uí Néill). It was in the ninth century, however, that Máelsechlainn mac Máile Ruanaid, who died in 862, expanded Southern Uí Néill power and control sufficiently to give weight to the long-standing claim that kings of Tara were kings of Ireland. His son, Flann Sinna, is described as *Rí Érenn*, 'king of Ireland', in an inscription on the Cross of the Scriptures at Clonmacnoise.

The celebrated hill is situated about mid-way between the towns of Dunshaughlin and Navan in south central Meath. The archaeological monuments lie on a low ridge some 2km long and about 155m above sea level (pl. 10). The ridge drops steeply to the west with dramatic views over the central plain of the Irish midlands.[1]

The earliest account of the sites on its summit is found in the *dindshenchas* and was compiled for a political reason to enhance the claims of the Southern Uí Néill, and of Máelsechlainn mac Domhnaill (king of Tara who died in 1022) in particular, against those of his rival Brian Bórú of Munster. These topographical texts are attributed to the Uí Néill court poet Cúán úa Lothcháin. He, in emphasizing the symbolic importance of Tara, linked its monuments to ancestral figures, heroes, or kings such as Cormac mac Airt or Lóegaire son of Niall Noígíallach (Niall of the Nine Hostages)

Written in Middle Irish and dating to about AD1000, there is an unusually detailed description of the monuments on the hill, which George Petrie and John O'Donovan attempted to correlate with the visible archaeological remains some eight centuries later in 1836 in the course of their work for the Ordnance Survey.

---

1 On Tara, see C. Newman, *Tara, an archaeological survey* (1997); 'Re-composing the archaeological landscape of Tara' in E. Bhreathnach (ed.), *The kingship and landscape of Tara* (2005), pp 361–409; 'The sacral landscape of Tara' in R. Schot et al. (eds), *Landscapes of cult and kingship* (2011), pp 22–43. E. Bhreathnach, *Tara: a select bibliography* (1995); E. Bhreathnach (ed.), *The kingship and landscape of Tara* (2005); M. O'Sullivan et al. (eds), *Tara from the past to the future* (2013).

The text *Dindgnai Temrach* (The Remarkable Places of Tara) is in effect a medieval survey of the hill clearly compiled from a quite detailed topographical scrutiny of the monuments visible at the time and following a route from south to north. It lists natural features, such as springs and streams, and archaeological monuments such as *duma* or burial mounds, earthworks called *ráith* which are enclosures or ramparts, as well as other sites. The following is just a part of a translation published by Petrie in 1839:

> Of the remarkable remains of Temur ...
>
> The *Rath of Laoghaire, the son of Niall,* lies to the north of this. There are four principal doors on it, facing the cardinal points. The body of Laoghaire was interred with his shield of valor in the external rampart, in the south-east of the royal *Rath* of Laoghaire at Temur, with his face to the south, [as if] fighting with the Lagenians ...
>
> *Rath Righ* is by the side of *Rath Laoghaire* to the north. There are three *deccra* here, viz.; the ruins of the *House of Cormac* in the south-east side of the Rath, facing *Rath Laoghaire* to the south. The ruins of the *Forradh* alongside the ruins of the *House of Cormac* to the east ...
>
> *Dumha na n-giall* (the Mound of the Hostages) lies to the north-east of the ruins of the *Forradh.*
>
> *Fal* lies by the side of *Dumha na n-giall* to the north, i.e., the stone that roared under the feet of each king that took possession of [the throne of] Ireland. *Fal,* the name of this stone, means fo ail, the *under* stone, i.e., the stone *under* the king ...
>
> *Rath na Seanadh* (fort of the synods) lies opposite *Dumha* na *n-giall,* and to the north of *Fal.*
>
> The site of *Pupall Adumnain* (pavilion or tent of Adamnan) is in this Rath, and his (Adamnan's) cross is opposite the fort to the east, and his *Seat* and his *Mound* are to the south of the cross ...
>
> *Long na m-ban,* i.e., *Teach Midhchuarta,* is to the north-west of the eastern mound. The ruins of this house are situate thus: the lower part to the north and the higher part to the south; and walls are raised about it to the east and to the west. The northern side of it is enclosed and small; the lie of it is north and south. It is in the form of a long house, with twelve doors upon it, or fourteen, seven to the west, and seven to the east. It is said, that it was here the *Feis Teamhrach* was held, which seems true; because as many men would fit in it as would form the choice part of the men of Ireland. And this was the great house of a thousand soldiers ...
>
> *Rath Grainne* (Grania's fort) is west of the *Sheskin* on the height of the hill ...
>
> The two *Claenfearts* are to the west of *Rath Grainne.* It was in the southern *Claenfeart* that the virgins were slaughtered by the Lagenians

on Samain's day (1st of November). It is in the northern *Claenfeart* that Lughaidh mac Con pronounced the false sentence concerning the green field being eaten by the sheep ...[2]

The southernmost monument mentioned in this text is a partly destroyed enclosure named Ráth Laoghaire in modern Irish. Lóegaire is an early medieval king of Tara who figures in Patrician legend and some of the material about him is evidently unhistorical. According to genealogical tradition he was son of Niall Noígíallach, Niall of the Nine Hostages. It was the latter who mated with the goddess of sovereignty who appeared in the guise of an ugly hag but was transformed into a beautiful woman by the rightful candidate for the kingship of Tara in *Echtra mac nEchach Muigmedóin* (The Adventure of the Sons of Eochaid Muigmedón).

The largest enclosure on the hill is Ráth na Rí (the Fort of the Kings). It is an earthwork of approximately oval plan measuring about 310m north–south and 210m east–west and is one of those fairly rare hilltop enclosures characterized by an internal ditch and external bank, as found at Navan. Various monuments occur within it and include *Dumha na nGiall* (the Mound of the Hostages), the Forrad (An Forrad: the King's Seat or inauguration mound) and Teach Cormaic (Cormac's House), named after Cormac mac Airt, one of the most famous of Tara's kings, often portrayed as the ideal ruler.

In places, the rampart of Ráth na Rí departs from its elliptical curve and it seems that some deviations were created intentionally to accommodate earlier monuments including the Mound of the Hostages (fig. 7.1). That the rampart had to be realigned to enclose earlier sites might suggest poor design, but it seems much more likely that the deviations were intended to visibly proclaim the inclusion of these monuments by exaggerating the effect of their presence on the later enclosure. This was a deliberate reference to ancestral acts real or imagined; older monuments were perceptibly re-employed.

A section through the internal ditch was excavated in the 1950s and showed it to be a deep, V-shaped fosse dug to a depth of 3m into the bedrock; it had a deep vertical-sided palisade trench several metres inside it. More recent limited excavation revealed extensive traces of ironworking and bronzeworking sealed beneath the bank and possibly dating as early as the second century BC. This activity extended across the area where the ditch was later dug. The ditch-fill contained few artefacts, but animal bones were found at almost every level, representing a sequence of deposition spanning several centuries. These bones were mainly those of mature cattle, pig, sheep or goat, horse and dog, and the broken nature of the remains suggested that all of these animals were eaten. Human bones were found and included skull fragments and the skeleton

2 G. Petrie, 'On the history and antiquities of Tara Hill', *Transactions of the Royal Irish Academy* 18 (1839), 25–232.

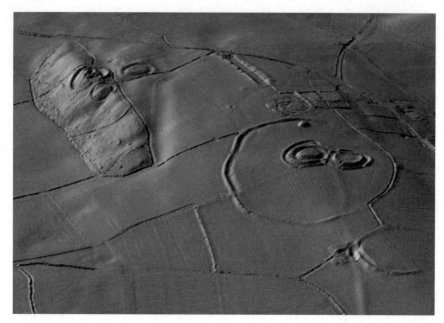

7.1. A LiDAR image of the Hill of Tara. This high resolution computer model of the summit of the hill was obtained by the Discovery Programme. The internal ditch of the large enclosure of Ráth na Rí is clearly visible in the centre-right of the image with the Mound of the Hostages and the conjoined Forrad and Cormac's House within it. The ring-barrows known as Ráth Ghráinne and the Claoinfhearta (the 'Sloping Trenches' – with vegetation removed) are on the upper left. The parallel banks of the Banqueting Hall are visible just beyond the Rath of the Synods. Ráth Laoghaire is on the lower right.

of an infant. The animal bones were interpreted as food debris, the remains of ceremonial feasts.[3]

This fairly functional explanation, however, probably underestimates the significance of this material and its context. In this situation, a variety of animals and horses in particular may have been killed and consumed as a part of kingship inauguration rites.[4] The ancient name of Tara, *temair*, is cognate with words like the Greek *temenos* meaning sacred enclosure and the Latin *templum* or sacred precinct, its Indo-European root, **tem-*, meaning to cut.[5] The cutting of the great ditch of the principal enclosure on the hill in the first century BC may have been a profoundly important act not just demarcating the hilltop sanctuary but also creating a liminal boundary that itself intersected with the paranormal and was infused with magico-religious significance.[6]

3 H. Roche, 'Excavations at Ráith na Ríg, Tara, Co. Meath', *Discovery Programme Reports* 6 (2002), 19–82.   4 F. McCormick, 'The horse in early Ireland', *Anthropozoologica* 42 (2007), 91.   5 D. Mac Giolla Easpaig, 'The significance and etymology of the placename *Temair*' in E. Bhreathnach (ed.), *The kingship and landscape of Tara* (2005), pp 423–49.   6 G. Dowling, 'The liminal boundary', *Journal of Irish Archaeology* 15 (2006), 15–37.

Two conjoined earthworks are among the most visible monuments in Ráth na Rí. The circular earthwork now called Teach Cormaic is a bivallate ringfort. The enclosed area is flat with a low sub-rectangular mound (traces of a house?) just off centre and is surrounded by two earthen banks with an intervening ditch. The Forrad, the inauguration mound, is a prominent flat-topped mound surrounded by a ditch and – for most of its circumference – two banks with an intervening ditch. The internal arrangement of the ditches indicates that this is a large bivallate ring-barrow. Three small circular burial mounds have been deliberately incorporated into the larger inner bank. The outer bank is noticeably narrower and may be a later addition. Since its size is similar to the outer bank of the adjacent ringfort, it seems that it represents an attempt to physically link the later habitation site to the burial complex.

A pillar stone of Newry granite on the summit of the Forrad is said to have been originally located near the Mound of the Hostages to the north. For this reason, it is today believed, possibly erroneously, to be the Lia Fáil, the stone of destiny, a stone that uttered a cry at the inauguration of a legitimate king of Tara. But this may have been a recumbent flagstone rather than this standing stone.[7]

The medieval name Dumha na nGiall (the Mound of the Hostages) is applied to a large circular mound at the northern end of Ráth na Rí. Excavation by Seán P. Ó Ríordáin in the 1950s has shown that it is an early prehistoric monument. A small passage tomb possibly built around 3000BC was covered by a cairn that was later enveloped in a mantle of earth containing numerous later burials of the late third and early second millennia BC. A curving segment of ditch was found beneath this monument and is the earliest identified feature on the hill. Radiocarbon dating suggests it is part of a late fourth-millennium-BC enclosure.

The Mound of the Hostages is also situated within a huge but somewhat later oval enclosure measuring 210m north–south and 175m east–west revealed by geophysical survey. A strong curving magnetic signature about 5m wide represents a sizeable ditch flanked by large pits on either side.[8] The pits form pairs placed about 8m from each other across the ditch. If, as seems possible, they once contained large timbers, then this enclosure was a truly monumental construction comparable in scale to some very large later Neolithic palisaded enclosures in Britain. A huge number of oak trees may have been felled to construct an edifice that was several times larger than Stonehenge. Situated as it was towards the eastern side of the hill, it was meant to be seen from the east, emphasizing the importance of the Gabhra Valley between Tara and Skreen at this early date.

---

7 T. Ó Broin, 'Lia Fáil: fact and fiction in the tradition', *Celtica* 21 (1990), 393–401. J. Carey, 'Ferp Cluche', *Ériu* 50 (1999), 165–8.   8 J. Fenwick & C. Newman, 'Geomagnetic survey on the Hill of Tara, Co. Meath, 1998–9', *Discovery Programme Reports* 6 (2002), 1–17.

The name of Ráth na Seanaid (the Rath of the Synods) commemorates the ecclesiastical synods supposed to have been held at Tara in the early medieval period. The site suffered considerable damage between 1899 and 1902 when some lunatic diggings were undertaken by a group called the British Israelites in an attempt to find the Ark of the Covenant.[9] Though the monument has the appearance of a much-disturbed multivallate ringfort, excavation by Ó Ríordáin in 1952–3 demonstrated that it had a complicated history that included a ditched enclosure, several arcs of timber palisade trenches, and a funerary phase with burials. The final phase was the construction of the ringfort, whose remains are visible today. It is dated to between the late second and the early fourth century AD. This has been described as a residential enclosure with various post-holes possibly representing a small subrectangular house, and traces of fires, pits and animal bones, evidence of ironworking and other material interpreted as habitation debris.[10]

The finds were unusual and for the most part consisted of fragments of imports from the Roman world or copies of Roman types made locally. They included a lead seal, glass beads, pieces of glass vessels, pottery sherds and an iron barrel padlock and bolt. The pottery included some Samian ware and many of the sherds, like the glassware, seem to be from fine drinking vessels. Cattle and pig bones, some from large animals, were common, but since they seem not to have been preserved no modern analysis has been possible. Given the complex ritual history of the site and the unusual nature of many of the finds, it does seem likely that the multivallate enclosure had a ceremonial role.

Ráth Ghráinne is an earthwork named after Gráinne, daughter of Cormac mac Airt. She was the legendary lover of Diarmaid in a famous elopement tale in the Fenian cycle associated with Finn mac Cumaill. It is a large ring-barrow with central circular mound surrounded by a ditch with external bank (pl. 10). Geophysical and aerial survey has demonstrated a remarkable sequence of ring-barrow construction here. A whole series of burial mounds intersect with each other, providing evidence of carefully planned ritual continuity. Several other low-profile circular sites are located to the north and north-east.

Over a dozen small burial mounds and two very large ring-barrows lie a short distance to the west and this northern portion of the hill was evidently a very significant necropolis. The large ring-barrows are named the Claoinfhearta or the 'Sloping Trenches', so-called because they are situated on the steep western slope of the hill (fig. 7.1). The northernmost was supposedly the dwelling of the king named Lugaid mac Con that collapsed catastrophically when he delivered a false judgment.

Figures that are best described as of varying degrees of historicity, such as Lóegaire, Cormac mac Airt and Lugaid mac Con, have been mentioned

9 M. Carew, *Tara and the Ark of the Covenant* (2003).   10 E. Grogan, *The Rath of the Synods, Tara, Co. Meath* (2008), pp 97, 108.

because they are kings whose names are linked with particular monuments on the summit of the hill. Among the many other personages associated with Tara are Conaire Mór, described as more purely mythical, the primordial just king who unwittingly breaks his taboos and is therefore hounded to his doom, and Conn of the Hundred Battles, who in *Baile in Scáil* had that vision on Tara of the god Lug and the young woman, the 'eternal Sovereignty of Ireland' (ch. 6).[11] Lug is of course associated with the large ringfort called Rath Lugh, 2.5km to the north-east of Tara in the Gabhra Valley. This earthwork is now flanked by the M3 motorway that today cleaves through the Tara landscape and its very name obviously links it to the mythology of Tara.

Some of the stories attached to Lug and the other figures serve in different ways to illustrate one or more aspects of the tradition of sacral kingship. The sacred king is a widespread phenomenon around the world and has been the subject of an enormous body of literature since the time of James Frazer's nineteenth-century *The Golden Bough*. As Frazer showed, a large body of ethnographical and historical evidence demonstrates that this is a kingly institution that is not primarily political, that to reign does not mean to govern but to guarantee the order of the world and society.[12]

There are many different models recorded in literary and anthropological studies and it is necessary to clearly distinguish between a king who is considered to be a god and one, in an Irish context, that is a sacred figure of unblemished physique, bound by ritual prescriptions and invested with quasi-divine qualities in that sacred marriage.

EARLY MEDIEVAL KINGSHIP

While early medieval law tracts, such as the *Críth Gablach* (Forked Purchase), are silent about the sacral nature of Irish kingship in the historical period, the concept of the sacred marriage between king and goddess that survived in features of medieval royal inauguration ceremony is the most significant indication of the king's originally sacred character. It is just one of a range of themes that repeatedly provide a glimpse of archaic beliefs, some of great antiquity with Indo-European antecedents.

Thanks to the law tracts and other sources, the social and political institutions of early medieval Ireland are reasonably well known and it is evident that the nature of kingship changed and developed in historical times.

---

11 On kingship, see D.A. Binchy, *Celtic and Anglo-Saxon kingship* (1970); F.J. Byrne, *Irish kings and high-kings* (1973); B. Jaski, *Early Irish kingship and succession* (2000); C. Doherty, 'Kingship in early Ireland' in E. Bhreathnach (ed.), *The kingship and landscape of Tara* (2005), pp 3–31.   12 L. Scubla, 'Sacred king, sacrificial victim, surrogate victim' in D. Quigley (ed.), *The character of kingship* (2005), p. 39.

Any summary risks oversimplification and there is no shortage of scholarly debate about many aspects. In general, it is true to say that in the early medieval period the island was divided into a large number of tribal groups or petty kingdoms, the *túath*, each perhaps comprising several thousand people.

There may have been as many as a hundred or more of these *túath* at any one time, the term meaning either people or territory (Indo-European **teutā* with its cognates found in almost all central and western Indo-European languages). The *túath* was ruled by a king, and its people comprised, in Binchy's words, 'a group of kindreds inhabiting a particular area and bound together by subjection to a common *rí*, not by descent (real or fictitious) from a common ancestor, still less by communal ownership of the land'.[13]

Whatever about the legal reality, clear claims to descent from mythical deities are evident in royal pedigrees and in the enormous corpus of genealogies, where, as Ó Corráin indicates, 'descent' and 'kinship' may be metaphors for other processes such as dynastic replacement, geographical contiguity or establishment of hierarchy.[14] The basic kin-group in the *túath* was the *fine*, which in its widest sense might include the descendants of a common great-great-great grandfather. Society was hierarchical, and is often said to have been divided essentially into kings, lords and commons. While this tripartite picture summarizes the social order, it does oversimplify the situation.

At the bottom of a complex social structure was a considerable slave population. The use of the word *cumal* (a female slave) as a unit of value in early Irish law indicates slaves were traded. Commoners were freemen and included the prosperous farmer and certain craftsmen. Above them in status were nobles, scholars, poets and churchmen. These (including some craftsmen) were classed as *nemed* or privileged persons (a term cognate with the Gaulish sacred *nemeton*). Individual rights and responsibilities varied according to status. The institution of clientship, an arrangement of reciprocal duties and obligations, created a bond between these grades of society. A lord, for example, received certain services and in return provided security and protection for a client.

In no way an absolute monarch, king and people had a contractual relationship. The king, *rí* (cognate with Gaulish *rīx* and Latin *rēx*), was the supreme lord of a *túath* and had the heads of the main noble families as clients. They in turn held minor lords and commoners in clientship. There were several grades of king: above the *rí* (the *rí tuaithe*), there were two types of over-king, the *ruiri* or superior king and above him the *rí ruirech* or king of superior kings.

---

13 D.A. Binchy, *Celtic and Anglo-Saxon kingship* (1970), p. 7.   14 D. Ó Corráin, 'Creating the past: the early Irish genealogical tradition', *Peritia* 12 (1998), 534.

As Binchy explained, the former was a king who was recognized as an overlord by the kings of at least two other tribes and this was a personal relationship only, a tie of fealty, he having no sovereignty over their tribesmen. The latter, the *rí ruirech*, had a number of superior kings bound to him in a similar fashion. These were relationships that involved tribute, hostages and military assistance.

Binchy wryly remarks that many of the inter-tribal wars noted in the annals may have been just punitive expeditions against a recalcitrant subordinate.[15] While 'there was little warfare but much violence in early medieval Ireland', a client who was a layman and free was obliged to take up arms and supply military service when required. Kings, who themselves might be war leaders, would have a retinue of household warriors or bodyguards.[16]

Mention should be made of the *fían*, a war- and hunting-band composed mainly of unmarried, landless and unsettled young men yet to become property-owning members of the *túath*.

They were preoccupied with hunting and raiding and this propensity finds an interesting metaphor in the numerous allusions to wolf-like behaviour and wolfish names. In providing a role for these early juvenile delinquents, the *fían* fulfilled the same social function as the type of male-bonding community or *Männerbund* found in various Indo-European societies.[17] Their deeds are romanticized in the exploits of the Fianna and Finn mac Cumaill in later tradition.

It was this hierarchical society composed of king, a noble class of warriors and skilled men, and a class of freemen, that Barry Cunliffe tentatively applied to the social organization of the hillfort of Danebury many years ago. He recognized that Celtic social structure may have differed considerably from place to place and time to time, but – reasonably enough – thought this historical model might be marginally more relevant in later prehistoric times than African or Asian analogies.[18]

Certainly, Celtic society was not uniform and did change. This was the case in Gaul by the time of Julius Caesar in the first century BC. In Ireland, the expansion of the major royal dynasties, well underway by the eighth century, hastened the process of detribalization and the desacralization of kingship, and led to the gradual disappearance of the *túath*. We have seen how the changing nature of kingship is reflected in Marion Deane's reading of *Compert*

---

15 D.A. Binchy, *Celtic and Anglo-Saxon kingship* (1970), p. 32.   16 T.M. Charles-Edwards, 'Irish warfare before 1100' in T. Bartlett & K. Jeffery (eds), *A military history of Ireland* (1996), p. 26. F. Kelly, *A guide to early Irish law* (1988), pp 66, 97.   17 K. McCone, 'Werewolves, cyclopes, *díberga* and *fíanna*', *Cambridge Medieval Celtic Studies* 12 (1986), 1–22; 'The Celtic and Indo-European origins of the *fían*' in S.J. Arbuthnot & G. Parsons (eds), *The Gaelic Finn tradition* (2012), pp 14–30. J.F. Nagy, *The wisdom of the outlaw* (1985). 18 B. Cunliffe, *Danebury*, 1 (1984), p. 560.

Conculainn (The Birth-tale of Cú Chulainn), in which the king, Conchobar, is credited with initiating clientship as a royal institution.

In rejecting Cunliffe's use of the picture we have of the hierarchical nature of early medieval society in Ireland to explain Danebury, various writers emphasized the thousand-year gap between the two worlds. Yet few would deny that the archaeology of the prehistoric Iron Age of southern England – or that of many other parts of the Celtic world – does indeed offer compelling evidence for a ruling class, a warrior caste, skilled craftsmen and strong farmers. To start at the top, a good case can be made that sacral kingship was once a feature of the social structure of parts of prehistoric Ireland – and Britain and Continental Europe.

THE CHARACTER AND RITUALS OF SACRAL KINGSHIP

The essential aspects of sacral kingship, encapsulated in certain mythic themes associated with some of those kings of Tara, have been mentioned already but can be summarized as follows:

– a central theme is the idea that the king was wedded to a woman who personified his kingdom as seen in those encounters between the goddess of sovereignty and the kings Niall and Conn respectively. We know of some of the inauguration rites associated with the symbolic marriage;
– the king is identified with the land and the cosmos, and is a mediator between this world and the Otherworld. Tara, identified particularly with the kingship of Ireland, was a special focus of supernatural threat;
– the maintenance of the cosmic order and the prosperity of the land were dependant on a just ruler who abided by his pact with the Otherworld. He was an unblemished individual who observed each and every Otherworldly *geis* or taboo imposed on him.

Conaire Mór, whose conception was the result of the impregnation of his divine mother by an Otherworldly figure in the guise of a bird (ch. 4), had his kingship of Tara foretold in a vision. This took place at a bull sacrifice reported in *Togail Bruidne Dá Derga* (The Destruction of Dá Derga's Hostel):

> Then the king, namely Eterscél, died. A bull-feast (*tairbfheis*) was convened by the men of Ireland: that is, a bull used to be killed by them, and one man would eat his fill of it and drink its broth and a spell of truth was chanted over him in his bed. Whoever he would see in his sleep would be king; and the sleeper would perish if he uttered a falsehood.[19]

19 Translation in Koch & Carey, *The Celtic heroic age*, p. 158.

There is also an account of a bull-feast held by Ailill and Medb to see who will be king of Tara in *Serglige Con Culainn* (The Wasting Sickness of Cú Chulainn). It has been considered to be a borrowing from the description of Conaire's divinatory rite, but in *Serglige Con Culainn* there is some additional detail. A white bull is specifically mentioned, as are four chanting druids. Mac Cana would prefer to see both tales, like the report of druidic sacrifice of white bulls in Pliny's *Historia Naturalis*, as a part of the common inheritance of Gauls and Irish.[20]

This bull ritual may once have been a more widespread practice even in Ireland. A small circular cairn now known as Carnfree, some six kilometres south-south-east of Rathcroghan, is believed to be the traditional burial place of the legendary Fraoch, hero of the *Táin Bó Fraích* (The Cattle Raid of Fraoch) who, as we saw (ch. 4), was probably associated with Oweynagat.

This cairn is one of the medieval inauguration sites of the O'Conor kings of Connacht and in the Annals of Connacht there is a famous but all-too-brief description of the inauguration of Feidhlim Ó Conchobhair as king there in AD1310. This medieval event was described as a *banais rígi* or kingship marriage, a surprising attempt to re-enact that archaic rite:

> Maelruanaid Mac Diarmata, seeing the exclusion of his foster-son from his patrimony … determined, like the warrior he was, to take his foster-son boldly and make him king by force. So he carried him to Carnfree and installed him on the mound according to the practice of the saints, and of Da Conna of Assylin in particular; and he, Fedlimid mac Aeda meic Eogain, was proclaimed in a style as royal, as lordly and as public as any of his race from the time of Brian son of Eochu Muigmedoin till that day. And when Fedlimid mac Aeda meic Eogain had married the Province of Connacht his foster-father waited upon him during the night in the manner remembered by the old men and recorded in the old books; and this was the most splendid kingship marriage ever celebrated in Connacht down to that day.[21]

F.J. Byrne has drawn attention to the interesting detail in *Táin Bó Fraích* in which Carnfree's eponymous hero is placed, on the orders of Ailill and Medb, in a bath of 'broth of fresh bacon, and flesh of a heifer chopped under adze and axe'. This, as he remarks, is the earliest example of a common motif of a hero being given a curative bath of broth, but, because it is associated with an inauguration place, it might represent a confused tradition of a ritual akin to the Tara *tairbfheis*.[22] The latter may have been a part of the *feis Temro* (the *feis*

20 P. Mac Cana, 'Conservation and innovation in early Irish literature', *Études celtiques* 13 (1973), 92.   **21** A.M. Freeman, *Annala Connacht* (1944), p. 223.   **22** F.J. Byrne, *Irish kings and high-kings* (1973), p. 19.

or feast of Tara) held once in the reign of each king. A number of Tara's kings are recorded as having held the *feis*, the last being Diarmait Mac Cerbaill in AD560.

According to Binchy, at Tara it signified the apotheosis of the sacred king and was held to mark the culmination of his reign perhaps when he had proven himself in battle and enforced his authority over all the subject tribes within the area of his rule.[23]

Another ritual of enkinging at Tara had equine associations. Some of the ordeals faced by a candidate for the kingship are described in *De Shíl Chonairi Móir* (Of the Seed of Conaire Mór).[24] Conaire Mór has to pass various tests:

> There was a king's chariot at Tara. To the chariot were yoked two steeds of the same colour, which had never before been harnessed. It would tilt up before any man who was not destined to receive the kingship of Tara, so that he could not control it, and the horses would spring at him. And there was a king's mantle in the chariot; whoso might not receive Tara's sovereignty the mantle was ever too big for him. And there were two flag-stones in Tara: 'Blocc' and 'Bluigne'; when they accepted a man, they would open before him until the chariot went through. And Fál was there, the *ferp cluche* at the head of the chariot course; when a man should have the kingship of Tara, it screeched against his chariot axle, so that all might hear. But the two stones Blocc and Bluigne would not open before one who should not hold the sovereignty of Tara, and their usual position was such, that one's hand could not pass sideways between them; also he who was not to hold Tara's kingship, the Fál would not screech against his axle.

According to Heinrich Wagner, the symbol of kingship in Iranian, Thracian and possibly Roman tradition was the chariot drawn by (white) horses[25] and, as we have also seen, the use of untamed horses in the ordeal is reminiscent of the practice recorded by Tacitus in which the neighs and snorts of wild horses, sometimes yoked to a sacred cart or chariot, were interpreted as divine omens by priests and kings (ch. 5). Also, Newman has noted that the crucial role of horses, unpolluted by earthly work, to test the prospective sacral king might indicate that an equine sovereignty goddess oversaw and guaranteed that institution at Tara.

---

23 D.A. Binchy, 'The fair of Tailtiu and the feast of Tara', *Ériu* 18 (1958), 113–38.   24 Text and trans.: L. Gwynn, 'De Síl Chonairi Móir', *Ériu* 6 (1912), 130–43, who translates *ferp cluche* as stone penis, but J. Carey, 'Ferp Cluche', *Ériu* 50 (1999), 165–8, argues that the oracular stone, Fál, was a flagstone on which the wheel rim and not the axle screeched. For further comments on Gwynn's translation, see J. Carey, 'Tara and the supernatural' in E. Bhreathnach (ed.), *The kingship and landscape of Tara* (2005), pp 32–48.   25 H. Wagner, *Studies in the origins of the Celts* (1971), p. 17.

Conaire is successful and enters Tara in 'the chariot of sovereignty' to be acclaimed by the oracular stone of Fál:

> The chariot and its steeds awaited him with the cloak of kingship in the chariot. The steeds stayed behind there for Conaire ... He stands in the chariot and it moves under him. He goes towards the two stones and they open before him. He goes to the Fál with all the host around him and his mother before him. The Fál cries out. 'Fál has accepted him!' cry the hosts. The hosts in Tara decline to give them battle; and make submission to Conaire and render to him his father's heritage. They acknowledge him as son of Éterscél Mór and give him the sovereignty and his father's territories; he makes seizures (of lands) for his hosts and till the ninth day from then he provides for them. They leave a bidding with him: that the sun should neither set nor rise on him in Tara.[26]

It is clear that the hosts mentioned are from the Otherworld and the injunction that the sun should neither set nor rise on Conaire in Tara is just one of the *geissi* or taboos placed on his kingship. These are effectively contracts with the Otherworld and are related in *Togail Bruidne Dá Derga* (The Destruction of Dá Derga's Hostel), which gives a different version of how he became king. Interestingly enough, it does not include the command that the sun should neither set nor rise on him in Tara. Possibly because this was a reference to the solar characteristics of Tara's rulers, it was thought an inappropriate allusion to include in a tale of a doomed king.

Just as the Otherworld favoured his accession to the kingship in the bull-feast and in the cries of Fál, it was Némglan from the Otherworld (ch. 3) who enunciated the series of taboos that would ensure the success of his reign:

> You shall not go righthandwise around Tara and lefthandwise around Brega. The evil beasts of Cerna must not be hunted by you. And you must not go out every ninth night beyond Tara. You must not sleep in a house from which firelight is visible after sunset and in which [light] is visible from outside. And three Reds shall not go before you into a Red's house. And no raiding shall be done in your reign. And after sunset a company of one woman or one man shall not enter the house in which you are. And you shall not settle the quarrel of your two slaves.[27]

His reign was prosperous, there was 'such abundance of good will that no one slew any other in Ireland', there was plenty of fish in the rivers Bush and

---

26 L. Gwynn, 'De Síl Chonairi Móir', *Ériu* 6 (1912), 139. On the taboos of Conaire Mór, see T. Sjöblom, *Early Irish taboos* (2000), p. 152.   27 Koch & Carey, *The Celtic heroic age*, p. 159.

Boyne, there were no thunderstorms; in fact 'from mid-spring to mid-autumn no wind disturbed a cow's tail'. However, Conaire's foster brothers and their companions took to thieving and marauding and he failed to stop them, thereby infringing one of the taboos, namely that there should be no plundering in his reign. He eventually took action, sparing his beloved foster brothers but condemning their companions to death. Recognizing the unfairness of his decision, he revoked it and ordered all of them to be banished to Britain. With this injustice, he violated *fír flathemon*, the 'prince's truth'.

This combination of breaking a taboo and delivering an unjust judgment is, in Ó Cathasaigh's opinion, an Irish instance of the Indo-European theme that Dumézil called 'the single sin of the sovereign', an irreparable act that destroys the very *raison d'être* of sovereignty.[28] Observing one's taboos is being true to one's obligations. The doomed Conaire broke his other taboos one after the other, even failing to prevent three horsemen with red tunics, mantles and weaponry and riding red horses, from preceding him to Dá Derga's hostel. Catastrophe follows and he and his followers die in its violent destruction.

The concept of *fír flathemon*, the 'prince's truth', is an integral element in the ideology of sacral kingship. Myles Dillon has compared it to the Hindu 'Act of Truth' (Sanskrit *satyā -kriyā*) for in both the Indian and Irish traditions there are tales in which the formal pronouncement of the truth is a magical act. The coincidences of idiom and episode suggest a common inheritance.[29]

The belief that truth was sacred is expressed in the eighth-century text *Audacht Morainn* (The Testament of Morann), described by Binchy as the oldest *speculum principis*, or 'mirror of princes' in western Europe. Here, a mythical judge addresses a mythical king at great length and reminds him of the beneficial consequences of just rule.

As summarized by Binchy:

> through *fír flathemon* comes prosperity and fertility for man, beast and crops; the seasons are temperate, the corn grows strong and heavy, mast and fruit are abundant on the trees, cattle give milk in plenty, rivers and estuaries teem with fish; plagues, famines and natural calamities are warded off; internal peace and victory over external enemies are guaranteed. The opposite of *fír flathemon* is *gáu flathemon* 'the injustice (lit. falsehood) of the prince', and this provokes all the corresponding disadvantages for his *tuath*.[30]

28 T. Ó Cathasaigh, '*Gat* and *Díberg* in *Togail Bruidne Da Derga*' in A. Ahlqvist et al. (eds), *Celtica Helsingiensia* (1996), pp 203–13.   29 M. Dillon, 'The Hindu Act of Truth in Celtic tradition', *Modern Philology* 44 (1947), 137–40; 'The archaism of Irish tradition', *Proceedings of the British Academy* 33 (1947), 245–64.   30 D.A. Binchy, *Celtic and Anglo-Saxon kingship* (1970), p. 10. Translation in Koch & Carey, *The Celtic heroic age*, p. 178; C. Watkins, '*Audacht Morainn*', *Ériu* 30 (1979), 181–98.

The just king guaranteed the order of the cosmos in the Indo-European world. Calvert Watkins cites several examples of this, including in *Audacht Morainn* 'It is through the ruler's truth that he secures peace ...', in the *Rig Veda* 'By Truth, Mitra and Varuna, increasers of Truth, embracers of Truth, you have reached great insight' and in a Vedic hymn 'By Truth, the earth is supported, (and) the sky is supported, along with the sun'.[31]

Cormac's predecessor as king of Tara was Lugaid mac Con and one day the youthful and precocious Cormac, who was in fosterage there, was present when Lugaid delivered a judgment on a relatively minor matter of trespassing sheep. The story is told in the ninth-century *Cath Maige Mucrama* (The Battle of Mag Mucrama):

> Now on one occasion sheep ate the woad of Lugaid's queen. The matter was brought to Mac Con for decision. 'I pronounce', said Mac Con, 'that the sheep be forfeited for it'. Cormac, a little boy, was on the couch beside him. 'No, foster-father', said he, 'the shearing of the sheep for the cropping of the woad would be more just, for the woad will grow and the wool will grow on the sheep'. 'That is the true judgment', said all. 'Moreover, it is the son of the true prince who has given it'. With that one side of the house falls down the cliff, namely the side in which the false judgment was given. It will remain for ever like that, the Clóenferta of Tara.[32]

The Claoinfhearta, as already noted, are two exceptionally large burial mounds situated on the steep western slope of the hill, a position of some significance since burial mounds elsewhere have this western-facing aspect too (fig. 7.1). Their funerary nature would have been clear even to a medieval antiquarian, but their unusual inclined location made one of them the ideal illustration of a collapsed dwelling. In an interesting instance of the malleability of myth, in one text the collapse of these 'Sloping Trenches' was claimed by the church to have been the consequence of an earthquake-inducing curse by St Patrick when his charioteer was killed.[33]

The collapse of his house was not the only result of Lugaid mac Con's misjudgment, however, for the account continues:

> After that he was a year in the kingship of Tara and no grass came through the earth, nor leaf on tree, nor grain in corn. So the men of Ireland expelled him from his kingship for he was an unlawful ruler.

31 C. Watkins, '*Audacht Morainn*', *Ériu* 30 (1979), 183, 184, 186.   32 M. O Daly, *Cath Maige Mucrama* (1975), p. 59 with emendation.   33 J. Carey, 'The two laws in Dubthach's judgement', *Cambridge Medieval Celtic Studies* 19 (1990), 2.

As we saw in *Compert Conculainn* (The Birth-tale of Cú Chulainn), when those birds laid waste the territory of Conchobar at Emain Macha (ch. 1), this image of the wasteland was a telling indication that the goddess of sovereignty had withdrawn her favour. Clearly, a series of bad harvests or famine or plague might have disastrous consequences for a sacred ruler.

When Cormac mac Airt became king in place of Lugaid mac Con cosmic equilibrium was restored and the fertility of the land returned. This may have been the sort of significant prosperity that impressed the historian Livy when he recorded that the semi-legendary Ambigatus, king of the Bituriges, ruled a part of Gaul some centuries earlier, a land remarkable for being 'so rich in corn and so populous'.[34]

When, over a millennium later, the productive seasons of the reign of the much-maligned MacBeth were thought worthy of note (*fertile tempus erat*), was this a Scottish statement on one of the ancient marks of a just ruler?[35] While the exceptional storage capacity of hillforts like Danebury might well indicate they were central places and centres for the redistribution of goods, could it be that the very visible display of wealth in commodities such as grain and livestock on sites like these was also intended to be a very public expression of a successful reign?

Physical perfection was another essential quality of a sacral king. The most famous example is the mythical Nuadu of the Tuatha Dé Danann who lost an arm and was provided with a silver replacement, hence his epithet *Argatlám* 'silver hand'. This blemish disqualified him from the kingship. The only king cited in a law-tract as losing the kingship of Tara is the seventh-century Congal Cáech who was blinded in one eye by a bee.[36] Cormac mac Airt is portrayed as the ideal king in early Irish literature. He was renowned for his wisdom and justice, and the country became 'a Land of Promise' in his reign. His death, however, was preceded by his exile a year before to Achaill, the Hill of Skreen to the east of Tara, because he lost an eye in a confrontation.[37]

A memory of royal mutilation also survives in elements of the legend of the Breton saint Melor. His father, the king, brought great prosperity to the land but was killed by Melor's uncle Rivod who proceeded to cut off Melor's right hand and left foot to disqualify him from the kingship. Rivod's unjust reign was disastrous and Melor was miraculously given a silver hand and a bronze foot by an angel. Despite all this, he was eventually decapitated but posthumously became a noted wonder-working saint.[38]

34 Livy, *Ab Urbe Condita*, 5.34; see M. Peacock, *The early history of Rome* (2005), p. 388.
35 A verse in the *Chronicle of Melrose* quoted by E.J. Cowan, 'The historical MacBeth' in W.D.H. Sellar (ed.), *Moray: province and people* (1993), p. 123.   36 F. Kelly, *A guide to early Irish law* (1988), p. 19.   37 T. Ó Cathasaigh, *The heroic biography of Cormac Mac Airt* (1977), p. 69.   38 G. Hily, *Le dieu celtique Lugus* (2012), p. 245; A.Y. Bourgès, 'Melor' in J.T. Koch (ed.), *Celtic culture*, 4 (2006), p. 1288.

KINGLY MONUMENTS

Not surprisingly, archaeological evidence for sacral kingship is difficult to identify. It is a possibility that the so-called Banqueting Hall on Tara had a role in rituals of inauguration. This linear earthwork consists of long pair of parallel earthen banks just over 70m north of the Rath of the Synods. It was identified as the Teach Miodchuarta or Mead Hall by medieval scholars and was the subject of much speculation even to the nature of the seating arrangements.

The parallel banks are slightly curved and run downslope from south to north for some 203m and are set about 25m apart. Both banks were seemingly raised from material dug from the interior, which is now below ground level. There are at least five gaps in the western bank and five or six in the eastern. Newman has suggested that the Banqueting Hall (fig. 7.1) is one of the later monuments on the celebrated hill (possibly dating to the fifth to eighth century AD). In an imaginative reading of the landscape, he has proposed that it was a processional way designed to unite the remains on Tara into a formal, religious arena, the hill and its monuments in effect constituting a sacral theatre.[39]

A semi-subterranean space, this is the one monument on the hill where the views to the outside world are denied. Starting at the north (that is the lower) end, it offers a ceremonial routeway to the summit sanctuary of Ráth na Rí along which the visitor, in an almost literal sense, enters Tara. Proceeding along the avenue, glimpses of the tombs of the ancestral kings and queens of Tara are caught through the gaps on the right-hand side. Reflecting on the lives of the ancestors, the royal party is reminded of the burden of responsibility that comes with world kingship, and of the fact that in re-enacting an inauguration they are about to take their place in history. The Hill of Skreen is visible to the east. This is the limbo that awaits those who break the taboos of kingship or fail to live up to the principle of the ideal just ruler. Cormac mac Airt was banished to Skreen after being physically blemished.

To the west lie the Claoinfhearta associated with the misfortunate Lugaid mac Con. Emerging from the processional way ten centuries ago, the royal party would have moved around the ramparts of Ráth na Rí and into the inner sanctuary through its entrance on the east. The climax of the inauguration ceremony then took place beside the Mound of the Hostages when the king placed his foot on the Lia Fáil, which would announce his rightful reign. While the earthwork is undated at present, this stimulating theory is in part testable by excavation. In addition, it is a theory that reminds us of the possible significance of processional avenues leading to circular enclosures.

---

39 C. Newman, 'Procession and symbolism at Tara: analysis of Tech Midhchúarta (the "Banqueting Hall") in the context of the sacral campus', *Oxford Journal of Archaeology* 26 (2007), 415–38.

Kingship ceremonies of some description may be reflected in the architecture of some early medieval ringforts that seem to have had some special function or form of occupation. Warner has suggested that a ringfort at Sessiamagaroll, near Benburb, Co. Tyrone, was a royal site. Its large size, commanding hilltop location and deep enclosing ditch are some indications of its former importance but it also has within it, abutting the rampart on the west, an imposing mound that Warner believes might be an inauguration mound.[40]

This association of ringfort and mound has been noted elsewhere. For example, one of a pair of imposing conjoined ringforts at Rathbrennan near the summit of a hill just east of Roscommon town overlooks the site of the sixth-century ecclesiastical foundation of St Commán, now in the town centre just over 3km away. The eastern fort has a circular mound in its interior near the rampart and a penannular depression in the mound's summit indicates that it was modified for some purpose.

Rathbrennan would appear to be the fort and mound referred to in the late twelfth- or early thirteenth-century *Acallam na Senórach* (Tales of the Elders of Ireland), on which St Patrick and Caílte were said to have sat when journeying through Roscommon. There they tell the story of how the fort was named and other tales:

> ... They continued to the south of the Wood of the Kin-Slaying, now called the Forest of Commán [Roscommon], where the nine sons of Úar, son of Indast, had killed each other, for which reason it was called the Wood of Kin-Slaying. They then continued on to the Fort of Glas, now called the Fort of Brénainn [Rathbrennan]. A tent was erected there for the King of Connaught, and Patrick and Caílte went and sat on an earthen mound by the perimeter of the fort.[41]

This may be a medieval recollection of the ceremonial use of this mound and, by introducing St Patrick, may even be an attempt to give a Christian gloss to the memory. Other examples of this juxtapositioning of mound and ringfort include a large multivallate enclosure at Rathra, near Castlerea, Co. Roscommon, that contains two mounds in its interior and the larger of these has a small penannular summit enclosure opening to the east-south-east.[42] Ceremonial associated with early medieval kingship is a distinct possibility at sites such as these.

As far as earlier times are concerned, archaeological traces of kingship rituals in prehistoric Ireland are presumably represented at Navan Fort (ch. 5),

40 R.B. Warner, 'The fort of Sessiamagaroll, Co. Tyrone', *Dúiche Néill* 14 (1983), 9–23.
41 A. Dooley & H. Roe, *Tales of the Elders of Ireland* (1999), pp 38–41. 42 J. Waddell, 'Continuity, cult and contest' in R. Schot et al. (eds), *Landscapes of cult and kingship* (2011),

where horse sacrifice may have been one important element. Such ¿
have been practised at Rathcroghan, too, where geophysical survey has re¿ay
broadly similar monumental architecture. The repetitive constructio¿
circular structures on the one spot, their entombment in a mound, and ev¿
the intriguing radial lines on the mound's summit (that recall those in the cairn
at Navan), all imply that some events there were approximately coeval with
those at Navan.

The trapezoidal eastern avenues approaching both Rathcroghan Mound
and the nearby northern enclosure are particularly interesting (pl. 7). Possibly
processional ways, they are larger versions of features found both at Navan and
at Knockaulin. It will be recalled that Newman in his discussion of the role of
the Banqueting Hall on Tara has noted that it too forms an approach-way to a
circular enclosure, in this case Ráth na Rí. It replicates and retains an
intriguing degree of asymmetry that is also evident in these features at
Rathcroghan, Navan, Knockaulin and the Glauberg, near Frankfurt (below).

Mention has already been made of the interpretation of the multivallate
ringfort at the Rath of the Synods on Tara as a residential enclosure dated to
between the late second and the early fourth century AD. Post-holes were
thought to represent a small subrectangular house and the material evidence
was interpreted as habitation debris. Others offer a different view, and the
assemblage of finds has been compared to similar material from British Iron
Age and Romano-British shrines such as the Uley shrines in Gloucestershire
and the rectangular structure to shrines like that at Heathrow. At Uley, where
much of the material was commonplace and even domestic, it was deemed to
be of ritual import because of its context.[43]

As Newman has said, writing of Tara:

> key elements of the mythology and rituals of sacral kingship are, by their
> very nature, beyond the range of scientific detection. Archaeologists
> should be alert, however, to the fact that in highly charged religious
> contexts such as this, even the mundane is potentially pregnant with
> magico-religious significance: how else, indeed, would the routines and
> objects of everyday life be brought into the benign orbit of religion?[44]

This is probably true of sites like Rathgall, Co. Wicklow, which has been
described as a major late Bronze Age settlement. This multivallate hillfort was
partly excavated by Barry Raftery and evaluation will have to await its full

p. 206.   **43** E. Bhreathnach, 'Transforming kingship and cult: the provincial ceremonial
capitals in early medieval Ireland' in R. Schot et al. (eds), *Landscapes of cult and kingship*
(2011), p. 127; G. Dowling, 'The architecture of power: an exploration of the origins of
closely spaced multivallate monuments in Ireland', in R. Schot et al. (eds), *Landscapes of cult
and kingship* (2011), p. 229.   **44** C. Newman, 'Procession and symbolism at Tara', *Oxford
Journal of Archaeology* 26 (2007), 430.

ation.[45] Preliminary reports indicate that four more-or-less concentric parts enclosed an area of some 7.3 hectares and excavations in the central one-built enclosure (possibly of medieval date) exposed a prehistoric annular ditched enclosure. This surrounded a circular structure interpreted as a large house that produced evidence for occupation and bronzeworking.

The quantity of metalworking evidence, including weapon manufacturing, goldwork, exotic glass beads, cremated burials and a hoard of bronzes, all combine to set Rathgall apart from other settlements of the time. These factors, the large size of the supposed house, its prominent hilltop location, and unusual ritual evidence all denote a site of considerable status. But it is one for which a purely functionalist explanation seems inadequate. The very name 'hillfort' is possibly misleading, for if the ramparts are of late Bronze Age date, they may have demarcated, rather than defended in any military sense, a great ceremonial enclosure with a sacred centre.

There is little doubt that sacral kingship was a feature of pre-Christian Ireland and it is likely that it was a prehistoric institution elsewhere in Europe too, wherever analogous tribal rural polities existed. Elites are often defined in the archaeological record by the construction of monumental structures, elaborate funerary practices or access to finely crafted or exotic goods. There is good historical evidence to show that this is a reasonable assumption at times, even if the term elite, more often than not, is just a useful but vague concept in the large body of literature on the study of social hierarchy in archaeology.

The quest for greater precision is more challenging. Various sorts of elites have been claimed in prehistoric Europe. Inspired by ethnographic analogies, chiefdoms emerged as a popular interpretation in the 1970s to explain the complexity of the archaeological record in the Bronze Age and earlier Iron Age in particular. This has proved to be a resilient though debated concept.

FUNERARY EVIDENCE

Material culture studies, notably of arms and armour, have inspired the identification of warrior aristocracies. In the burial sphere, the label 'royal' does lurk in the archaeological undergrowth. There is reference to the occasional royal grave – some high-status chariot graves in Yorkshire have been called royal burials for instance.[46] On the Continent, terms such as princely grave, *tombe princière* or *Fürstengrab* are commonly used. The latter, along with contemporary princely settlements or *Fürstensitzen*, are a well-known feature of parts of the Hallstatt and early La Tène Iron Age. Much has been written

---

45 Summary account in J. Waddell, *Prehistoric archaeology of Ireland* (2010), p. 285.   46 M. Parker Pearson, 'Food, sex and death', *Cambridge Archaeological Journal* 9 (1999), 56.

about the territories controlled by these elites, their rise and fall, [147] economic relationship with the Mediterranean world.

In the different sorts of chiefdoms that have been proposed in the evolu of complex societies, kings are rarely acknowledged. Perhaps this is because the understandable association of kingship with state formation and with absolute monarchy, an anointed sovereign ruling by the grace of God. Yet the linguistic evidence would suggest that all Indo-European peoples were, at one time or another, ruled by tribal kings. Indo-European **rēg-s*, the ancestor of Sanskrit *rāj-*, Latin *rēx* and Irish *rí*, with Welsh *rhi* and Gaulish *-rīx*, all point to this.[47]

A very general definition of these polities or chiefdoms is provided by the Irish structure with the *túath* meaning either people or territory, which, as we have seen, was a tribal group or petty kingdom comprising thousands of people ruled by a *rí tuaithe*. This twofold picture of a primary political unit ruled by a king and larger groups controlled by over-kings is reminiscent of the simple and complex chiefdoms found in the anthropological literature.

This Irish hierarchical model could conceivably embrace both the smaller polities that were a feature of parts of Britain and Ireland in later prehistory and the larger and more complex aggregations found in parts of the Continent. More importantly, it permits us to consider the real possibility that the elites in some of these different chiefdom societies included sacral kings. Though kings are occasionally mentioned, the relatively late classical sources are for the most part silent on this point. That foundation myth of the Greek colony of Massalia recorded by Aristotle may be an allusion to this institution and, as already pointed out, the memory of the great prosperity of part of Gaul under the rule of Ambigatus might have been seen as the mark of a sacred king.

Though Julius Caesar has little or no detail to offer on the nature of kingship, a decline in traditional kingship is generally believed to have occurred by his time. However, over a century later, when Tacitus belittled Mariccus of the Boii for pretending to be divine and calling himself a god, he may unwittingly have chronicled an important detail:

> I am ashamed to say that a certain Mariccus, a commoner of the tribe of the Boii, boldly endeavoured to thrust himself into greatness and to challenge the armies of Rome, pretending to be divine. This champion of Gaul, and god, as he had entitled himself, had already gathered a force of 8,000 men, and was beginning to influence the neighbouring Aeduan cantons. But the chief community of the Aedui wisely sent out a picked force, and Vitellius provided auxiliaries in support; they scattered the mob of fanatics. Mariccus was captured in the engagement, and later

---

47 D.A. Binchy, *Celtic and Anglo-Saxon kingship* (1970), p. 3. For a sceptical view, see K. McCone, *Pagan past and Christian present* (1990), p. 14.

thrown to wild beasts. As they refused to devour him, the common
people stupidly believed him invulnerable, until he was executed in the
presence of Vitellius.[48]

This was not just a peasant revolt in the territory of the Boii in western Gaul in
AD69, and it was more than a messianic protest.[49] Notwithstanding the
contempt of Tacitus for both Mariccus and his followers, it is quite possible
that the unfortunate Mariccus, at a time of great crisis, was very deliberately
invoking the old order to encourage his followers in his desperate challenge.
Vestiges of sacral kingship may have survived the Roman conquest.

There may be earlier clues, however. The possibility that representations of
horses with human heads were allusions to equine invocations that were a part
of kingship rituals has been mentioned (fig. 5.4). John Creighton has made the
interesting suggestion that the persistent imagery of a combination of male
heads and horses on British and Continental Iron Age coinage symbolize the
sacred marriage fundamental to sacral authority.[50] The same may be said of the
horse and warrior imagery that is represented in various sorts of stone carving
at sites like Roquepertuse and Entremont in southern France.[51] It is possible
that one place to find some archaeological trace of these elusive individuals, be
they sacral kings or sacral chiefs, is in older contexts that appear to have a
sacred character.

The Glauberg is a princely settlement of the Hallstatt and earlier La Tène
periods on the eastern edge of the fertile Wetterau, north of Frankfurt in
western Germany. A hillfort overlooks a ceremonial complex on lower ground
to the south, comprising at least two burial mounds with an associated processional way.[52] It was the latter configuration of circular monument and avenue
with nearby burial mounds that Newman compared to the enclosure and avenue
at Tara and at Rathcroghan in 2007. At the Glauberg, one of the burial mounds
was a huge monument some 50m in diameter surrounded by a deep ditch
approached on the south-east by a pair of parallel 10m-wide ditches forming
an avenue some 400m in length. As Newman noted, an interesting detail at all

---

48 Tacitus Histories 2:61; see W.H. Fyfe & D.S. Levene, *Tacitus* (1997), p. 93. **49** This
passage has been studied by M. Gwyn Morgan, 'The three minor pretenders in Tacitus',
Latomus 52 (1993), 770. For the suggestion of a messianic protest, see J. Webster, 'Druidic
and other revitalization movements', *Britannia* 30 (1999), 15. **50** J. Creighton, *Coins and
power* (2000), p. 22; 'Gold, ritual and kingship' in C. Haselgrove & D. Wigg-Wolf (eds), *Iron
Age coinage and ritual practices* (2005), pp 69–84. As Creighton (*Coins and power*, p. 24) notes,
the personal name Epomeduos is found on a number of Gaulish coins and has been thought
to combine the words for horse (as in Epona) and mead and thus be a Continental allusion
to the royal horse sacrifice. In this context, however, according to G.-J. Pinault, 'Gaulois
Epomeduos' (2007), p. 301, it seems that *-meduos* derives from **med-wo-* 'to rule' and the name
means 'master of horses'. **51** For which, see I. Armit, *Headhunting and the body* (2012), p. 143.
52 F.-R. Hermann, 'Der Glauberg, Fürstensitz, Fürstengräber und Heiligtum' in H. Baitinger
& B. Pinsker (eds), *Das Ratsel der Kelten von Glauberg* (2002), pp 90–111.

of these sites is the fact that the alignment of the avenue or the narrowing of enclosure entrance seems to be a deliberate feature to obscure or redirect access and to manipulate the experience of the participants in the process.

A wooden chamber was discovered in this burial mound and found to contain the corpse of an adult male with rich grave goods. These included a highly decorated bronze flagon that once held a honey-based drink, an iron sword and three spears, a bow with quiver and arrows, a shield made of wood, leather and iron, and gold personal ornaments including earrings, a bracelet, a finger ring and a torc.

Perhaps the most spectacular discovery, however, was a life-sized sandstone statue of an adult male found beside the mound on the north-west. He is apparently depicted as wearing leather body armour and carrying a shield. He is also wearing several bracelets, a finger ring and a torc that closely resembles the one found in the grave nearby. It is possible that this is an image of the individual buried there (pl. 8). If this is so, then the exceptional grave goods may provide a clue to the insignia appropriate to a person of sacral status at this time. Variously described as depicting a warrior, a stone knight, a hero, a mortal or a god, the statue is a piece of sculpture laden with symbolism.

The prominent leaf-crown is a striking detail and quite a number of explanations have been offered for this well-known device in Celtic art. It has been seen, for instance, as a version of the horns of Mediterranean goddesses such as Hathor and Astarte, a portrayal of the hero's light that emanated from the head of Cú Chulainn and a representation of the leaves of the sacred mistletoe used by the druids. Whatever its inspiration, given the context of its various representations in stone and on metalwork, most commentators would see it as a symbol of divinity.

Again, there has been much comment on the marked contrast between the upper and lower limbs of the Glauberg figure. His arms are stylized, almost atrophied and held in a ritual pose. In contrast, the legs have well-defined musculature recalling the naturalistic and athletically youthful style of Greek *kouros* statuary. Bearing in mind the qualities that a sacral king should have, it is conceivable that the stylized arms and associated weaponry represent the restrained power of a just ruler, the strongly delineated thighs and calves evoke that person's central relationship with strength and fertility.

This may be the case as far as another celebrated male statue is concerned. A stone figure found beside a tumulus at Hirschlanden (Baden-Württemberg) is naked but for a conical hat, a neck-ring, dagger and belt (pl. 8). Its arms and legs are carved in the Glauberg manner, with the same marked contrast between upper and lower body. Clearly ithyphallic, however, its fertility symbolism is evident and it too is doubtless charged with sacral connotations.[53]

---

[53] I. Armit & P. Grant, 'Gesture politics and the art of ambiguity: the Iron Age statue from Hirschlanden', *Antiquity* 82 (2008), 409–22.

The stylized nature of the Glauberg statue contrasts with the more naturalistic depiction of a seated male on the rim of the bronze flagon found in the nearby grave. This large vessel was certainly a ceremonial drinking piece and the bronze figurine was a highly symbolic component of whatever cult practices occurred. The man, with a curling hairstyle, wears clothing and body armour and is seated in a cross-legged position. He is flanked by a pair of fantastic sphinx-like animals with their heads turned towards him. The style and posture of this male figure is comparable to the stone sculptures of seated warriors known in the south of France, particularly at sites such as Roquepertuse. This must bring to mind the exceptional suite of stone carvings of seated warriors, women and drinking vessels at nearby Entremont that recall aspects of the rituals of sacral kingship (ch. 6).

Both the Glauberg and the Hirschlanden statues are almost complete and the fact that both just lack their feet can be explained in a prosaic fashion, the lower extremities were broken off where they once were inserted in sockets. Megaw has argued that this sort of breakage was, as with the smashing of other carvings with warlike attributes, the deliberate destruction of a hero figure, like the equally deliberate 'killing' of weaponry so often encountered in burials and in votive deposits.[54]

In each case, only the feet are missing, and this is a puzzling coincidence. Their footless nature possibly holds a particular message and, assuming they were once shod, their shoes may have had a special significance. Golden shoes were a symbolic attribute of kingship in Irish and Welsh tradition (ch. 4), and various Otherworldly figures were associated either with a golden sandal on whichever foot touched the ground or with a silver sandal on one foot and a golden one on the other. This might have been a motif ultimately related to the Indian taboo that prohibited a king treading the ground unshod lest his potency be drained away into the earth.

Megaw may have been correct in part, but, in these cases, in confining the iconoclastic destruction to the feet we may have an example, not of the decommissioning of a heroic warrior, but of the very visible statement, some time after his death and burial, of the deactivation of the powers of a sacral king by eliminating the protection provided by his special footwear. As we have seen in the case of the reversed shoes in the Hochdorf grave, these objects probably had a distinctive symbolism.

The argument that the Glauberg and Hirschlanden statues might be representations of sacred kings has the merit, at least, of offering an explanation for a range of different symbols that seem to embrace such diverse concepts as exalted status or divinity, martial competence and fertility. To the south, near Stuttgart, the Hirschlanden burial mound was located some 10km from the 'princely seat' of the Hohenasperg. It was one of a series of burial mounds

---

54 J.V.S. Megaw, 'Celtic foot(less) soldiers? An iconographic note', *Gladius* 23 (2003), 61–70.

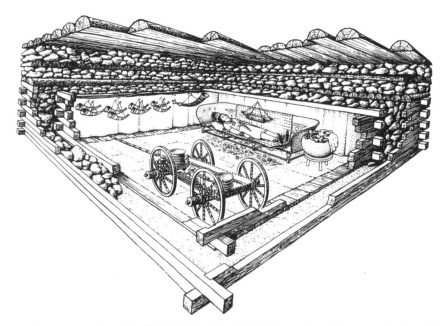

7.2. A reconstruction of the Hochdorf burial which had been placed in a great timber and stone vault. The body lay on a bronze couch supported by eight castors in the form of female figurines and was accompanied by the aristocratic status symbols common in graves of this type: a drinking and feasting set that included nine drinking horns, a four-wheeled wagon and personal ornaments.

associated with this settlement, and several, containing male burials with rich grave goods, are held to be 'princely burials'. But maybe 'prince' is a misnomer in some cases; it seems possible that the rulers of the Hohenasperg should be judged to have been sacral personages with all the status, obligations, ritual associations and constraints that early Irish tradition implies.

HOCHDORF

The Hochdorf burial mound lies about 10km from the Hohenasperg, a hilltop now enveloped in modern settlement and one that dominates the fertile plain north of Stuttgart and just north-west of Ludwigsburg. The Hochdorf excavation in the late 1970s revealed a great deal of information on funerary practice. A very large mound, some 6m high and 60m in diameter originally, contained the well-protected and undisturbed burial of a tall adult male.

He had been buried in a great timber-and-stone vault as a protection against grave robbers. It was evident that the funerary activity took several weeks and some five years are estimated to have passed before the construction of the mound was completed. It was a protracted and public affair in the mid-sixth century BC (fig. 7.2). The prolonged ritual lasting several years may even have been followed by acts of remembrance and all this suggests that highly significant events like the death of this individual may have been occasions when the social order was effectively reshaped.

The body had been placed on a decorated bronze couch supported by eight castors in the form of female figurines. This unique piece of furniture was modeled on north Italian fashions. The deceased was accompanied by the aristocratic status symbols common in graves of this type: a drinking and feasting set, a four-wheeled wagon and personal ornaments. The wooden wagon was a ceremonial vehicle clad in sheet iron. Items placed on top of it included harness fitments for two horses, nine bronze plates, three bronze basins (all showing signs of use), a heavy iron axe, a long iron knife and a socketed iron spike. In addition to the horse equipment, equine symbolism occurs on the bronze couch, where the decoration includes images of paired stallions drawing a wagon.

Nine drinking horns hung on the wall of the chamber; eight were made of cattle horn but the largest, hanging behind the head of the corpse, was of sheet iron. The body was clothed in woven fabrics with, behind the head, a broad conical hat made of birch bark (its shape like that depicted on the Hirschlanden statue).

Ornaments included a broad collar of sheet gold (again similar to that worn by the Hirschlanden figure), two gold fibulae, a gold armlet, a gold-covered bronze belt plaque and – of course – the sheet gold decoration on the pair of shoes (fig. 4.5). There was also sheet gold decoration on the scabbard of an iron dagger. A large bronze cauldron of Greek type, made in southern Italy, and a golden cup were placed at the foot of the corpse; the cauldron had once contained high-quality mead.

When compared to other graves that had a greater amount of imported exotica, it once seemed to some commentators that the Hochdorf male may not have been of the highest rank. But this is an assessment based on the assumption that status always correlates with the presence of prestige goods and it is now recognized that grave goods are not necessarily a measure of the wealth and social status of the deceased or of their kin. As one writer has observed, burials and their contents are not faithful 'mirrors of life'; if anything, they are a 'hall of mirrors of life'.[55] While status or gender may determine burial practice, this is not necessarily so. It is now accepted that social and religious concepts are reflected in such ritual and that the very selective process evident in the deposition of grave goods – that themselves have an inherent symbolism – is a real challenge to archaeological interpretation.

55 H. Härke, 'The nature of burial data' in C.K. Jensen & K.H. Nielsen (eds), *Burial and society* (1997), p. 27.

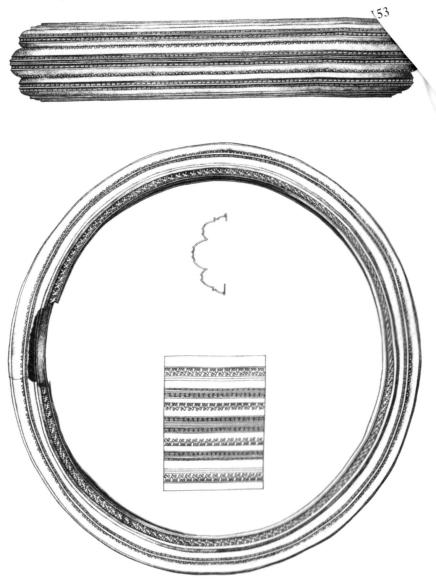

7.3. The Hochdorf sheet gold collar. Deliberately cut with a sharp implement, its decoration includes four very narrow zones of stamped images of winged horses forming a continuous frieze placed in two bands one above and one below the mid-point of the collar.

As we have seen, over thirty years ago Calvert Watkins, a specialist in early Indo-European linguistics and society, noted that golden shoes were a symbolic attribute of kingship in Irish tradition. Writing of the then recently excavated Hochdorf, he said:

What we are looking at, on the feet of a Hallstatt chieftain in the sixth century BC, would still be remembered in early Irish some 1,300 years later as *da assa co foraib óir impu*, 'two shoes with uppers of gold around them'. The golden shoes in which he was laid out were the insignia of his authority, as much a symbol of his kingship as the more familiar gold collar which he wore.[56]

The gold collar on the Hochdorf body was clearly an important object too, for it had been deliberately cut with a sharp implement in what presumably was an act of deconsecration. Also significant, surely, is the fact that it bears equine symbolism (fig. 7.3). Four very narrow zones of stamped images of horses forming a continuous frieze are placed in pairs of parallel bands one above and one below the mid-point of the collar. Edged by equally narrow zones of geometric motifs, the paired bands of horses are mirror images of each other.[57] This is the only gold item to bear anything other than abstract motifs and miniaturization is unlikely to be an inconsequential detail. If, as has been said, these are images of tiny horses with their riders, then there may be a great equestrian narrative memorialized here.

There is another possibility, however, because it seems more likely that winged horses rather than horses with riders are represented. A small winged horse was prominently placed on each of the terminals of the gold collar found at Vix.[58] As Green has said, depicting a winged horse (as on the Breton coin illustrated in fig. 5.4, 2) may be a reference to the animal's Otherworld status, for in many traditional societies flight is the mechanism by which a shaman or ritualist reaches the spirit-world.[59] Thus, the Hochdorf collar might be not just a mark of rank but an indication of the Otherworldly source of this individual's power.

The question of the social status of the Hochdorf 'prince' has, of course, led to much deliberation and a number of writers have alluded to the sacral character of such 'princely' persons. Dirk Krausse has argued that the iron axe, knife and spike found on the Hochdorf wagon close to the bronze plates and basins form a set of tools related to these eating utensils. Since iron axes have been found in other rich graves, he believes that it and the spike and knife were not just butchery equipment but implements for the sacrificial killing of animals and an indication of the religious status of the deceased.[60]

Stéphane Verger, in an ambitious and complex analysis of the symbolic significance of various aspects of the Hochdorf grave, has made the case that this individual's exalted status was the culmination of regional socio-political

56 C. Watkins, 'Language, culture or history?' in C.S. Masek et al. (eds), *Papers from the parasession on language and behavior* (1981), p. 246. **57** L. Hansen, *Hochdorf VIII* (2010), p. 36, Taf. 1. **58** S. Verger, 'L'utilisation du répertoire figuratif dans l'art celtique ancien', *Histoire de l'Art* 16 (1991), 7. **59** M. Green, *An archaeology of images* (2004), p. 163. **60** D. Krausse, 'Der "Keltenfürst" von Hochdorf', *Archäologisches Korrespondenzblatt* 29

developments.[61] He has proposed that elements in the grave such as the feasting vessels and even the eight females who support the bronze couch reflected the existence in the Hohenasberg region of eight tribal groups, these figurines possibly representing their mythical female ancestors. The same sort of ancestral myth is, he believes, represented in a pair of puzzling pendants attached to the end of the iron drinking horn, which are copies of ornaments worn by the wealthiest Hallstatt women. He has suggested that the feasting and drinking equipment in the grave had diverse purposes and symbolic significance.

Inspired by the detailed portrayal of the allocation of different portions of meat to different persons based on their rank and status found in the description of the Banqueting Hall on Tara, Verger has also claimed that differences in style and design of the nine bronze plates and the basins in the grave reflect distinctions in rank and in the provision of various cuts of meat to members of the Hochdorf retinue. This Irish account, preserved in the twelfth-century Book of Leinster and the later Yellow Book of Lecan, describes how meat was apportioned, pieces such as tenderloin going to the king and literati with the unlucky doorkeeper rewarded with the coccyx of the animal. Such feasting formalities were undoubtedly of great antiquity and survived after a fashion into the seventeenth century in Ireland and Scotland.[62]

According to Verger, three persons of the highest rank at Hochdorf were served from the three basins and each had a plate with geometric decoration on the rim, while five others of lesser nobility each had a plate with embossed decoration. A ninth person had an undecorated plate and may have had a special status, perhaps religious or scholarly. The differences in these feasting utensils seem to have been replicated in the different ways they were placed on the wagon. However, drinking ceremonies were dissimilar in his opinion, because here the only significant variation was between the one large iron drinking horn and the eight other smaller organic ones. This, he thought, indicated a certain equality among those assembled for drinking rites and these persons represented tribal leaders of the Hohenasperg complex. In these gatherings, the great iron horn was a communal drinking vessel. The bronze couch may at one time have been a throne for the three persons of highest status he has identified; they would have been seated side-by-side on the couch in the traditional cross-legged fashion.

In Verger's opinion, the wealth of goldwork associated with the Hochdorf individual and other insignia implied that he had acquired sacral characteristics specifically associated with kingship. The goldwork was intimately associated

(1999), 339–58. **61** S. Verger, 'La grande tombe de Hochdorf', *Siris* 7 (2006), 5–44; 'Partager la viande, distribuer l'hydromel. Consommation collective et pratique du pouvoir dans la tombe de Hochdorf' in S. Krausz et al. (eds), *L'âge du fer en Europe* (2013), pp 495–504. **62** F. McCormick, 'The distribution of meat in a hierarchical society' in P. Miracle & N. Milner (eds), *Consuming passions and patterns of consumption* (2002), p. 27.

with his person, as was the gold cup that would have touched his lips. This was found with the bronze cauldron and these objects marked his ultimate achievement of royal power sanctioned by the drink offered by the goddess of sovereignty (like the young woman in *Baile in Scáil* who granted rulership to Conn of the Hundred Battles). Other feminine elements such as the pendants on the iron horn and the figurines supporting the couch also evoked this incarnation of sovereignty in the person of this one individual whose rule now had divine sanction.

Whatever about Verger's interpretation of the significance of the bronze plates and basins and of the nature of the drinking rituals and usage of the great drinking horn, he is right to stress the sacral character of the Hochdorf personage. Remembering that story of the foundation of Massalia and the role of a sovereignty goddess-like figure who offered a bowl of wine to the chosen ruler, each drink of mead presented to the Hochdorf individual in his lifetime may have been a ceremonial re-enactment of his inauguration and an acknowledgment of his status. At the very least, the drinking horns and plates in the grave were, as is usually admitted, a part of a collective feasting set, but the very special status of the dead person may have been reflected in the deposition of nine particular items.

This detail has been noted elsewhere and may have a special meaning. A burial mound at Kappel am Rhein north of Freiburg (Baden Württemberg) was excavated in 1976 and contained a timber chamber with a richly furnished male burial dated to the later seventh century BC. Nothing survived of the corpse, but grave goods included a dismantled four-wheeled wagon, an iron dagger, two iron spears and two large pottery vessels. A bronze cauldron had a huge bronze bucket over 1m tall standing in it and within the bucket were fourteen other bronze vessels and the mounts of a large drinking horn. Eight of these vessels were almost identical small ribbed cylindrical buckets and, along with the drinking horn, could have formed another noteworthy set of nine items (fig. 7.4).[63]

Irish evidence indicates the number nine had a particular importance. The Rees brothers, in a study of the significance of numbers, have shown how early Irish literature has many references to 'companies of nine' sometimes consisting of a leader and eight others. In *Fled Bricrenn* (Bricriu's Feast), with its competition for the champion's portion, eight swordsmen guarded Bricriu on his way to the feast. In the *Táin*, Medb's chariot is accompanied by eight others.

Lóegaire, king of Tara, commanded nine chariots to be equipped as he prepared to challenge St Patrick.[64] The latter reference occurs in Muirchú's life of the saint written in the seventh century, in which the pagan king is

63 R. Dehn et al., *Das Hallstattzeitliche Fürstengrab im Hügel 3 von Kappel am Rhein in Baden* (2005).   64 A. & B. Rees, *Celtic heritage* (1961), p. 193.

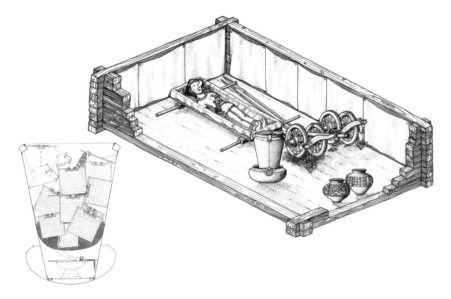

7.4. Right: a reconstruction of a rich burial at Kappel am Rhein in which a timber chamber contained a burial with grave goods that included a dismantled four-wheeled wagon, an iron dagger, two iron spears and two large pottery vessels. A bronze cauldron had a huge bronze bucket over 1m tall standing in it and within the bucket (left) were fourteen other bronze vessels and the mounts of a large drinking horn.

unflatteringly compared to Nebuchadnezzar of Babylon. As he prepares to confront the saint, Lóegaire ordered 'nine chariots yoked therefore according to the tradition of the gods' (*Iunctis ergo nouem curribus secundum deorum traditionem*). His meeting with Patrick is probably the stuff of legend, but Muirchú's allusion to a pagan belief in the symbolic importance of a gathering of nine warriors is revealing.[65]

There are other fleeting references to a similar occurence. It seems likely that king Conchobar and his charioteer were in one of the nine chariots harnessed to pursue the birds in *Compert Conculainn* (The Birth-tale of Cú Chulainn), and when the charioteers who accompanied Lug in the epic battle in *Cath Maige Tuired* (The Second Battle of Moytura) are named, they are eight in number.[66] It is an arrangement that also occurs in the *Iliad*, where Menestheus and Hector, for instance, each go to battle with eight companions.[67] Whether the eight female figures that supported the Hochdorf corpse should be included as related symbolism is not clear, but the archaeological evidence

65 D. Howlett, *Muirchú Moccu Macthéni's 'Vita Sancti Patricii' Life of Saint Patrick* (2006), p. 73. This episode is the legend of the lighting of the Easter fire by Patrick questioned by D.A. Binchy, 'The fair of Tailtiu and the feast of Tara', *Ériu* 18 (1958), 130.   **66** E.A. Gray, *Cath Maige Tuired* (1982), p. 65.   **67** *Iliad* XIII:689–700 and 790–802; H.W. Singor, 'Nine against Troy', *Mnemosyne* 44 (1991), 43.

indicates that this eight-plus-one configuration is an ancient element of European warrior ideology and not just a literary conceit.

With few exceptions, like Verger, the idea that the Hochdorf person may have been a sacred king has not found favour among most commentators. Neither ethnographic analogy nor Indo-European evidence has been employed to any extent.[68] Given this unproductive methodological reluctance in French and German archaeological studies, it is not surprising that so little consideration has been given to early Irish tradition in this debate. To be fair, this may be because much of this material is, as we have seen, relatively inaccessible in medieval texts.

While any attempt to reconstruct the social institutions of a prehistoric people must be a speculative exercise to a great degree, the concept of sacral kingship deserves to be a factor in the continuing discussion on the rank and role of exceptional personages like the Hochdorf male.

Mention has been made of the difficulties posed by questions of status or gender in the burial record. While an association between weaponry and male burials is frequently manifest, it is often the case that gender is not so clearly marked by other associated artefacts such as personal ornaments. Recent years have seen a growing interest in the exploration of the gendered status of individuals in various communities and a recognition that the binary biological male–female distinction is not the same as culturally constructed gender differences that may vary in time and place.

The incidence of ostensibly female ornaments in male burials has prompted suggestions that they might denote the practice of 'ritual transvestism' or the presence of 'rule-breaking rulers' in Iron Age Europe.[69] Some of the items in the Hochdorf grave might be considered more appropriate in a female context: decorated belt plates and amber beads are often found in women's graves, for example.

But, once again, early Irish literature reminds us that there are other possibilities. Rather than a reference to the deceased's gender, it is conceivable that the presence of essentially feminine items of adornment were an expression of the ruler's all-embracing beauty. It is worth recalling that there is good archaeological evidence, reflected in toilet articles in burials for instance, that an aesthetic of male beauty was an important part of warrior identity as early as the Bronze Age.[70]

Early Irish tradition indicates that claims of gender ambiguity in a male dominated warrior society should be treated with the greatest caution. It is true that Cú Chulainn's well-known fight with Fer Diad in the *Táin* has been

68 M.K.H. Eggert, 'Der Tote von Hochdorf', *Archäologisches Korrespondenzblatt* 29 (1999), 211–22; U. Veit, 'König und Hohepriester?', *Archäologisches Korrespondenzblatt* 30 (2000), 549–68. 69 Summarized by L. Hansen, *Hochdorf VIII* (2010), p. 97. 70 P. Treherne, 'The warrior's beauty', *Journal of European Archaeology* 3 (1995), 124.

viewed in homoerotic terms, in part because of the great affection displayed by Cú Chulainn for his foster brother and in part because of the brutal violation of Fer Diad's body.[71] It is also the case that the peculiar custom of a man kissing or sucking a male breast as a mark of submission or fealty, recorded by St Patrick in his *Confessio* and in the Old Irish story *Echtra Fergusa meic Léti* (The Adventure of Fergus mac Léti), has provoked the idea that in a male group, in which the leader was symbolically regarded as a maternal figure, a ritual reality was created in which women were redundant.[72]

The relationship of medieval poet and patron should be considered too, because this has occasioned comment. When a king or lord was addressed poetically, great emphasis was often given to the lord's beauty, his attractiveness to men and the poet's desire to be by his side. Ní Dhonnchadha has argued persuasively that fetishization of the beauty of a leader was a form of male homosocial bonding. It had an added dimension because the beauty of the king in earlier times and the lord thereafter is an expected aspect of a ruler who is the flawless bridegroom of the sovereignty goddess. Moreover, the rites of sacral marriage were a form of legitimation based on heterosexual symbolism, and yet another form of legitimation was associated with the ruler's unblemished body because he embodied all, both male and female.[73]

It may be added that the relationship of poet and patron was not just a medieval phenomenon but one of great antiquity. Mac Cana has written:

> That formal eulogy was regarded as central to the relation of poet or priest-poet and royal patron is evidenced abundantly in Celtic sources as it is in Indic and other Indo-European traditions, and in the light of the interpretative commentaries of modern Indo-European specialists … one might well say that in ancient times formal eulogy was the life-blood of sacral kingship.[74]

While flamboyant burials like Hochdorf are promising subjects to study in the search for elite persons like sacral kings, such rich and superbly excavated graves are not a widespread phenomenon in any period. Even though a number of very wealthy graves are known in the later Bronze Age (and some in central Europe have even been described as royal burials), the practice of cremation and a tendency to consign grave goods to a funeral pyre makes analysis difficult.[75]

---

71 S. Sheehan, 'Fer Diad De-flowered: homoerotics and masculinity in *Comrac Fir Diad*' in R. Ó hUiginn & B. Ó Catháin (eds), *Ulidia 2* (2009), pp 54–65. **72** J. Carey, 'The encounter at the ford: warriors, water and women', *Éigse* 34 (2004), 23. **73** M. Ní Dhonnchadha, 'Courts and coteries I, 900–1600', in A. Bourke et al. (eds), *The Field Day anthology of Irish writing*, 4 (2002), p. 296. **74** P. Mac Cana, *The cult of the sacred centre* (2011), p. 327. **75** M. Gimbutas, *Bronze Age cultures* (1965), p. 311; A.F. Harding, *European societies in the Bronze Age* (2000), pp 100, 169.

THE DEAL BURIAL

In general, it is also true to say that the later prehistoric funerary record is a fairly impoverished one in many parts of Europe, including Ireland and Britain. But, bearing in mind that some of the aristocratic metalwork with solar symbolism, like the Petrie Crown and the Battersea shield, may have been royal paraphernalia, the bronze crown found on the skull of an adult male at Mill Hill, near Deal in Kent, is worth considering too (fig. 7.5).

There is an allusion to the *mind suíthi*, the diadem or crown of wisdom, in *Audacht Morainn* (The Testament of Morann). In *Airne Fíngein* (Fingein's Night-watch), the wonders that marked the birth of Conn Cétchathach included the helmet or crown of Brión hidden in an Otherworld well and the diadem of Laegaire mac Luchta (ch. 3). It is not surprising that crowns or diadems should have been a special form of head-dress associated with status and wisdom.

Buried with sword and shield, the Mill Hill male was naturally described as a warrior. The grave was found near the summit of a ridge overlooking the sea on the outskirts of Deal.[76] A simple pit contained the extended skeleton of a 30–35-year-old man whose left arm lay slightly bent across his pelvis. His shield, represented by its bronze fitments and decorated plaque on the boss, covered the left side of the body. An iron sword in a decorated bronze scabbard rested on his left arm and, it is worth noting, the scabbard had been placed face down, in an inverted position.

There was a decorated bronze suspension ring nearby, also buried face down. A decorated bronze brooch (that may have once been attached to a cloak) lay on the left shin. The crown was found on the skull and comprised a decorated bronze band that was worn around the head with a plain bronze strip that covered the top of the head. The engraved decoration on the band is a slender symmetrical wave design with, at its centre, a rosette- or wheel-like motif that could be construed as a solar symbol (fig. 7.5).

Interestingly, various items in the grave appeared to have been old when buried and seemed to have had disparate life histories. The crown showed signs of wear and the sword did not fit well into the scabbard, for instance. This means that, rather than being the personal possessions of the individual, they might represent an assemblage designed to create an image of a warrior for someone who had some other special significance.[77]

This burial lay about 40m north-west of the site of a large Bronze Age barrow that must once have been a very prominent monument. It became the focus for at least two cemeteries of Iron Age burials and a later extensive series of Anglo-Saxon graves. The Iron Age burials were mostly simple elongated

---

76 K. Parfitt, *Iron Age burials from Mill Hill, Deal* (1995).   77 D. Garrow and C. Gosden, *Technologies of enchantment?* (2012), p. 226.

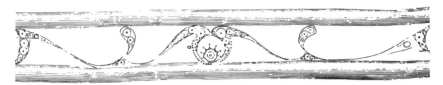

7.5. A male burial at Mill Hill, Deal, Kent, was accompanied by an iron sword, a shield and a bronze brooch. A bronze crown was found on the skull with engraved decoration that comprised a wave design with, at its centre, a rosette- or wheel-like motif perhaps a solar symbol.

pits containing unburnt skeletons; only a few had grave goods such as brooches of the mid-second to mid-first centuries BC. The largest burial group, the south-west cemetery, also contained a horse burial, the complete skeleton of a 6- to 7-year-old mare. The nearest grave held the remains of a young adult male and, not unreasonably, it was suggested this was the burial of a horse and rider. Both these were about 50m south of the burial with the crown, but, of course, there may be no connection between the two.

An unusual find was a subterranean shrine 30m south-east of the barrow site. This consisted of a 2.5m-deep chalk-cut vertical shaft leading to an underground chamber that, judging from Roman pottery sherds, had been filled in some time in the second century AD. A small chalk carving of a human figure found in the fill may once have stood in a niche in the north-western chamber wall. The figure had a rectangular body with no limbs featured. The head – on a slender neck – had a stylized face with schematic eyes, wedge-shaped nose and simple mouth in a style found on many Iron Age carvings throughout much of the Celtic world.[78]

The relative simplicity of the cemetery burials serves to emphasize the exceptional nature of the crowned burial. It has been described as one of the most important collections of metal artefacts from any Iron Age grave in Britain, given the range and quality of the decorated objects.[79] In fact, the whole complex and its chronological span, the crowned burial, the horse burial and the subterranean shrine, all imply that this region on the Kent coast was of special importance, and those who ruled it may have been equally distinctive.

It may never be possible to demonstrate that the Hochdorf and Mill Hill individuals were rulers with a sacral dimension. Indeed, because the correlation of grave-type or goods with status is often problematic, it may never be possible to do more than acknowledge their elite status in a very general way. Just as the funerary record sometimes appears as a less than reliable guide in the reconstruction of social ranking in prehistory, so too with settlement evidence. The absence of clear settlement hierarchies has been another concern in the debate about the stratified nature of Iron Age societies, for example, and has encouraged the exploration of alternative social models.[80]

However, an acceptance of the institution of sacral kingship as an interpretative option allows us to consider new or different possibilities. Social power and status may not rest on material goods, conspicuous display or monumental construction. It may find expression in complex symbolic ways.

78 K. Parfitt, 'The Deal man', *Current Archaeology* 101 (1986), 166–8; K. Parfitt & M. Green, 'A chalk figurine from Upper Deal, Kent', *Britannia* 18 (1987), 295–8. **79** I.M. Stead, 'The metalwork' in K. Parfitt, *Iron Age burials from Mill Hill, Deal* (1995), p. 88. **80** T. Moore & X.-L. Armada, 'Crossing the divide' in T. Moore & X.-L. Armada (eds), *Atlantic Europe in the first millennium BC* (2011), p. 46; J.D. Hill, 'How did British Middle and Late Pre-Roman Iron Age societies work (if they did)?' in T. Moore & X.-L. Armada

Given the equine associations of the Indo-European institution of sacral kingship and the Irish evidence, equine imagery and burial may have special meaning. Perhaps the function of that great white horse carved in the chalk on the upper slope of White Horse Hill on the Berkshire Downs at Uffington should be reconsidered (ch. 6)?

Splendid burials, solar imagery and fine metalwork all offer promising lines of enquiry, but white mares and equine rituals are hard to find. It is fair to say, in Scotland, Sterckx's intriguing suggestion notwithstanding, the legend of the role of the nomadic ass in the selection of the rightful location for the medieval castle of the Thane of Cawdor (ch. 5) is rather far removed from the wandering stallions of Hindu kingly ceremony.

Scotland does present another interesting avenue for research. In Ireland, the study of the archaeology of Tara has immeasurably broadened our understanding of this major royal site and its landscape. The very term 'royal site' is a narrow misnomer, for these are landscapes with ancient pedigrees. Newman has shown

> that in later prehistory, if not before, Tara was conceived as a sacralized landscape associated with hierogamy and the installation of sacral kings, and that this development coloured the kingship of Tara for many generations to come, bequeathing to them a legacy that is still evident in the landscape around Tara. Conceived of through the prism of religion and myth, sacral landscapes can have cosmogonic symbolism. Through the medium of ritual they are cosmicized by the building of shrines, temples and residences, the erection of mounds and stones, the creation of burial grounds, the naming of places, and more ...[81]

The study of the landscapes of medieval royal sites like Dunadd and Forteviot is producing exciting results. Research in the environs of Forteviot has revealed an exceptional Neolithic and Bronze Age ceremonial landscape. Stephen Driscoll was doubtless correct to argue that the siting of early medieval structures there was informed by the geography established by some of the pre-existing monuments.[82]

In arguing the case that Dunadd had a prehistory to match its eminence in historic times (in his Rhind Lectures in 1992), Bradley was aware that there was virtually no archaeological evidence to show that there was any prehistoric activity on the prominent site of the royal stronghold, but he too made the point that monuments are encountered by successive generations who see them

---

(eds), *Atlantic Europe* (2011), pp 242–63.   81 C. Newman, 'The sacral landscape of Tara' in R. Schot et al. (eds), *Landscapes of cult and kingship* (2011), p. 22.   82 G. Noble & K. Brophy, 'Ritual and remembrance at a prehistoric ceremonial complex in central Scotland', *Antiquity* 85 (2011), 787–804; S.T. Driscoll, 'Picts and prehistory', *World Archaeology* 30

from different perspectives. This, of course, was a feature of the archaeology of the Boyne Valley, as he rightly pointed out.[83]

Many of the monuments in the exceptional concentration of prehistoric sites in the Kilmartin Valley to the north of Dunadd could still have been identifiable in the first millennium AD. In addressing the phenomenon of royal sites located near prominent prehistoric monuments, Driscoll took the argument further, reminding us that the mythological qualities of these monuments made them attractive sources of supernatural legitimacy for emerging political entities.

As both writers noted, the Irish evidence, both archeological and historical, is instructive. Just as the Uí Néill kings of Tara saw some of the monuments there as memorials to mythical ancestors, so too must the kings of Dunadd have been conscious of the mythical qualities of the cairns in the Kilmartin Valley. This was a sacralized landscape that, like Tara, began as early as the fourth millennium BC.[84]

The prehistoric linear cemetery there, for example, must have had an extraordinary tale to tell to anyone who journeyed along the western banks of Kilmartin Burn. The great central chambered cairn at Nether Largie is now a shadow of its former self; it originally had a diameter of some 40m – over twice the size of the Mound of the Hostages on Tara. Dunadd was chosen as an inauguration site of the kings of Dál Riata for other reasons too. It was, as Ewan Campbell has emphasized, a high place with wide commanding views, like other royal sites, and may even have been considered a giant cairn mimicking the smaller sites in its vicinity.[85] Many of the myths of sovereignty and kingship we have contemplated probably animated the lives of those who lived there in early medieval times.

(1998), 152.   83 R. Bradley, *Altering the earth* (1993), pp 91, 119.   84 A. Sheridan, 'Contextualizing Kilmartin' in A.M. Jones et al., *Image, memory and monumentality* (2012), pp 163–83.   85 E. Campbell, 'Royal inauguration in Dál Riata and the Stone of Destiny' in R. Welander et al. (eds), *The Stone of Destiny* (2003), p. 54.

Epilogue

The case that sacral kingship deserves to be seriously considered in any discussion of possible socio-political structures in prehistoric Europe may be a challenge to archaeologists unaccustomed to grappling with monuments and landscapes, like celebrated Tara, enhanced by a complex mythic past. The archaeological evidence, at present, may seem as elusive as some solar imagery. The argument was prompted, however, by the prominence of this institution in early Irish tradition and by the claim that all Indo-European peoples, at one time or another, were probably tribal polities ruled in this way. When and where this may have happened may be a difficult question to answer, but there may be clues in the later prehistoric record in elite metalwork and in rich male burials in particular. Solar symbolism, equine ritual, drinking ceremonial and some evidence of a preoccupation with an Otherworld may all be important evidential threads. Of course, the correspondences drawn between early Ireland and Vedic India, the two geographical extremes of the Indo-European world, have not gone unquestioned, but the cumulative evidence that Irish tradition retains Indo-European characteristics lost or feebly reflected elsewhere in the west is impressive. These include horse sacrifice, those elements of sacral kingship such as the concept of the 'prince's truth' (akin to the Hindu 'Act of Truth'), and the recognition of an Irish instance of the Indo-European theme 'the single sin of the sovereign'.[1]

The shared association between kingship and equine activity is especially important and equine imagery may be valuable in attempts to identify the institution of sacral kingship. It is possible, for example, that representations of horses with human heads may be allusions to equine invocations that were a potent part of kingly rituals. No less significant is the evidence for a sacred marriage with a goddess whose name and association with a sacramental drink also have Indo-European roots. There may have been a widespread prehistoric rite in which authority was affirmed by the proffering of a drink by a woman of special status. The serving of drink was 'a special gift' of the Otherworldly sovereignty goddess whose earthly female mediators had the capability to mystically validate the authority of a ruler. The pairing of drinking vessels in rich female graves may indicate that the woman buried there once had this function and, though neither goddess nor wife, she was so important that her role deserved to be commemorated in death. This sovereignty figure was also

1 Other themes that may be added to this list include boundless generosity (*potlatch*) and magical vessels (including cauldrons): S. Zimmer, 'Indo-Celtic connections', *Journal of Indo-European Studies* 29 (2001), 379–405.

the female personification of the land and this is a reminder that landscape features might be experienced as animate entities influencing cultural practice and beliefs – a process by no means confined to Ireland. If she was ever venerated, she may have been the object of votive offerings.

Other themes with an Indo-European dimension include that relationship between the Boyne story and Indo-Iranian myth and, of course, the significant connection between kingship and solar imagery. That some fine metalwork such as bronze vessels or shields bearing solar symbolism should be kingly paraphernalia is an intriguing possibility. It is true that complex solar imagery surfaces at different times and in different places in prehistoric Europe, but the longevity of the motif of the voyage of the sun is a testimony to the long lifespan of a fundamentally important cosmological belief that can be clearly traced for nearly two thousand years. Since some of the motifs employed appear to reflect the nocturnal voyage of the sun through a subterranean Otherworld from west to east where it was reborn, this is without doubt an illustration of a question that was once foremost in the pre-modern mind. The rebirth of the sun at propitious moments in its yearly round was an occasion of ceremony at least since the time of Newgrange over five millennia ago. The mythology of the River Boyne and Newgrange is especially interesting, because there seems to be some agreement here between myth and archaeology. They each appear to offer complimentary references to the part the river played in the creation of the monument and its role as a source of the esoteric wisdom that was the foundation of the solar rituals there.

The supernatural creatures that were said to emerge from Oweynagat at Rathcroghan wreaking havoc on the surrounding land and the image of the wasteland created by the Otherworldly birds around Navan are mythic themes that speak of the consequences of a kingly inability to maintain cosmic equilibrium. Like that royal misjudgment now forever linked to the northern-most of the 'Sloping Trenches' on the western hillside of Tara, the catastrophic failure of a sacred king in the maintenance of both order and justice had grave results not only for him but for his people. The power and influence of the Otherworld was ever-present for both good and ill and this unwavering proximity of the supernatural was not restricted to Ireland either.

There is an abundance of evidence that the Otherworld was a major concern of the prehistoric mind and is not as obscure and archaeologically elusive as one might think. There are numerous cult practices with a subterranean focus at different times, not just in Ireland, Scotland and England, but across a wide area of northern and western Continental Europe. Time and again, the digging of pits, shafts and ditches, and material offerings placed in the earth or in watery places, appear to testify to an interest in those chthonic powers that had an impact on human affairs. Burial places, of course, were portals to this world, but we should be alert to the possibility that Otherworldly references could sometimes be reflected not just in burial goods like reversed swords or shoes or inverted pottery, but in grave architecture as well. This Otherworld was also an element of Indo-European belief and was a fluid concept that took various forms. In early Ireland, it was seen as a prosperous and peaceful land, the dwelling place of malevolent creatures, a land of the dead, and a mirror world that might provide the outer world in winter with wild garlic and primroses and buttercups, those 'fruits of summer'.

Importantly, this Otherworld was the source of the authority of sacral kingship affirmed by that sacred marriage. Like those chains that linked magical bird-flocks, there is a connection between solar imagery and the Otherworld and there is the evident bond between the Otherworld and sacred kings that brings us full circle – just like that diurnal and nocturnal voyage of the sun that must have raised so many questions in ancient Europe.

Bibliography

Aguirre, M., 'The riddle of sovereignty', *Modern Language Review* 88 (1993), 273–82.

Aitchison, N.B., 'The Ulster Cycle: heroic image and historical reality', *Journal of Medieval History* 13 (1987), 87–116.

—— *Armagh and the royal centres in early medieval Ireland: monuments, cosmology and the past* (Woodbridge, 1994).

Alexinsky, G., 'Slavonic mythology' in R. Aldington & D. Ames (trans.), *New Larousse encyclopedia of mythology* (London, 1968), pp 281–98.

Allen, D.F., 'Temples or shrines on Gaulish coins', *Antiquaries Journal* 53 (1973), 71–4.

Aner, E. & K. Kersten, *Die Funde der älteren Bronzezeit des nordischen Kreises in Dänemark, Schleswig-Holstein und Niedersachsen*, 2 (Copenhagen, 1976).

Armit, I., *Towers in the north: the brochs of Scotland* (Stroud, 2003).

—— 'Janus in furs? Opposed human heads in the art of the European Iron Age' in G. Cooney et al. (eds), *Relics of old decency: archaeological studies in later prehistory. Festschrift for Barry Raftery* (Dublin, 2009), pp 279–86.

—— *Headhunting and the body in Iron Age Europe* (Cambridge, 2012).

—— & P. Grant, 'Gesture politics and the art of ambiguity: the Iron Age statue from Hirschlanden', *Antiquity* 82 (2008), 409–22.

Arthurs, J.B., 'Macha and Armagh', *Bulletin of the Ulster Place-name Society* 1 (1953), 25–9 (reprinted in *Ainm* 7 (1996–7), 152–7).

Auboyer, J., 'Le caractère royal et divin du trône dans l'Inde ancienne' in *La regalità sacra. The sacral kingship. Contributions to the central theme of the VIIIth International Congress for the History of Religions (Rome, April 1955)* (Leiden, 1959), pp 181–8.

Belier, W.W., *Decayed gods: origin and development of Georges Dumézil's 'idéologie tripartie'* (Leiden, 1991).

Bender, B., 'The politics of the past: Emain Macha (Navan), Northern Ireland' in R. Layton, P.G. Stone & J. Thomas (eds), *Destruction and conservation of cultural property* (London, 2001), pp 199–211.

Bendrey, R., N. Thorpe, A. Outram & L.H. van Wijngaarden-Bakker, 'The origins of domestic horses in northwest Europe: new direct dates on the horses of Newgrange, Ireland', *Proceedings of the Prehistoric Society* 79 (2013), 91–103.

Bennike, P., *Palaeopathology of Danish skeletons: a comparative study of demography, disease and injury* (Copenhagen, 1985).

Bergh, S., *Landscape of the monuments: a study of the passage tombs in the Cúil Irra region, Co. Sligo, Ireland* (Stockholm, 1995).

—— 'Design as message: role and symbolism of Irish passage tombs' in A. Rodríguez Casal (ed.), *O Neolítico Atlántico e as orixes do megalitismo, Actas do Coloquio Internacional (Santiago de Compostela, 1–6 de Abril de 1996)* (Santiago de Compostela, 1997), pp 141–50.

Bergin, O. & R.I. Best (eds), 'Tochmarc Étaíne', *Ériu* 12 (1938), 137–96.

Berrocal-Rangel, L., 'New interpretations on upright stone bands: "*chevaux-de-frise*" in western Europe', forthcoming.

Bhreathnach, E., *Tara: a select bibliography* (Dublin, 1995).

— 'Observations on the occurrence of dog and horse bones at Tara', *Discovery Programme Reports* 6 (2002), 117–22.

— (ed.), *The kingship and landscape of Tara* (Dublin, 2005).

— 'Transforming kingship and cult: the provincial ceremonial capitals in early medieval Ireland' in R. Schot et al. (eds), *Landscapes of cult and kingship* (Dublin, 2011), pp 126–48.

Bhreathnach, M., 'The sovereignty goddess as goddess of death?', *Zeitschrift für celtische Philologie* 39 (1982), 243–60.

Biel, J., 'Ein Fürstengrabhügel der späten Hallstattzeit bei Eberdingen-Hochdorf, Kr. Ludwigsburg, Baden-Württemberg', *Germania* 60 (1982), 61–104.

Binchy, D.A., 'The fair of Tailtiu and the feast of Tara', *Ériu* 18 (1958), 113–38.

— *Celtic and Anglo-Saxon kingship. The O'Donnell lectures for 1967–8* (Oxford, 1970).

Borsje, J., 'Druids, deer and "Words of Power": coming to terms with evil in medieval Ireland' in K. Ritari & A. Bergholm (eds), *Approaches to religion and mythology in Celtic studies* (Cambridge, 2008), pp 122–49.

— 'Supernatural threats to kings: exploration of a motif in the Ulster Cycle and in other medieval Irish tales' in R. Ó hUiginn & B. Ó Catháin (eds), *Ulidia 2. Proceedings of the Second International Conference on the Ulster Cycle of Tales, National University of Ireland Maynooth, 24–27 June 2005* (Maynooth, 2009), pp 173–94.

— *The Celtic evil eye and related mythological motifs in medieval Ireland* (Louvain, 2012).

Bourgès, A.Y., 'Melor' in J.T. Koch (ed.), *Celtic culture: a historical encyclopedia*, 4 (Santa Barbara, 2006), pp 1288–9.

Bourke, A., S. Kilfeather, M. Luddy, M. Mac Curtain, G. Meaney, M. Ní Dhonnchadha, M. O'Dowd & C. Wills (eds), *The Field Day anthology of Irish writing, 4, Irish women's writing and traditions* (Cork, 2002).

Bowman, S. & S. Needham, 'The Dunaverney and Little Thetford flesh-hooks: history, technology and their position within the later Bronze Age Atlantic Zone feasting complex', *Antiquaries Journal* 87 (2007), 53–108.

Bradley, R., *The passage of arms: an archaeological analysis of prehistoric hoards and votive deposits* (Cambridge, 1990).

— *Altering the earth: the origins of monuments in Britain and Continental Europe. The Rhind Lectures, 1991–2* (Edinburgh, 1993).

— 'Death by water: boats and footprints in the rock art of western Sweden', *Oxford Journal of Archaeology* 16 (1997), 315–24.

— *Rock art and the prehistory of Atlantic Europe: signing the land* (London, 1997).

— *An archaeology of natural places* (London, 2000).

— *The past in prehistoric societies* (London, 2002).

— 'Stuart Piggott, Ancient Europe and the prehistory of northern Britain' in I.A.G. Shepherd & G.J. Barclay (eds), *Scotland in ancient Europe: the Neolithic* and early *Bronze Age of Scotland in their European context* (Edinburgh, 2004), pp 3–11.

Brash, R.R., *The ogam inscribed monuments of the Gaedhil in the British Islands* (ed. G.M. Atkinson), (London, 1879).

Brothwell, D. & A.T. Sandison, *Diseases in antiquity: a survey of the diseases, injuries and surgery of early populations* (Springfield, IL, 1967).

Bruneau, P., 'L'impair de chaussures' in P.L. de Bellefonds (ed.), *Agathos Daimon. Mythes et cultes: études d'iconographie en l'honneur de Lilly Kahil* (Athens, 2000), pp 63–72.

Buckley, V.M. & P.D. Sweetman, *Archaeological survey of County Louth* (Dublin, 1991).

Burenhult, G., *The archaeological excavation at Carrowmore, Co. Sligo, Ireland: excavation seasons 1977–1979* (Stockholm, 1980).

Byrne, F.J., 'Clann Ollaman Uaisle Emna', *Studia Hibernica* 4 (1964), 54–94.

— 'Historical note on Cnogba (Knowth)', *Proceedings of the Royal Irish Academy* 66C (1968), 383–400.

— *Irish kings and high-kings* (London, 1973).

Byrne, M.E. & M. Dillon, 'Táin Bó Fraich', *Études celtiques* 2 (1937), 1–27.

Cahill, M. & M. Sikora (eds), *Breaking ground, finding graves*, 1 (Dublin, 2011).

Campbell, E., 'Royal inauguration in Dál Riata and the Stone of Destiny' in R. Welander, D.J. Breeze & T.O. Clancy (eds), *The Stone of Destiny: artefact and icon* (Edinburgh, 2003), pp 42–59.

Campbell, J.F.V., *The Book of the Thanes of Cawdor: a series of papers selected from the charter room at Cawdor, 1236–1742* (Edinburgh, 1859).

Card, N. & J. Downes, 'Mine Howe: the significance of space and place in the Iron Age' in J. Downes & A. Ritchie (eds), *Sea change* (Balgavies, 2003), pp 11–19.

Carew, M., *Tara and the Ark of the Covenant: a search for the Ark of the Covenant by British-Israelites on the Hill of Tara (1899–1902)* (Dublin, 2003).

Carey, J., 'The location of the Otherworld in Irish tradition', *Éigse* 19 (1982), 36–43.

— 'Notes on the Irish war-goddess', *Éigse* 19 (1983), 263–75.

— 'Origin and development of the Cesair legend', *Éigse* 22 (1987), 37–48.

— 'Myth and mythography in *Cath Maige Tuired*', *Studia Celtica* 24–5 (1990), 53–69.

— 'The two laws in Dubthach's Judgement', *Cambridge Medieval Celtic Studies* 19 (1990), 1–18.

— 'Time, memory and the Boyne necropolis', *Proceedings of the Harvard Celtic Colloquium* 10 (1990), 24–36.

— 'The sun's night journey: a Pharaonic image in Medieval Ireland', *Journal of the Warburg and Courtauld Institutes* 57 (1994), 14–34.

— 'Ferp Cluche', *Ériu* 50 (1999), 165–8.

— 'The encounter at the ford: warriors, water and women', *Éigse* 34 (2004), 10–24.

— 'An Old Irish poem about Mug Ruith', *Journal of the Cork Historical and Archaeological Society* 110 (2005), 113–34.

— 'Tara and the supernatural' in E. Bhreathnach (ed.), *The kingship and landscape of Tara* (Dublin, 2005), pp 32–48.

— 'Bresal/Bressual Beolíach' in J.T. Koch (ed.), *Celtic culture: a historical encyclopedia*, 1 (Santa Barbara, 2006), pp 246–7.
— 'Donn, Amairgen, Íth and the prehistory of Irish pseudohistory', *Journal of Indo-European Studies* 38 (2010), 319–41.
Carney, J., 'Language and literature to 1169' in D. Ó Cróinín (ed.), *A new history of Ireland, prehistoric and early Ireland*, 1 (Oxford, 2005), pp 451–510.
Carson, R.A.G. & C. O'Kelly, 'A catalogue of the Roman coins from Newgrange, Co. Meath, and notes on the coins and related finds', *Proceedings of the Royal Irish Academy* 77C (1977), 35–55.
Chapman, M., *The Celts: the construction of a myth* (Basingstoke, 1992).
Charles-Edwards, T.M., 'Irish warfare before 1100' in T. Bartlett & K. Jeffery (eds), *A military history of Ireland* (Cambridge, 1996), pp 26–51.
Chaume, B. & W. Reinhard, 'Les dépôts de l'enclos cultuel hallstattien de Vix "les Herbues" et la question des enceintes quadrangulaires', *Bulletin de la Société préhistorique française* 104 (2007), 342–67.
Clarke, G., *Archaeology and society: reconstructing the prehistoric past* (3rd ed., London, 1960).
Clinton, M., *The souterrains of Ireland* (Dublin, 2001).
Coe, P.P., 'Belisama' in J.T. Koch (ed.), *Celtic culture: a historical encyclopedia*, 1 (Santa Barbara, 2006), p. 201.
Coles, J., 'And on they went ... processions in Scandinavian Bronze Age rock carvings', *Acta Archaeologica* 74 (2003), 211–50.
— & A.F. Harding, *The Bronze Age in Europe* (London, 1979).
Collis, J., *The Celts: origins, myths and inventions* (Stroud, 2003).
Coomaraswamy, A.K., 'On the loathly bride', *Speculum* 20 (1945), 391–404.
Cooney, G., K. Becker, J. Coles, M. Ryan & S. Sievers (eds), *Relics of old decency: archaeological studies in later prehistory. Festschrift for Barry Raftery* (Dublin, 2009).
Corcoran, M. & G. Sevastopulo, 'The origin of the greywacke orthostats and kerbstones at Newgrange and Knowth, Brú na Bóinne', Heritage Council March 2008 Seminar, http://www.heritagecouncil.ie/seandalaiocht/hci-irish-page/bru-na-boinne-research-framework-project/march-2008-seminar/?L=3, accessed 17 Dec. 2012.
Corns. A., J. Fenwick & R. Shaw, 'More than meets the eye ... the Discovery Programme's high resolution LiDAR survey of Tara', *Archaeology Ireland* 22:3 (2008), 34–8.
Cowan, E.J., 'The historical MacBeth' in W.D.H. Sellar (ed.), *Moray: province and people* (Edinburgh, 1993), pp 117–41.
Creighton, J., 'Visions of power: imagery and symbols in late Iron Age Britain', *Britannia* 26 (1995), 285–301.
— *Coins and power in late Iron Age Britain* (Cambridge, 2000).
— 'Gold, ritual and kingship' in C. Haselgrove & D. Wigg-Wolf (eds), *Iron Age coinage and ritual practices* (Mainz, 2005), pp 69–84.
Cross, T.P. & A.C.L. Brown, 'Fingen's Night-watch. Airne Fingein', *Romanic Review* 9 (1918), 29–47.
— & C.H. Slover, *Ancient Irish tales* (London, 1935).

Crowell, A.L. & W.K. Howell, 'Time, oral tradition and archaeology at Xakwnoowú, a Little Ice Age fort in southeastern Alaska', *American Antiquity* 78 (2013), 3–23.

Cunliffe, B., *Danebury. An Iron Age hillfort in Hampshire, 1: the excavations, 1969–1978* (London, 1984).

— 'Pits, preconceptions and propitiation in the British Iron Age', *Oxford Journal of Archaeology* 11 (1992), 69–83.

— *Danebury. An Iron Age hillfort in Hampshire, 6: a hillfort community in perspective* (York, 1995).

Davidson, H.E. & P. Fisher (ed. & trans.), *Saxo Grammaticus. The history of the Danes, books I–IX* (Woodbridge, 1996).

Deane, M., 'Dangerous liaisons', *Proceedings of the Harvard Celtic Colloquium* 23 (2003), 52–79.

— '*Compert Conculainn:* possible antecedents?' in J.E. Rekdal & A. Ó Corráin (eds), *Proceedings of the Eighth Symposium of Societas Celtologica Nordica. Studia Celtica Upsaliensia* 7 (2007), 61–85.

— 'Kingship: a valedictory for the sacred marriage' in R. Ó hUiginn & B. Ó Catháin (eds), *Ulidia* 2 (Maynooth, 2009), pp 326–42.

— 'From sacred marriage to clientship: a mythical account of the establishment of kingship as an institution' in R. Schot et al. (eds), *Landscapes of cult and kingship* (Dublin, 2011), pp 1–21.

de Blácam, A., *Gaelic literature surveyed* (Dublin, 1929).

Dehn, R., M. Egg & R. Lehnert, *Das Hallstattzeitliche Fürstengrab im Hügel 3 von Kappel am Rhein in Baden* (Mainz, 2005).

de Loos-Dietz, E.P., 'Le *monosandalos* dans l'Antiquité', *Babesch. Bulletin Antieke Beschaving* 69 (1994), 175–97.

de Pontfarcy, Y., 'The historical background to the pilgrimage to Lough Derg' in M. Haren & Y. de Pontfarcy (eds), *The medieval pilgrimage to St Patrick's Purgatory Lough Derg and the European tradition* (Enniskillen, 1998), pp 7–34.

— 'The sovereignty of Paeonia' in M. Richter & J.-M. Picard (eds), *Ogma: essays in Celtic studies in honour of Próinséas Ní Chatháin* (Dublin, 2002), pp 145–50.

de Vries, J., *La religion des Celtes* (Paris, 1963).

Dillon, M., 'The archaism of Irish tradition: the Sir John Rhys memorial lecture', *Proceedings of the British Academy* 33 (1947), 245–64.

— 'The Hindu Act of Truth in Celtic tradition', *Modern Philology* 44 (1947), 137–40.

— *Lebor na Cert. The Book of Rights* (London, 1962).

— *Celts and Aryans: survivals of Indo-European speech and society* (Simla, 1975).

Dixon-Kennedy, M., *Encyclopedia of Russian and Slavic myth and legend* (Santa Barbara, 1998).

Doherty, C., 'Kingship in early Ireland' in E. Bhreathnach (ed.), *The kingship and landscape of Tara* (Dublin, 2005), pp 3–31.

Dooley, A., *Playing the hero: reading the Irish saga Táin Bó Cúailnge* (Toronto, 2006).

— & H. Roe, *Tales of the Elders of Ireland: a new translation of Acallam na Senórach* (Oxford, 1999).

Dorson, R.M., 'The eclipse of solar mythology', *Journal of American Folklore* 68 (1955), 393–416.

Dowden, K., *European paganism: the realities of cult from antiquity to the late Middle Ages* (London, 2000).

Dowling, G., 'The liminal boundary: an analysis of the sacral potency of the ditch at Ráith na Ríg, Tara, Co. Meath', *Journal of Irish Archaeology* 15 (2006), 15–37.

— 'The architecture of power: an exploration of the origins of closely spaced multivallate monuments in Ireland' in R. Schot et al. (eds), *Landscapes of cult and kingship* (Dublin, 2011), pp 213–31.

Downes, J. & A. Ritchie (eds), *Sea change: Orkney and northern Europe in the later Iron Age, AD300–800* (Balgavies, 2003).

Drescher, H., 'Neue Untersuchungen am Sonnenwagen von Trundholm und über die Gusstechnik bronzezeitlichen Tierfiguren', *Acta Archaeologica* 33 (1962), 39–62.

Driscoll, S.T., 'Picts and prehistory: cultural resource management in early medieval Scotland', *World Archaeology* 30 (1998), 142–58.

Duignan, M., 'The Turoe Stone: its place in insular La Tène art' in P.-M. Duval & C. Hawkes (eds), *Celtic art in ancient Europe, five protohistoric centuries* (London, 1976), pp 201–17.

Dumézil, G., *Horace et les Curiaces* (Paris, 1942).

— 'Le trio des Macha', *Revue de l'histoire des religions* 146 (1954), 5–17.

— 'Le puits de Nechtan', *Celtica* 6 (1963), 50–61.

— *Mythe et épopée*, 1 (Paris, 1968).

— *Mythe et épopée*, 3 (Paris, 1973).

— *The destiny of a king* (Chicago, 1973) (translation of *Mythe et épopée*, 2, part 3 by A. Hiltebeitel).

Dumville, D.N., 'Echtrae and immram: some problems of definition', *Ériu* 27 (1976), 73–94.

Duncan, L., 'Altram Tige Dá Medar', *Ériu* 11 (1932), 184–225.

Duval, P.-M., *Les Celtes* (Paris, 1977).

— *Monnaies Gauloises et mythes celtiques* (Paris, 1987).

Echt, R., *Das Fürstinnengrab von Reinheim. Studien zur Kulturgeschichte der Früh-La-Tène-Zeit* (Bonn, 1999).

Eggert, M.K.H., 'Der Tote von Hochdorf: Bemerkungen zum Modus archäo-logischer Interpretation', *Archäologisches Korrespondenzblatt* 29 (1999), 211–22 (English translation: M.K.H. Eggert, 'The Hochdorf dead: comments on the mode of archaeological interpretation' in R. Karl & D. Stifter (eds), *The Celtic world: critical concepts in historical studies, 2, Celtic archaeology* (London, 2007), pp 180–96).

Eliade, M., *The myth of the eternal return or, cosmos and history* (Princeton, NJ, 1971).

Ellis, H.R., *The road to Hel: a study of the conception of the dead in Old Norse literature* (Cambridge, 1943).

Enright, M.J., *Lady with a mead cup: ritual, prophecy and lordship in the European warband from La Tène to the Viking Age* (Dublin, 1996).

Eogan, G., 'A composite late Bronze Age object from Roscommon, Ireland' in W.H. Metz, B.L. van Beek & H. Steegstra (eds), *Patina: essays presented to Jay*

Jordan Butler on the occasion of his 80th birthday (Groningen, 2001), pp 231–40.

Eriksen, P., 'The great mound of Newgrange: an Irish multi-period mound spanning from the megalithic tomb period to the early Bronze Age', *Acta Archaeologica* 79 (2008), 250–73.

Euskirchen, M., 'Epona', *Bericht der Römisch-Germanischen Kommission* 74 (1993), 607–838.

Fenwick, J. & C. Newman, 'Geomagnetic survey on the Hill of Tara, Co. Meath, 1998–9', *Discovery Programme Reports* 6 (2002), 1–17.

Ferguson, S., 'Account of ogham inscriptions in the cave at Rathcroghan, County of Roscommon', *Proceedings of the Royal Irish Academy* 9 (1864), 160–70.

Findly, E.B., 'The "Child of the Waters": a revaluation of Vedic Apam Napat', *Numen* 26 (1979), 164–84.

Fitzpatrick, A.P., 'Night and day: the symbolism of astral signs on later Iron Age anthropomorphic short swords', *Proceedings of the Prehistoric Society* 62 (1996), 373–98.

FitzPatrick, E., *Royal inauguration in Gaelic Ireland, c.1100–1600: a cultural landscape study* (Woodbridge, 2004).

— , E. Murphy, R. McHugh, C. Donnelly & C. Foley, 'Evoking the white mare: the cult landscape of *Sgiath Gabhra* and its medieval perception in Gaelic *Fir Mhanach*' in R. Schot et al. (eds), *Landscapes of cult and kingship* (Dublin, 2011), pp 163–91.

Fontijn, D.R. *Sacrificial landscapes: cultural biographies of persons, objects and 'natural' places in the Bronze Age of the southern Netherlands, c.2300–600BC* (Leiden, 2002).

Ford, P.K., 'The Well of Nechtan and "La Gloire Lumineuse"' in G.J. Larson (ed.), *Myth in Indo-European antiquity* (Berkeley, CA, 1974), pp 67–74.

— (ed.), *The Mabinogi and other medieval Welsh tales. Edited with an introduction by Patrick K. Ford* (Berkeley, CA, 2008).

Frank, R., *Old Norse court poetry: the Dróttkvætt stanza* (Ithaca, NY, 1978).

Freeman, A.M. (ed.), *Annala Connacht. The Annals of Connacht (AD1224–1544)* (Dublin, 1944).

Freeman, P., *The philosopher and the druids: a journey among the ancient Celts* (London, 2006).

Fyfe, W.H. & D.S. Levene (ed. & trans.), *Tacitus. The histories* (Oxford, 1997).

Garrow, D. & C. Gosden, *Technologies of enchantment? Exploring Celtic art: 400BC to AD100* (Oxford, 2012).

Geertz, C., *Local knowledge: further essays in interpretive anthropology* (New York, 1983).

Gerloff, S., *Atlantic cauldrons and buckets of the late Bronze and early Iron Ages in western Europe* (Stuttgart, 2010).

Giles, M., *A forged glamour: landscape, identity and material culture in the Iron Age* (Oxford, 2012).

Gimbutas, M., *Bronze Age cultures in central and eastern Europe* (The Hague, 1965).

Gray, E.A., *Cath Maige Tuired. The second battle of Mag Tuired* (London, 1982).

Green, M., *Symbol and image in Celtic religious art* (London, 1989).

— *The sun-gods of ancient Europe* (London, 1991).

— *Celtic goddesses. Warriors, virgins and mothers* (London, 1995).

— 'Images in opposition: polarity, ambivalence and liminality in cult repr
sentation', *Antiquity* 71 (1997), 898–911.

— 'Back to the future: resonances of the past in myth and material culture' in A.
Gazin-Schwartz & C. Holtorf (eds), *Archaeology and folklore* (London, 1999),
pp 48–66.

— 'Pagan Celtic iconography and the concept of sacral kingship', *Zeitschrift für
celtische Philologie* 52 (2000), 102–17.

— 'Cosmovision and metaphor: monsters and shamans in Gallo-British cult-
expression', *European Journal of Archaeology* 4 (2001), 203–32.

— *An archaeology of images: iconology and cosmology in Iron Age and Roman Europe*
(London, 2004).

Gregory, A., *Cuchulain of Muirthemne: the story of the men of the Red Branch of
Ulster* (London, 1902).

Gricourt, D. & D. Hollard, 'Lugus et le cheval', *Dialogues d'histoire ancienne* 28
(2002), 121–66.

Gricourt, J., 'Epona – Rhiannon – Macha', *Ogam* 6 (1954), 25–40, 75–86, 137–8,
165–88.

Grinsell, L.V., *Folklore of prehistoric sites in Britain* (Newton Abbot, 1976).

Grogan, E., *The Rath of the Synods, Tara, Co. Meath: excavations by Seán P. Ó
Ríordáin* (Dublin, 2008).

Guizot, F., *L'histoire de France depuis les temps les plus reculés jusqu'en 1789 racontée
à mes petits-enfants par M. Guizot*, 1 (Paris, 1872).

Guyonvarc'h, C.-J., 'Nemos, Nemetos, Nemeton', *Ogam* 12 (1960), 185–97.

— 'Annexes étymologiques du commentaire. Nechtan (*Nept-ono-*) ou "le fils de la
sœur"', *Celticum 15. Supplément à Ogam-Tradition celtique* 106 (1966), 377–82.

Gwynn, E., *The Metrical Dindshenchas Part 3* (Dublin, 1913).

— *The Metrical Dindshenchas Part 4* (Dublin, 1924).

Gwynn, L., 'De Síl Chonairi Móir', *Ériu* 6 (1912), 130–43.

Hamel, A.G. van, *Compert Con Culainn and other stories* (Dublin, 1933).

Hamlin, A. & C. Lynn (eds), *Pieces of the past: archaeological excavations by the
Department of the Environment for Northern Ireland, 1970–1986* (Belfast,
1988).

Hansen, L., *Hochdorf VIII. Die Goldfunde und Trachtbeigaben des späthallstatt-
zeitlichen Fürstengrabes von Eberdingen-Hochdorf (Kr. Ludwigsburg)* (Stuttgart,
2010).

Harding, A.F., *European societies in the Bronze Age* (Cambridge, 2000).

Härke, H., 'The nature of burial data' in C.K. Jensen & K.H. Nielsen (eds), *Burial
and society: the chronological and social analysis of archaeological burial data*
(Aarhus, 1997), pp 19–27.

Harrison, J.E., *Prolegomena to the study of Greek religion* (Cambridge, 1903).

Harrison, R.J., *Symbols and warriors: images of the European Iron Age* (Bristol,
2004).

Henderson, G. (ed.), *Fled Bricrend: the feast of Bricriu* (London, 1899).

y, R., 'The observance of light: a ritualistic perspective on "imperfectly" aligned passage tombs', *Time and Mind: the Journal of Archaeology, Consciousness and Culture* 1 (2008), 319–30.

Herbert, M., 'Goddess and king: the sacred marriage in early Ireland', *Cosmos* 7 (1992), 264–75.

— 'Society and myth, *c*.700–1300' in A. Bourke et al. (eds), *The Field Day anthology of Irish writing*, 4 (Cork, 2002), pp 250–72.

Herity, M. (ed.), *Ordnance Survey letters Roscommon* (Dublin, 2010).

Hermann, F.-R., 'Der Glauberg, Fürstensitz, Fürstengräber und Heiligtum' in H. Baitinger & B. Pinsker (eds), *Das Rätsel der Kelten von Glauberg: Glaube, Mythos, Wirklichkeit* (Stuttgart, 2002), pp 90–111.

Hill, J.D., 'How did British middle and late pre-Roman Iron Age societies work (if they did)?' in T. Moore & X.-L. Armada (eds), *Atlantic Europe in the first millennium BC: crossing the divide* (Oxford, 2011), pp 242–63.

Hily, G., *Le dieu celtique Lugus* (Rennes, 2012).

Hingley, R., 'Ancestors and identity in the later prehistory of Atlantic Scotland: the reuse and reinvention of Neolithic monuments and material culture', *World Archaeology* 28 (1996), 231–43.

Hofeneder, A., 'Vestiges of sun worship among the Celts', *Pandanus '10* 4:2 (2010), 85–107.

Howlett, D., *Muirchú Moccu Machténi's 'Vita Sancti Patricii' Life of Saint Patrick* (Dublin, 2006).

Hull, E., *Cuchulain: the hound of Ulster* (London, 1909).

— 'Legends and traditions of the Cailleach Bheara or Old Woman (Hag) of Beare', *Folklore* 38 (1927), 225–54.

Hull, V., 'De Gabáil in t-Sída (concerning the seizure of the fairy mound)', *Zeitschrift für celtische Philologie* 19 (1933), 53–8.

— 'Early Irish Segais', *Zeitschrift für celtische Philologie* 29 (1962–4), 321–4.

Irwin, J., '"Asokan" pillars: a reassessment of the evidence – 4: symbolism', *Burlington Magazine* 118:884 (1976), 734–53.

Jackson, K.H., 'The adventure of Laeghaire Mac Crimhthainn', *Speculum* 17 (1942), 377–89.

— *The international popular tale and early Welsh tradition* (Cardiff, 1961).

— *The oldest Irish tradition: a window on the Iron Age* (Cambridge, 1964).

James, E.O., 'The sacred kingship and the priesthood' in *La regalità sacra. The sacral kingship: contributions to the central theme of the VIIIth International Congress for the History of Religions (Rome, April 1955)* (Leiden, 1959), pp 63–70.

James, S., *The Atlantic Celts: ancient people or modern invention?* (London, 1999).

Jaski, B., *Early Irish kingship and succession* (Dublin, 2000).

Jendza, C., 'Theseus the Ionian in Bacchylides 17 and Indo-Iranian Apām Napāt', *Journal of Indo-European Studies* 41 (2013), 431–57.

Jones, G., *A history of the Vikings* (2nd ed., Oxford, 1984).

Jope, E.M., *Early Celtic art in the British Isles* (Oxford, 2000).

Joy, J., 'Reflections on Celtic art: a re-examination of mirror decoration' in D. Garrow, C. Gosden & J.D. Hill (eds), *Rethinking Celtic art* (Oxford, 2008), pp 78–99.

— *Iron Age mirrors: a biographical approach* (Oxford, 2010).

Kaul, F., *Ships on bronzes: a study in Bronze Age religion and iconography* (Copenhagen, 1998).

— 'Bronze Age tripartite cosmologies', *Praehistorische Zeitschrift* 80 (2006), 235–46.

Kelly, F., *A guide to early Irish law* (Dublin, 1988).

— 'The beliefs and mythology of the early Irish with special reference to the cosmos' in C. Ruggles (ed.), *Astronomy, cosmology and landscape* (Bognor Regis, 2001), pp 167–72.

Kelly, P., 'The Táin as literature' in J.P. Mallory (ed.), *Aspects of the Táin* (Belfast, 1992), pp 69–102.

Killeen, J.F., 'Fear an énais', *Celtica* 9 (1971), 202–4.

Kimmig, W., *Das Kleinaspergle. Studien zu einem Fürstengrabhügel der frühen Latènezeit bei Stuttgart* (Stuttgart, 1988).

Knüsel, C.J., 'More Circe than Cassandra: the princess of Vix in ritualized social context', *European Journal of Archaeology* 5 (2002), 275–308.

Koch, J.T., 'A Welsh window on the Iron Age: Manawydan, Mandubracios', *Cambridge Medieval Celtic Studies* 14 (1987), 17–52.

— 'Further to *Tongu do dia toinges mo thuath* etc.', *Études celtiques* 29 (1992), 249–61.

— 'Windows on the Iron Age: 1964–1994' in J.P. Mallory & G. Stockman (eds), *Ulidia: proceedings of the First International Conference on the Ulster Cycle of Tales* (Belfast, 1994), pp 229–42.

— (ed.), *Celtic culture: a historical encyclopedia*, 1–5 (Santa Barbara, CA, 2006).

— & J. Carey (eds), *The Celtic heroic age: literary sources for ancient Celtic Europe and early Ireland and Wales* (Malden, MA, 1995).

Krausse, D., 'Der "Keltenfürst" von Hochdorf: Dorfältester oder Sakralkönig? Anspruch und Wirklichkeit der sog. kulturanthropologischen Hallstatt-Archäologie', *Archäologisches Korrespondenzblatt* 29 (1999), 339–58 (English trans.: D. Krausse, 'The "Celtic Prince" of Hochdorf: village-elder or sacred king? Pretence and reality of the so-called "cultural anthropological" Hallstatt archaeology' in R. Karl & D. Stifter (eds), *The Celtic world: critical concepts in historical studies*, 2, *Celtic archaeology* (London, 2007), pp 197–229).

Kristiansen, K., 'Rock art and religion. The sun journey in Indo-European mythology and Bronze Age rock art' in A.C. Fredell, K. Kristiansen & F. Criado Boado (eds), *Representations and communications: creating an archaeological matrix of late prehistoric rock art* (Oxford, 2010), pp 93–115.

— & T.B. Larsson, *The rise of Bronze Age society: travels, transmissions and transformations* (Cambridge, 2005).

Kruta, V., *La cruche celte de Brno. Chef-d'oeuvre de l'art: miroir de l'Univers* (Dijon, 2007).

Kvilhaug, M., *The maiden with the mead: a goddess of initiation rituals in Old Norse mythology?* (Saarbrücken, 2009).

Kyriakidis, E. (ed.), *The archaeology of ritual* (Los Angeles, 2007).

Lambert, P.-Y., 'Deux mots Gaulois, *Souxtu* et *Comedovis*', *Comptes-rendus des séances de l'Académie des Inscriptions et Belles-Lettres* (2006), 1507–24.

Lambot, B. & P. Méniel, 'Le centre communautaire et cultuel du village gaulois d'Acy-Romance dans son contexte régional' in S. Verger (ed.), *Rites et espaces en pays celte et méditerranéen: étude comparée à partir du sanctuaire d'Acy-Romance (Ardennes, France)* (Rome, 2000), pp 7–139.

La regalità sacra. The sacred kingship: contributions to the central theme of the VIIIth International Congress for the history of religions (Rome, April 1955) (Leiden, 1959).

Le Roux, F. & C.-J. Guyonvarc'h, *Mórrígan – Bodb – Macha: la souveraineté guerrière de l'Irlande* (Rennes, 1983).

Lincoln, B., 'On the imagery of paradise', *Indogermanische Forschungen* 85 (1980), 151–64.

— *Priests, warriors and cattle: a study in the ecology of religions* (Los Angeles, 1981).

— *Theorizing myth: narrative, ideology and scholarship* (Chicago, 1999).

Lindsey, A.W., 'The Dunalis souterrain and ogham stone', *Proceedings of the Belfast Natural History and Philosophical Society* (1934–5), 61–70.

Linduff, K.M., 'Epona: a Celt among the Romans', *Latomus* 38 (1979), 817–37.

Lucas, A.T., 'The sacred trees of Ireland', *Journal of the Cork Historical and Archaeological Society* 68 (1963), 16–54.

Lynch, R., *The Kirwans of Castlehacket, Co. Galway: history, folklore and mythology in an Irish horseracing family* (Dublin, 2006).

Lynn, C.J., 'Navan Fort: a draft summary of D.M. Waterman's excavations', *Emania* 1 (1986), 11–19.

— 'The Iron Age mound in Navan Fort: a physical realization of Celtic religious beliefs?', *Emania* 10 (1992), 32–57.

— 'House-urns in Ireland?', *Ulster Journal of Archaeology* 56 (1993), 70–7.

— 'Hostel, heroes and tales: further thoughts on the Navan Mound', *Emania* 12 (1994), 5–20.

— 'That mound again: the Navan excavations revisited', *Emania* 15 (1996), 5–9.

— *Excavations at Navan Fort, 1961–71, by D.M. Waterman* (Belfast, 1997).

— 'Navan Fort site C excavations, June 1999, interim report', *Emania* 18 (2000), 5–16.

— 'Navan Fort site C excavations, May 2000, interim report no. 2', *Emania* 19 (2002), 5–18.

— *Navan Fort: archaeology and myth* (Bray, 2003).

— 'Suggested archaeological and architectural examples of tripartite structures', *Journal of Indo-European Studies* 34 (2006), 111–41.

— & D. Miller, 'Crossing boundaries: literary and archaeological evidence for early Irish royal inauguration rites and sites', *Studia Indo-Europaea* 2 (2002–5), 161–75.

Macalister, R.A.S., 'Temair Breg: a study of the remains and traditions of Tara', *Proceedings of the Royal Irish Academy* 34C (1919), 231–404.

— *Corpus Inscriptionum Insularum Celticarum*, 1 (Dublin, 1945).

Mac Cana, P., *Celtic mythology* (London, 1970).

— 'Conservation and innovation in early Irish literature', *Études celtiques* 13 (1973), 61–118.

— 'The *topos* of the single sandal in Irish tradition', *Celtica* 10 (1973), 160–6.

— 'Placenames and mythology in Irish tradition: places, pilgrimages and things' in G.W. MacLennan (ed.), *Proceedings of the First North American Congress of Celtic Studies* (Ottawa, 1988), pp 319–41.

— 'The Irish analogues of Mélusine' in P. Lysaght, S. Ó Catháin & D. Ó hÓgáin (eds), *Islanders and water-dwellers: proceedings of the Celtic-Nordic-Baltic Symposium held at University College Dublin, 16–19 June 1996* (Dublin, 1999), pp 149–64.

— *The cult of the sacred centre: essays on Celtic ideology* (Dublin, 2011).

Mac Giolla Easpaig, D., 'The significance and etymology of the placename *Temair*' in E. Bhreathnach (ed.), *The kingship and landscape of Tara* (Dublin, 2005), pp 423–49.

MacNeill, E., *Phases of Irish history* (Dublin, 1919).

Mallory, J.P., 'The literary topography of Emain Macha', *Emania* 2 (1987), 12–18.

— (ed.), *Aspects of the Táin* (Belfast, 1992),

— 'The world of Cú Chulainn: the archaeology of *Táin Bó Cúailnge*' in J.P. Mallory (ed.), *Aspects of the Táin* (Belfast, 1992), pp 103–59.

— 'Excavations of the Navan Ditch', *Emania* 18 (2000), 21–35.

— & M.G.L. Baillie, '*Tech ndaruch:* the fall of the house of oak', *Emania* 5 (1988), 27–33.

— & T.E. McNeill, *The archaeology of Ulster from colonization to plantation* (Belfast, 1991).

—, D.M. Brown & M.G.L. Baillie, 'Dating Navan Fort', *Antiquity* 73 (1999), 427–31.

Marazov, I., *The Rogozen treasure* (Sofia, 1989).

— 'Philomele's tongue: reading the pictorial text of Thracian mythology' in L. Bonfante (ed.), *The barbarians of ancient Europe: realities and interactions* (Cambridge, 2011), pp 132–89.

Marstrander, C., 'A new version of the Battle of Mag Rath', *Ériu* 5 (1911), 226–47.

Martin, B.K., '"Truth" and "Modesty": a reading of the Irish Noinden Ulad', *Leeds Studies in English* 20 (1989), 99–117.

Mattingly, H., *Tacitus. The Agricola and the Germania: translated with an introduction by H. Mattingly, revised by S.A. Handford* (London, 1970).

McCafferty, P. & M. Baillie, *The Celtic gods: comets in Irish mythology* (Stroud, 2005).

McCone, K., 'Werewolves, cyclopes, *díberga* and *fianna*: juvenile delinquency in early Ireland', *Cambridge Medieval Celtic Studies* 12 (1986), 1–22.

— *Pagan past and Christian present in early Irish literature* (Maynooth, 1990).

— 'The Celtic and Indo-European origins of the *fían*' in S.J. Arbuthnot & G. Parsons (eds), *The Gaelic Finn tradition* (Dublin, 2012), pp 14–30.

McCormick, F., 'The distribution of meat in a hierarchical society: the Irish evidence' in P. Miracle & N. Milner (eds), *Consuming passions and patterns of consumption* (Cambridge, 2002), pp 25–31.

— 'The horse in early Ireland', *Anthropozoologica* 42 (2007), 85–104.

McKenna, C.A., 'The theme of sovereignty in *Pwyll*', *Bulletin of the Board of Celtic Studies* 29 (1980), 35–52 (also published in C.W. Sullivan III (ed.), *The Mabinogi: a book of essays* (New York, 1996), pp 303–30).

McTurk, R., *Chaucer and the Norse and Celtic worlds* (London, 2005).

Meduna, J. & I. Peskar, 'Ein latènzeitlicher Fund mit Bronzebeschlägen von Brno-Maloměřice (Kr. Brno-Stadt)', *Bericht der Römisch-Germanischen Kommission* 73 (1992), 181–267.

Megaw, J.V.S., *Art of the European Iron Age: a study of the elusive image* (Bath, 1970).

— 'Celtic foot(less) soldiers? An iconographic note', *Gladius* 23 (2003), 61–70.

— & M.R. Megaw, 'Cheshire cats, Mickey Mice, the new Europe and ancient Celtic art' in C. Scarre & F. Healy (eds), *Trade and exchange in prehistoric Europe: proceedings of a conference held at the University of Bristol, April 1992* (Oxford, 1993), pp 219–32.

Megaw, R. & V. Megaw, 'Through a window on the European Iron Age darkly: fifty years of reading early Celtic art', *World Archaeology* 25 (1994), 287–302.

Meid, W., *Die Romanze von Froech und Findabair* (Innsbruck, 1970).

Meller, H. (ed.), *Der geschmiedete Himmel: Die weite Welt im Herzen Europas vor 3600 Jahren* (Stuttgart, 2004).

Méniel, P., *Les sacrifices d'animaux chez les Gaulois* (Paris, 1992).

Metzner-Nebelsick, C., 'Wagen- und Prunkbestattungen von Frauen der Hallstatt- und frühen Latènezeit in Europa. Ein Beitrag zur Diskussion der sozialen Stellung der Frau in der älteren Eisenzeit' in J.M. Bagley, C. Eggl, D. Neumann & M. Schefzik (eds), *Alpen, Kult und Eisenzeit. Festschrift für Amei Lang zum 65. Geburtstag* (Rahden, 2009), pp 237–70.

Meyer, K., 'The adventures of Nera', *Revue celtique* 10 (1889), 212–28.

— 'Baile in Scáil', *Zeitschrift für celtische Philologie* 3 (1901), 457–66.

Milcent, P.-Y., 'Statut et fonctions d'un personnage féminin hors norme' in C. Rolley (ed.), *La tombe princière de Vix* (Paris, 2003), pp 312–27.

Miles, B., *Heroic saga and classical epic in medieval Ireland* (Woodbridge, 2011).

Miles, D., S. Palmer, G. Lock, C. Gosden & A.M. Cromarty, *Uffington White Horse and its landscape: investigations at White Horse Hill, Uffington, 1989–95, and Tower Hill, Ashbury, 1993–4* (Oxford, 2003).

Miller, D.A., 'Georges Dumézil: theories, critiques and theoretical extensions', *Religion* 30 (2000), 27–40.

Moore, T. & X.-L. Armada, 'Crossing the divide: opening a dialogue on approaches to western European first millennium BC studies' in T. Moore & X.-L. Armada (eds), *Atlantic Europe in the first millennium BC: crossing the divide* (Oxford, 2011), pp 3–77.

Morgan, M. Gwyn, 'The three minor pretenders in Tacitus, "Histories" II', *Latomus* 52 (1993), 769–96.

Moroney, A., 'Winter sunsets at Dowth', *Archaeology Ireland* 13:4 (1999), 29–31.

Morris, H., 'Ancient graves in Sligo and Roscommon', *Journal of the Royal Society of Antiquaries of Ireland* 59 (1929), 99–115.

— 'Dun na mBarc and the Lady Ceasiar', *Journal of the Royal Society of Antiquaries of Ireland* 63 (1933), 69–87.

Muhr, K., 'The early place-names of County Armagh', *Seanchas Ardmhacha: Journal of the Armagh Diocesan Historical Society* 19 (2002), 1–54.

— 'Place-names and the understanding of monuments' in R. Schot et al. (eds), *Landscapes of cult and kingship* (Dublin, 2011), pp 232–55.

Müller-Lisowski, K., 'La légende de St Jean dans la tradition irlandaise et le druide Mog Ruith', *Études celtiques* 3 (1938), 46–70.

— 'Contributions to a study in Irish folklore: traditions about Donn', *Bealoideas* 18 (1948), 142–99.

Nagy, J.F., *The wisdom of the outlaw: the boyhood deeds of Finn in Gaelic tradition* (Berkeley, CA, 1985).

Needham, S. & S. Bowman, 'Flesh-hooks, technological complexity and the Atlantic Bronze Age feasting complex', *European Journal of Archaeology* 8 (2005), 93–136.

Newman, C., *Tara: an archaeological survey* (Dublin, 1997).

— 'Re-composing the archaeological landscape of Tara' in E. Bhreathnach (ed.), *The kingship and landscape of Tara* (Dublin, 2005), pp 361–409.

— 'Misinformation, disinformation and downright distortion: the battle to save Tara, 1999–2005' in C. Newman & U. Strohmayer, *Uninhabited Ireland: Tara, the M3 and public spaces in Galway* (Galway, 2007), pp 61–101.

— 'Procession and symbolism at Tara: analysis of Tech Midhchúarta (the "Banqueting Hall") in the context of the sacral campus', *Oxford Journal of Archaeology* 26 (2007), 415–38.

— 'The sacral landscape of Tara: a preliminary exploration' in R. Schot et al. (eds), *Landscapes of cult and kingship* (Dublin, 2011), pp 22–43.

— 'In the way of development: Tara, the M3 and the Celtic Tiger' in R. Meade & F. Dukelow (eds), *Defining events: power, resistance and identity in 21st-century Ireland* (Manchester, 2014), forthcoming.

Ní Bhrolcháin, M., *An introduction to early Irish literature* (Dublin, 2009).

— 'Death-tales of the early kings of Tara' in R. Schot et al. (eds), *Landscapes of cult and kingship* (Dublin, 2011), pp 44–65.

Ní Chatháin, P., 'Traces of the cult of the horse in early Irish sources', *Journal of Indo-European Studies* 19 (1991), 124–31.

Ní Dhonnchadha, M., 'On Gormfhlaith daughter of Flann Sinna and the lure of the sovereignty goddess' in A.P. Smyth (ed.), *Seanchas: studies in early and medieval Irish archaeology, history and literature in honour of Francis J. Byrne* (Dublin, 2000), pp 225–37.

— 'Gormlaith and her sisters, *c.*750–1800 (Noínden Ulad – The Debility of the Ulidians)' in A. Bourke et al. (eds), *The Field Day anthology of Irish writing*, 4 (Cork, 2002), pp 173–4.

— 'Courts and coteries 1, 900–1600' in A. Bourke et al. (eds), *The Field Day anthology of Irish writing*, 4 (Cork, 2002), pp 293–303.

Noble, G. & K. Brophy, 'Ritual and remembrance at a prehistoric ceremonial complex in central Scotland: excavations at Forteviot, Perth and Kinross', *Antiquity* 85 (2011), 787–804.

Nordberg, A., 'The grave as a doorway to the Other World', *Temenos: Nordic Journal of Comparative Religion* 45 (2009), 35–63.

Oaks, L.S., 'The goddess Epona: concepts of sovereignty in a changing landscape' in M. Henig & A. King (eds), *Pagan gods and shrines of the Roman Empire* (Oxford, 1986), pp 77–83.

Ó Broin, T., '"Craebruad": a spurious tradition', *Éigse* 15 (1974), 103–13.

— 'Lia Fáil: fact and fiction in the tradition', *Celtica* 21 (1990), 393–401.

Ó Buachalla, B., 'Irish Jacobite poetry', *Irish Review* 12 (1992), 40–9.

Ó Cathasaigh, T., *The heroic biography of Cormac Mac Airt* (Dublin, 1977).

— 'The semantics of "Síd"', *Éigse* 17 (1979), 137–55.

— 'Pagan survivals: the evidence of early Irish narrative' in P. Ní Chatháin & M. Richter (eds), *Irland und Europa. Ireland and Europe. Die Kirche im Früh-mittelalter. The early church* (Stuttgart, 1984), pp 291–307.

— 'The eponym of Cnogba', *Éigse* 23 (1989), 27–38.

— '*Gat* and *Díberg* in *Togail Bruidne Da Derga*' in A. Ahlqvist et al. (eds), *Celtica Helsingiensia: proceedings from a Symposium on Celtic Studies* (Helsinki, 1996), pp 203–13.

Ó Corráin, D., 'Creating the past: the early Irish genealogical tradition', *Peritia* 12 (1998), 530–60.

— 'Historical need and literary narrative' in D. Ellis Evans, J.G. Griffith & E.M. Jope (eds), *Proceedings of the Seventh International Congress of Celtic Studies held at Oxford, from 10th to 15th July 1983* (Oxford, 1986), pp 141–58.

— 'Early medieval law, *c.*700–1200' in A. Bourke et al. (eds), *The Field Day anthology of Irish writing*, 4 (Cork, 2002), pp 6–44.

Ó Cróinín, D. (ed.), *A new history of Ireland, prehistoric and early Ireland*, 1 (Oxford, 2005).

O Daly, M., *Cath Maige Mucrama. The Battle of Mag Mucrama* (Dublin, 1975).

Ó Duinn, S., *Forbhais Droma Dámhgháire. The siege of Knocklong* (Cork, 1992).

Ó Floinn, R., 'Notes on some Iron Age finds from Ireland' in G. Cooney et al. (eds), *Relics of old decency: archaeological studies in later prehistory. Festschrift for Barry Raftery* (Dublin, 2009), pp 199–210.

Ó hÓgáin, D., *Fionn mac Cumhaill: images of the Gaelic hero* (Dublin, 1988).

Ó hUiginn, R., 'The background and development of *Táin Bó Cúailnge*' in J.P. Mallory (ed.), *Aspects of the Táin* (Belfast, 1992), pp 29–67.

— 'Fergus, Russ and Rudraige: a brief biography of Fergus Mac Róich', *Emania* 11 (1993), 31–40.

— & B. Ó Catháin (eds), *Ulidia 2: proceedings of the Second International Conference on the Ulster Cycle of Tales, National University of Ireland Maynooth, 24–27 June 2005* (Maynooth, 2009).

Ó Máille, T., 'Medb Chruachna', *Zeitschrift für celtische Philologie* 17 (1928), 129–46.

Ó Mainnín, M.B., '"Co mBeith a Ainm Asa": the eponymous Macha in the place-names *Mag Macha*, *Emain Macha* and *Óenach Macha*' in R. Ó hUiginn & B. Ó Catháin (eds), *Ulidia 2* (Maynooth, 2009), pp 195–207.

Ó Riain, P., 'Early Irish literature' in G. Price (ed.), *The Celtic connection* (Gerrards Cross, 1992), pp 65–80.

O'Brien, S., 'Dioscuric elements in Celtic and Germanic mythology', *Journal of Indo-European Studies* 10 (1982), 117–36.

O'Brien, W., *Sacred ground: megalithic tombs in coastal south-west Ireland* (Galway, 1999).

O'Connell, A., *Harvesting the stars: a pagan temple at Lismullin, Co. Meath* (Dublin, 2013).

O'Curry, E., *Lectures on the manuscript materials of ancient Irish history* (Dublin, 1861).

O'Flaherty, W. Doniger, *Textual sources for the study of Hinduism* (Chicago, 1990).

O'Kelly, M.J., *Newgrange: archaeology, art and legend* (London, 1982).

— & C. O'Kelly, 'The tumulus of Dowth, County Meath', *Proceedings of the Royal Irish Academy* 83C (1983), 135–90.

O'Leary, A.M., 'Mog Ruith and apocalypticism in eleventh-century Ireland' in J.F. Nagy (ed.), *The individual in Celtic literatures* (Dublin, 2001), pp 51–60.

O'Meara, J.J., *The first version of the Topography of Ireland by Giraldus Cambrensis* (Dundalk, 1951).

O'Rahilly, C., *Táin Bó Cúalnge from the Book of Leinster* (Dublin, 1967).

— *Táin Bó Cúailnge Recension 1* (Dublin, 1976).

O'Rahilly, T.F., *Early Irish history and mythology* (Dublin, 1946).

— 'On the origin of the names *Erainn* and *Ériu*', *Ériu* 14 (1946), 7–28.

Olivier, L., 'The Hochdorf "princely grave" and the question of the nature of archaeological funerary assemblages' in T. Murray (ed.), *Time and archaeology* (London, 1999), pp 109–38.

Olmsted, G.S., 'The Gundestrup version of *Táin Bó Cuailnge*', *Antiquity* 50 (1976), 95–103.

— *The Gundestrup cauldron: its archaeological context, the style and iconography of its portrayed motifs, and their narration of a Gaulish version of Táin Bó Cúailnge* (Brussels, 1979).

— *The Gods of the Celts and the Indo-Europeans* (Budapest, 1994).

O'Sullivan, M., C. Scarre & M. Doyle (eds), *Tara from the past to the future* (Dublin, 2013).

Parfitt, K., 'The Deal man', *Current Archaeology* 101 (1986), 166–8.

— *Iron Age burials from Mill Hill, Deal* (London, 1995).

— & M. Green, 'A chalk figurine from Upper Deal, Kent', *Britannia* 18 (1987), 295–8.

Parker Pearson, M., *Bronze Age Britain* (London, 1993).

— 'Food, sex and death: cosmologies in the British Iron Age with particular reference to east Yorkshire', *Cambridge Archaeological Journal* 9 (1999), 43–69.

Patay, P., *Die Bronzegefässe in Ungarn* (Munich, 1990).

Payne, A., M. Corney & B. Cunliffe, *The Wessex hillforts project: extensive survey of hillfort interiors in central southern England* (London, 2006).

Peacock, M. (ed.), *The early history of Rome: books I–V of the Ab Urbe Condita* (trans. B.O. Foster, New York, 2005).

Pertlwieser, M., 'Frühhallstattzeitliche Wagenbestattungen in Mitterkirchen' in M. Pertlwieser (ed.), *Prunkwagen und Hügelgrab. Kultur der frühen Eisenzeit von Hallstatt bis Mitterkirchen* (Linz, 1987), pp 55–65.

Petrie, G., 'On the history and antiquities of Tara Hill', *Transactions of the Royal Irish Academy* 18 (1839), 25–232.

Piggott, S., *Ancient Europe from the beginnings of agriculture to classical antiquity* (Edinburgh, 1965).

Pinault, G.-J., 'Gaulois *Epomeduos*, le maître des chevaux' in P.-Y. Lambert & G.-J. Pinault (eds), *Gaulois et celtique continental* (Geneva, 2007), pp 291–307.

Power, M., 'Cnucha cnoc os cionn Life', *Zeitschrift für celtische Philologie* 11 (1917), 39–55.

Pralon, D., 'La légende de la fondation de Marseille', *Éudes Massaliètes* 3 (1992), 51–6.

Prendergast, F. & T. Ray, 'Ancient astronomical alignments: fact or fiction?', *Archaeology Ireland* 16:2 (2002), 32–5.

Prüssing, G., *Die Bronzegefässe in Österreich* (Stuttgart, 1991).

Puhvel, J., 'Aspects of equine functionality' in J. Puhvel (ed.), *Myth and law among the Indo-Europeans: studies in Indo-European comparative mythology* (Berkeley, CA, 1970), pp 159–72.

— *Comparative mythology* (Baltimore, MD, 1987).

Py, M., *La sculpture Gauloise méridionale* (Paris, 2011).

Raftery, B., *A catalogue of Irish Iron Age antiquities* (Marburg, 1983).

— *Pagan Celtic Ireland: the enigma of the Irish Iron Age* (London, 1994).

— 'Iron Age Ireland' in D. Ó Cróinín (ed.), *A new history of Ireland, prehistoric and early Ireland*, 1 (Oxford, 2005), pp 134–81.

Randsborg, K., 'Opening the oak-coffins: new dates – new perspectives', *Acta Archaeologica* 77 (2006), 1–162.

Rapin, A., 'Une épée celtique damasquinée d'or du Vᵉ s. av. J.-C. au Musée des Antiquités Nationales', *Antiquités Nationales* 34 (2002), 155–71.

Rees, A.D., 'Modern evaluations of Celtic narrative tradition', *Proceedings of the Second International Congress of Celtic Studies held in Cardiff, 6–13 July, 1963* (Cardiff, 1966), pp 31–61.

— & B. Rees, *Celtic heritage: ancient tradition in Ireland and Wales* (London, 1961).

Reinach, S., *Bronzes figurés de la Gaule romaine* (Paris, 1894).

— *Catalogue illustré du Musée des antiquités nationales au Château de Saint-Germain-en-Laye*, 2 (Paris, 1921).

Renfrew, C., *Prehistory: the making of the human mind* (London, 2007).

Ridgeway, W., 'The date of the first shaping of the Cuchulainn saga', *Proceedings of the British Academy* 2 (1906), 135–68.

Ritchie, A., *Prehistoric Orkney* (London, 1995).

— 'Paganism among the Picts and the conversion of Orkney' in J. Downes & A. Ritchie (eds), *Sea change* (Balgavies, 2003), pp 3–10.

Roche, H., 'Excavations at Ráith na Ríg, Tara, Co. Meath, 1997', *Discovery Programme Reports* 6 (2002), 19–82.

Rolley, C. (ed.), *La tombe princière de Vix* (Paris, 2003).

Roosevelt, T., 'The ancient Irish sagas', *Century Magazine* 73 (1907), 327–36.

Ross, A., 'Chain symbolism in pagan Celtic religion', *Speculum* 34 (1959), 39–59.

— *Pagan Celtic Britain: studies in iconography and tradition* (London, 1967).

Roymans, N., 'The cultural biography of urnfields and the long-term history of a mythical landscape', *Archaeological Dialogues* 1 (1995), 2–24.

Sartori, P., 'Der Schuh im Volksglauben', *Zeitschrift des Vereins für Volkskunde* 4 (1894), 41–54, 148–80, 282–305, 412–47.

Savory, H.N., *Guide catalogue of the early Iron Age collection* (Cardiff, 1976).

Scheers, S., 'Celtic coin types in Britain and their Mediterranean origins' in M. Mays (ed.), *Celtic coinage: Britain and beyond. The eleventh Oxford Symposium on coinage and monetary history* (Oxford, 1992), pp 33–46.

Schjødt, J.P., 'Ibn Fadlan's account of a Rus funeral: to what degree does it reflect Nordic myths?' in P. Hermann, J.P. Schjødt & R.T. Kristensen (eds), *Reflections on Old Norse myths* (Turnhout, 2007), pp 133–48.

— 'Ideology of the ruler in pre-Christian Scandinavia: mythic and ritual relations', *Viking and Medieval Scandinavia* 6 (2010), 161–94.

Schot, R., C. Newman & E. Bhreathnach (eds), *Landscapes of cult and kingship* (Dublin, 2011)

Scott, A.B. & F.X. Martin, *Expugnatio Hibernica. The Conquest of Ireland, by Giraldus Cambrensis* (Dublin, 1978).

Scott, B.G., *Early Irish ironworking* (Belfast, 1990).

Scubla, L., 'Sacred king, sacrificial victim, surrogate victim or Frazer, Hocart, Girard' in D. Quigley (ed.), *The character of kingship* (Oxford, 2005), pp 39–62.

Sheehan, S., 'Fer Diad De-flowered: homoerotics and masculinity in *Comrac Fir Diad*' in R. Ó hUiginn & B. Ó Catháin (eds), *Ulidia* 2 (Maynooth, 2009), pp 54–65.

Sheridan, A., 'Contextualising Kilmartin: building a narrative for developments in western Scotland and beyond, from the early Neolithic to the late Bronze Age' in A.M. Jones, J. Pollard, M.J. Allen & J. Gardiner (eds), *Image, memory and monumentality: archaeolological engagements with the material world* (Oxford, 2012), pp 163–83.

Sims-Williams, P., 'Celtomania and Celtoscepticism', *Cambrian Medieval Celtic Studies* 36 (1998), 1–35.

Singor, H.W., 'Nine against Troy. On epic ΦΑΛΑΓΓΕΣ, ΠΡΟΜΑΧΟΙ, and an old structure in the story of the "Iliad"', *Mnemosyne* 44 (1991), 17–62.

Sjöblom, T., *Early Irish taboos: a study in cognitive history* (Helsinki, 2000).

Sjoestedt, M.-L., 'Forbuis Droma Damhghaire', *Revue celtique* 43 (1926), 1–123.

— *Gods and heroes of the Celts, translated by Myles Dillon* (London, 1949).

Slavin, B., 'Supernatural arts, the landscape and kingship in early Irish texts' in R. Schot et al. (eds), *Landscapes of cult and kingship* (Dublin, 2011), pp 66–86.

Sprockhoff, E., 'Central European Urnfield Culture and Celtic La Tène: an outline', *Proceedings of the Prehistoric Society* 21 (1955), 257–81.

Stead, I.M., 'The metalwork' in K. Parfitt, *Iron Age burials from Mill Hill, Deal* (London, 1995), pp 59–111.

— & K. Hughes, *Early Celtic designs* (London, 1997).

Sterckx, C., *Mythes et dieux celtes: essais et études* (Paris, 2010).

Stokes, Wh., 'Cóir Anmann (Fitness of Names)' in Wh. Stokes & E. Windisch (eds), *Irische Texte mit Übersetzungen und Wörterbuch* 3:2 (Leipzig, 1891), pp 285–444.

— 'The Edinburgh Dinnshenchas', *Folklore* 4 (1893), 471–96.

— 'The Voyage of the Huí Corra', *Revue celtique* 14 (1893), 22–69.

— 'The Prose Tales of the Rennes Dindsenchas', *Revue celtique* 15 (1894), 272–336.

— 'The Prose Tales of the Rennes Dindsenchas', *Revue celtique* 16 (1895), 31–83.

— 'The Annals of Tigernach: fourth fragment', *Revue celtique* 17 (1896), 337–420.

— 'Echtra mac Echach Muigmedóin', *Revue celtique* 24 (1903), 190–203.

— 'The Evernew Tongue', *Ériu* 2 (1905), 96–162.

Stout, G., *Newgrange and the Bend of the Boyne* (Cork, 2002).

Stutley, M., 'The asvamedha or Indian horse sacrifice', *Folklore* 80 (1969), 253–61.

Sundqvist, O., '"Religious ruler ideology" in pre-Christian Scandinavia' in C. Raudvere & J.P. Schjødt (eds), *More than mythology: narratives, ritual practices and regional distribution in pre-Christian Scandinavian religions* (Lund, 2012), pp 225–61.

Sveinsson, E. Ól., 'Celtic elements in Icelandic tradition', *Béaloideas* 25 (1957), 3–24.

Swift, C., 'The gods of Newgrange in Irish literature and Romano-Celtic tradition' in G. Burenhult & S. Westergaard (eds), *Stones and bones: formal disposal of the dead in Atlantic Europe during the Mesolithic–Neolithic interface, 6000–3000BC* (Oxford, 2003), pp 53–63.

— 'Commentary: the Knowth oghams in context' in F.J. Byrne, W. Jenkins, G. Kenny & C. Swift, *Excavations at Knowth 4: historical Knowth and its hinterland* (Dublin, 2008), pp 120–32.

Thomas, J., 'The identity of place in Neolithic Britain: examples from south-west Scotland' in A. Ritchie (ed.), *Neolithic Orkney in its European context* (Cambridge, 2000), pp 79–87.

— *Archaeology and modernity* (London, 2004).

Toner, G., 'Emain Macha in the literature', *Emania* 4 (1988), 32–5.

— 'Macha and the invention of myth', *Ériu* 60 (2010), 81–109.

Treherne, P., 'The warrior's beauty: the masculine body and self-identity in Bronze Age Europe', *Journal of European Archaeology* 3 (1995), 105–44.

Tymoczko, M., 'The semantic fields of early Irish terms for black birds' in A.T.E. Matonis & D.F. Melia (eds), *Celtic language, Celtic culture: a Festschrift for Eric P. Hamp* (Van Nuys, CA, 1990), pp 151–71.

Uckelmann, M., *Die Schilde der Bronzezeit in Nord-, West- und Zentraleuropa* (Stuttgart, 2012).

Ucko, P.J., 'Ethnography and archaeological interpretation of funerary remains', *World Archaeology* 1 (1969), 262–80.

Ustinova, Y., *Caves and the ancient Greek mind: descending underground in the search for ultimate truth* (Oxford, 2009).

Veit, U., 'Des Fürsten neue Schuhe – Überlegungen zum Befund von Hochdorf', *Germania* 66 (1988), 162–9.

— 'König und Hohepriester? Zur These der sakralen Gründung der Herrschaft in der Hallstattzeit', *Archäologisches Korrespondenzblatt* 30 (2000), 549–68 (English translation: U. Veit, 'King and high priest? On the theory of a sacral foundation of Hallstatt leadership' in R. Karl & D. Stifter (eds), *The Celtic world: critical concepts in historical studies, 2, Celtic archaeology* (London, 2007), pp 230–60).

Vendryes, J., *Airne Fíngein* (Dublin, 1953).

Verger, S., 'L'utilisation du répertoire figuratif dans l'art celtique ancien', *Histoire de l'Art* 16 (1991), 3–17.

— 'Qui était la Dame de Vix? Propositions pour une interprétation historique' in M. Cébeillac-Gervasoni & L. Lamoine (eds), *Les élites et leurs facettes: les élites locales dans le monde hellénistique et romain* (Rome, 2003), pp 583–625.

— 'La grande tombe de Hochdorf, mise en scène funéraire d'un *cursus honorum* tribal hors pair', *Siris: studi e ricerche della Scuola di specializzazione in archeologia di Matera* 7 (2006), 5–44.

— 'La Dame de Vix: une défunte à personnalité multiple' in J. Guilaine (ed.), *Sépultures et sociétés: du Néolithique à l'histoire* (Paris, 2009), pp 285–309.

— 'Archéologie du couchant d'été' in J.-P. Le Bihan & J.-P. Guillaumet (eds), *Routes du monde et passages obligés de la Protohistoire au haut Moyen Âge* (Quimper, 2010), pp 293–337.

— 'Partager la viande, distribuer l'hydromel: consommation collective et pratique du pouvoir dans la tombe de Hochdorf' in S. Krausz, A. Colin, K. Gruel, I. Ralston & T. Dechezleprêtre (eds), *L'âge du fer en Europe: mélanges offerts à Olivier Buchsenschutz* (Bordeaux, 2013), pp 495–504.

Waddell, J., 'Irish Bronze Age cists: a survey', *Journal of the Royal Society of Antiquaries of Ireland* 100 (1970), 91–139.

— *The prehistoric archaeology of Ireland* (2nd ed., Bray, 2000).

— 'The elusive image' in G. Cooney et al. (eds), *Relics of old decency: archaeological studies in later prehistory. Festschrift for Barry Raftery* (Dublin, 2009), pp 341–9.

— *The prehistoric archaeology of Ireland* (3rd ed., Dublin, 2010).

— 'Continuity, cult and contest' in R. Schot et al. (eds), *Landscapes of cult and kingship* (Dublin, 2011), pp 192–212.

— 'The Tal-y-llyn plaques and the nocturnal voyage of the sun' in W.J. Britnell & R.J. Silvester (eds), *Reflections on the past: essays in honour of Frances Lynch* (Welshpool, 2012), pp 337–50.

— 'The Cave of Crúachain and the Otherworld' in J. Borsje, A. Dooley, S. Mac Mathúna & G. Toner (eds), *Celtic cosmology: perspectives from Ireland and Scotland* (Toronto, 2014), pp 77–92.

—, J. Fenwick & K. Barton, *Rathcroghan, Co. Roscommon: archaeological and geophysical survey in a ritual landscape* (Dublin, 2009).

Wagner, H., *Studies in the origins of the Celts and of early Celtic civilization* (Belfast, 1971) (also published in *Zeitschrift für celtische Philologie* 31 (1970), 1–58).

— 'Studies in the origins of early Celtic traditions', *Ériu* 26 (1975), 1–26.

— 'Origins of pagan Irish religion', *Zeitschrift für celtische Philologie* 38 (1981), 1–28.

Warmenbol, E., 'Miroirs et mantique à l'âge du Bronze' in C. Burgess, P. Topping & F. Lynch (eds), *Beyond Stonehenge: essays on the Bronze Age in honour of Colin Burgess* (Oxford, 2007), pp 377–96.

Warner, R.B., 'The fort of Sessiamagaroll, Co. Tyrone: an *airthir* royal site', *Dúiche Néill, Journal of the O Neill Country Historical Society* 14 (1983), 9–23.

— 'The Drumconwell ogham and its implications', *Emania* 8 (1991), 43–50.

— 'Emania varia 1', *Emania* 12 (1994), 66–72.

— 'Keeping out the Otherworld: the internal ditch at Navan and other Iron Age "hengiform" enclosures', *Emania* 18 (2000), 39–44.

— 'The Tamlaght hoard and the Creeveroe axe', *Emania* 20 (2006), 20–8.

Watkins, C., '*Is tre fír flathemon*: marginalia to *Audacht Morainn*', *Ériu* 30 (1979), 181–98.

— 'Language, culture, or history?' in C.S. Masek, R.A. Hendrick & M.F. Miller (eds), *Papers from the parasession on language and behavior. Chicago Linguistic Society* (Chicago, 1981), pp 238–48 (reprinted in L. Oliver (ed.), *Calvert Watkins. Selected writings, 2* (Innsbruck, 1994), pp 663–73).

— *How to kill a dragon: aspects of Indo-European poetics* (Oxford, 1995).

Webster, J., 'At the end of the world: druidic and other revitalization movements in post-conquest Gaul and Britain', *Britannia* 30 (1999), 1–20.

West, M.L., *Indo-European poetry and myth* (Oxford, 2007).

Whitehouse, H., 'Rites of terror: emotion, metaphor and memory in Melanesian initiation cults', *Journal of the Royal Anthropological Institute* 2 (1995), 703–15.

Wiley, D.M., 'The politics of myth in *Airne Fíngein*' in J.F. Eska (ed.), *Narrative in Celtic tradition: essays in honor of Edgar M. Slotkin* (New York, 2011), pp 276–87.

Windisch, E., *Compert Conculainn. Irische Texte mit Übersetzungen und Wörterbuch* 2:2 (Leipzig, 1880).

Wirth, S., 'Vogel-Sonnen-Barke' in H. Beck, D. Geuenich & H. Steuer (eds), *Reallexikon der Germanischen Altertumskunde* 32 (Berlin, 2006), pp 552–63.

— 'Le mystère de la barque solaire: quelques considérations à propos des décors sur les situles de type Hajdúböszörmény et sur une situle inédite du bronze final' in L. Baray (ed.), *Artisanats, sociétés et civilisations: hommage à Jean-Paul Thevenot* (Dijon, 2006), pp 331–45.

Yates, D. & R. Bradley, 'Still water, hidden depths: the deposition of Bronze Age metalwork in the English Fenland', *Antiquity* 84 (2010), 405–15.

Zaroff, R., 'Asvamedha: a Vedic horse sacrifice', *Studia Mythologica Slavica* 8 (2005), 75–86.

Ziegler, S., *Die Sprache der altirischen Ogam-Inschriften* (Göttingen, 1994).

Zimmer, H., *The art of Indian Asia: its mythology and transformations* (New York, 1955).

Zimmer, S., 'Indo-Celtic connections: ethic, magic and linguistic', *Journal of Indo-European Studies* 29 (2001), 379–405.

Index